THE ECONOMICS OF
SUBSISTENCE AGRICULTURE

The Economics of Subsistence Agriculture

COLIN CLARK

M.A. (Oxon.), M.A. (Cantab.), Hon. D.Sc. (Milan)
Hon. D.Ec. (Tilburg)

*Formerly Professorial Fellow of Brasenose College, Oxford, and
Director, Agricultural Economics Research Institute, Oxford*

AND

MARGARET HASWELL

B.Litt., M.A. (Oxon.)

*Fellow of St Hugh's College, Oxford
University Lecturer, Agricultural Economics Institute, Oxford*

Fourth Edition

MACMILLAN
ST MARTIN'S PRESS

First edition 1964
Second edition 1966
Third edition 1967
Fourth edition 1970

Published by
MACMILLAN AND CO LTD
London and Basingstoke
Associated companies in New York Toronto
Dublin Melbourne Johannesburg and Madras

Library of Congress catalog card no. 75-121341

SBN (boards) 333 03688 3
(paper) 333 11658 5

Printed in Great Britain by
ROBERT MACLEHOSE AND CO LTD
The University Press, Glagsow

Contents

List of Tables

List of Charts

Preface to the Fourth Edition

Although the post-Second World War development thrust has gained for the poorer countries an initial boost in rates of growth of total production, this has not led to sustained growth. Instead, we find that islands of relative prosperity have been created which have formed only small enclaves, while overwhelmingly large traditional sectors have stagnated. The 'Development Decade' of the sixties has not resolved the problems of farmers in low-productivity areas, and we enter the seventies with many millions of the world's population still living by subsistence agriculture on a monotonous diet, while the threat of famine remains ever present for countless numbers.

Other aspects of their poverty are lack of transport, clothing, housing, medicine and education, which often represent needs more urgent even than those for additional food. Industrialisation will inevitably continue to be a slow process, and many of these needs will have to be met by an expansion of the export and import trade of the subsistence agriculture countries, a problem to which little thought has yet been given.

The fourth edition of this book, which covers fifty-seven countries, assembles further evidence on the manner in which a subsistence cultivator produces, how he occupies his working hours, his methods of transport and exchange, how he owns or leases his land, and how he spends his small amount of money. Additional chapters have been added on wages and leisure, programming for full employment, and the role of agriculture in national economic development. There has been much updating of the evidence presented in the third edition, and new and valuable economic relationships are revealed — largely attributable to improvement in the supply of information. Even so, there still remains a neglected field of study, and that is for many more village and farm-level investigations from which precise measurements can be made to provide a body of information on factors affecting farmers' decisions. In the absence of such information, assumptions that agricultural education, extension services and credit institutions will induce change in the rate of absorption of new agricultural factors may be completely erroneous.

This edition sifts recent evidence in greater depths than has previously been possible with the data available to show the complexity of farmers' problems of land and labour use under different conditions of climate and soils in subsistence agriculture countries — which often leave subsistence cultivators idle over a considerable part of the year. National totals of agricultural production contained in Chapter V are supported by empirical evidence, which points to the need for re-programming output to provide for more regular employment. Attention is drawn to series of plans prepared for one or two countries; but the programmer who seeks to induce the subsistence cultivator to work much longer hours than he does now must offer him a high marginal return per hour in exchange. A number of production functions designed to throw light on the marginal productivity of labour are quoted in Chapter VI; they also indicate marginal productivities of land, which appear to be highly variable.

Important new material is included in this edition on food consumption covering a fifteen-fold range of incomes in rural Madagascar, which indicate that starchy staples are replaced with protein-rich foods with rising income. The Madagascar study also adds support to the considerable body of evidence appearing in earlier editions in a chapter on transport, that transport difficulties are checking economic development. In Madagascar, as elsewhere under similar conditions, this has led to concentration on high-value crops; an extreme case is quoted of one village where even the foot track is only open during the short dry season of two months of the year. The fact that traders are consequently forced to carry exceptionally large stocks, encouraging speculation in the necessities of life whose price may suddenly double or treble, driving poor farmers deeply into debt and to the pledging of future crops, is a further undesirable effect of the lack of transport. A much greater investment is called for in improved transport from major highways through to local farm-to-farm roads as a matter of absolute priority, without which the transition from a subsistence to a commercial economy cannot take place.

A determinant of the role of agriculture in national economic development is the extent to which labour can be transferred from agricultural to non-agricultural activities with increased agricultural productivity. Individual data on the growth of non-agricultural employment are presented, and causes explaining a decline in agricultural employment are examined.

Much of the final chapter on trade, aid and development is a reassessment by one of the authors on the acute economic problem for the developing countries which arises from their urgent need to import manufactured goods, most of which have to come from the developed countries. Values are quoted which show that the economic difficulties of subsistence agriculture countries are accentuated by the fact that many are substantial importers of food, raw materials and fuel, as well as manufactures.

Whatever arguments may be advanced against it, most of the increase in agricultural production will have to come in the developing countries, because they will not be able to increase their manufactured exports much faster than they are now doing; and it is only through increased agricultural production that they can produce enough exports to buy their urgently needed imports.

C. C.

M. R. H.

Acknowledgments

The authors gratefully acknowledge the research assistance which they have received from Mr. Peter Martin. They further wish to acknowledge his help in preparing the manuscript of the present edition for press, which contains much new material and further chapters. In addition, the numerous charts appearing in the book were prepared by Mr. Martin.

CHAPTER I

Food Requirements

'A lifetime of malnutrition and actual hunger is the lot of at least two-thirds of mankind.' This extraordinary mis-statement, which is in fact based on an arithmetical error, is believed by almost everyone, because they have heard it so often; people come to think that any statement which they have heard repeated frequently enough (as Hitler pointed out) must be true. This lack of critical sense however is particularly reprehensible in the prominent men of letters and scientists whose repetition of the statement has done so much to secure its acceptance, men accustomed in their own field to making the most careful and critical judgements, but apparently willing to accept any sort of statement without evidence as soon as they go outside them. Under these circumstances (as Hitler once again pointed out) it is both easier and more profitable to get people to believe a large falsehood than a small one.

Social psychologists may take this almost universal circulation of a statement demonstrably false as yet another example of the unbalanced state of mind of a generation prone to faction and extremism (now perhaps being replaced by a more rational younger generation?).

This statement was first made in 1950 by Lord Boyd Orr,[1] who had just retired from the post of Director-General of FAO (Food and Agriculture Organization of the United Nations). A search for the evidence on which this statement is supposed to have been based provides a most interesting intellectual detective story, and yields an astonishing result. This search was undertaken by M. K. Bennett,[2] Director of the Food Research Institute at Stanford University, and a recognized world authority in this field. In the years since 1954 no reply of any kind to Bennett has been made by Lord Boyd Orr, or by anyone speaking on his behalf.

Bennett carefully scrutinized the text of FAO's 'Second World Food Survey', which was not published until 1952, but which

---

[1] In *Scientific American*, New York, August 1950.
[2] In his book, *The World's Food*, Harper Brothers, New York, 1954.

appears to have contained the material on which Lord Boyd Orr was working. This survey included a statistical table, for which neither sources nor methods of compilation were given, purporting to show average calorie requirements per head of all the nations in the world, and comparing these with supposed data of calorie supplies — data which, for most of the countries in question, have not since been republished, because of serious doubts about their accuracy.

These very dubious calculations (which showed, for instance, that Portugal was seriously undernourished, but not Spain) nevertheless fixed figures for supposed calorie requirements well below FAO's earlier 'estimates'. But Bennett's examination of Lord Boyd Orr's text compels him to conclude — 'one cannot escape the inference' — that he had completely mixed up the statistics (inaccurate in any case) which had been placed before him; and had taken as supposed minimum requirements, below which people would actually suffer hunger, a set of figures of 'targets' for production at some time in the future (which targets FAO itself had in fact already abandoned).

The scientific measurement of man's food requirements is a task which was begun comparatively late in the history of physiology and biochemistry, and is yet far from complete. As in all branches of science, conclusions reached on the subject of human nutrition must be tentative, claiming only to summarize the best knowledge at present available. Many, however, have written on this subject with an extreme dogmatism, which will not stand up to scientific questioning.

Food — leaving aside questions of taste and enjoyment — has to serve a number of physiological purposes, the first and most immediate of which is to maintain bodily activity and warmth. This purpose is served in varying degree by all foods; the contribution to it of various foods can be measured precisely in terms of the single unit of energy, the calorie. (It used to be held that calories could not be regarded as entirely homogeneous as sources of our food energy, but that it was necessary for us to receive a certain proportion of them in the form of fat. This proposition is, however, very doubtful physiologically, although there may be a case for it on the grounds of taste and palatability.)

After the provision of energy, the next most important function of food, if we may use the analogy of the factory, is the performance of 'essential maintenance work'. All the muscles and organs of the body need repair, some almost continuously, others intermittently. The performance of these repairs is not primarily a function of the energy foods, but requires a large and highly differentiated group of chemical compounds, the proteins,[1] which depend upon the element nitrogen, organized into certain chemical structures. We pass tons of plain nitrogen through our lungs every year without being able to use any of it; it is only after some difficult chemical syntheses have been performed for us by plants or animals that we can get it into our diet.

As each muscle or organ of the body is repaired, the worn-out piece is broken up into what might be called 'scrap', large chemical molecules which go back into circulation in the bloodstream, from which they are used again to perform some of the simpler repairing tasks. So well organized is the biochemistry of the human body that each atom of nitrogen, it has been computed, can be used three or four times, in performing successively simpler tasks, until finally it has reached the chemical stage where it cannot be used further, and has to be excreted in the urine.

While not essential (beyond certain very small quantities), animal proteins are for certain purposes more efficacious than vegetable proteins. A person dependent upon vegetable protein may therefore have to consume more in the aggregate.

It has long been known that certain quantities of mineral elements, particularly iron and calcium, were required in the diet, though the precise amount is still debatable. Starting with Hopkins's discoveries in 1906, it has been found since that a great variety of 'accessory food factors' (now called vitamins) are necessary for health, though only required in small quantities. Later it was discovered that man, like plants and animals, requires very small quantities of a great variety of mineral 'trace elements'.

Research work now proceeding also indicates that, out of the great variety of edible fats, a certain limited number (belonging chemically to the 'unsaturated' group) are necessary for health, and that their absence may eventually lead to grave arterial disease; and at the same time it appears (though there is some division of medical opinion on this question) that certain other fats may do positive harm in this respect if consumed in too large quantities, particularly the fats found in the milk and the meat of ruminant animals.

[1] Named after the sea god Proteus, famous in Greek mythology for the bewildering variety of forms which he could assume. The chemist who discovered proteins was a classical scholar.

There is no doubt that shortages of vitamins and minerals in the diet may have serious effects upon health, and may sometimes be fatal. Though it cannot be said with complete finality, it seems however to be generally agreed among those who have studied this subject that such shortages (likewise shortages of unsaturated fats relative to other fats) are not very likely to arise in a primitive nomadic or peasant community whose food, scanty though it be, is nevertheless directly obtained from natural sources. Such peoples consume their cereals or meats in comparatively unprocessed form, and supplement them with a variety of other natural products, such as wild salad plants, seaweeds, snails, fungi and many others. Deficiencies of vitamins and minerals may occur through a more or less accidental event, as when the custom of polishing rice in certain Asian communities led to a spread of beriberi, or among the poorer sections of industrial communities, living upon foods which, by the nature of things, have been selected for their transportability and storability, and which may have been transported, processed and stored in ways which may have caused them to lose some of their mineral and vitamin components.

Another feature of deficiencies of vitamins and minerals is that most of such deficiencies known so far can be easily and cheaply remedied by the mixing of very small quantities of chemical preparations in other foods. However, in view of the possible existence of other such food factors which may not yet have been discovered, it is advisable to continue to include a wide range of variegated natural foods in the diet.

The meat, dairy produce, fruit, etc., which predominate in our diets, while much more agreeable — none of us would like to live on a diet computed to meet physiological minimum requirements, consisting mainly of porridge — nevertheless should be regarded as amenities rather than physiological necessities.

For poor peasant communities therefore our first question should be on the availability of calories and proteins.

FAO was once sardonically described by *The Economist*[1] as 'a permanent institution devoted to proving that there is not enough food in the world'. There is unfortunately a considerable element of truth in this accusation; though it is also true, as *The Economist* went on to admit, that FAO has rendered great service to the world by giving 'much useful practical advice and assistance'

[1] 23 August 1952.

regarding food production and distribution throughout the world.

FAO assembled a number of physiologists to estimate calorie requirements under various circumstances.[1] Their results, however, had to be adjusted, for reasons shown below; on the one hand, they seem to have underestimated the needs of men engaged in active physical work, but on the other hand to have overestimated the needs of children.

FAO's field staff have done valuable work throughout the world; but statements from FAO headquarters on world food requirements appear to come from public relations men rather than from statisticians. A little wary now of claiming that two-thirds of the world is starving, they nevertheless decided that it would give a good send-off to the Freedom from Hunger Campaign to state that half the world was suffering from malnutrition; and to get President Kennedy and the Duke of Edinburgh to repeat the statement for them. When FAO were asked to produce evidence for this statement, there ensued a long delay, during which they had to engage outside expert assistance to see whether they could find any definition of 'malnutrition' which would cover half the world. Eventually they came up with the conclusion (*Third World Food Survey*) that people were malnourished if they did not eat as well as the inhabitants of Britain, i.e. that they must derive at least 20 per cent of their calorie intake from animal products, fruits and vegetables, and fats and oils. No medical evidence whatever was adduced in support of this proposition, apart from the statement 'it is generally agreed' (p. 9). If doctors had been consulted they would probably have replied that the average British diet, far from representing the border-line of malnutrition, is more likely to expose its consumers to the dangers of over-nutrition.

An estimate of the amount of actual hunger in the world, in the sense of lack of the necessary calories, was prepared by FAO's Director of Statistics, Dr. Sukhatme.[2] Making a mathematical analysis of the information available on average food consumption in Asia, and its distribution about the mean, he concluded that 10–15 per cent of the world's population, at any one time, were actually lacking the necessary calories. In the discussion (the 1957 FAO standards of calorie requirements then being taken as given) this conclusion was generally confirmed, subject to the amount of

[1] FAO Nutritional Studies, *Calorie Requirements*, No. 5, 1950; No. 15, 1957.
[2] *Journal of the Royal Statistical Society*, Series A, Part 4, 1961.

hunger in China probably being greater, in the rest of Asia less than he had stated.

Sir Norman Wright, Chief Scientific Adviser to FAO, in an address to the British Association for the Advancement of Science at Cardiff in 1960, stated a very high minimum level of calorie requirements, much above that which FAO's expert committee had concluded in 1957.

But is it not the case, many people may ask, that it is possible to have a diet adequate in calories, or 'starchy foods', but still to suffer serious malnutrition through lack of adequate quantities of the (emotively named) 'protective foods'? When one of the writers was working with Lord Boyd Orr in the 1930s, this was clearly understood. We required 100 g. of fat per head per day, 68 g. of protein, at least half of which must be obtained from animal sources, 0·9 g. of calcium, which must be obtained from dairy products and vegetables, not by enriching flour; and so on. Subsequent advances in physiological science, fortified by the experience of medical administrators during the war years, when they had real famines to deal with, in both Europe and Asia, have caused all these figures to be abandoned; though of course there is always a time lag between scientific and popular knowledge, and a great many people (and governments) are still acting on the out-of-date information. It was Sir Norman Wright who stated, immediately after the war, that while a certain amount of fat undoubtedly made the diet more palatable, there was no physiological need for any fat consumption at all. During subsequent years, as many physiologists and doctors have proclaimed that the consumption of large quantities of fat, particularly in dairy produce and in meat from ruminant animals, and artificially hardened vegetable fats, is positively harmful, the consumption of such fats has already fallen heavily, particularly in the U.S.A.

Regarding protein requirements, FAO attempted to follow up its report on calorie requirements with a similar study for protein. With the best of learning and goodwill, the leading experts in this field were quite unable to come to anything like an agreed conclusion on this extremely complex subject. Some recent work, however,[1] has indicated that true protein needs may not be much more than half of what was previously supposed. If the protein is of good quality, Brock would put adult protein needs at as low as

[1] Professor Waterlow, Jamaica, and Professor Brock, Cape Town; private communications.

½ g./kg. body weight/day (with higher figures for children, rising to a maximum of 3). Other requirements he would also put much lower than previously supposed; calcium at 0·3 instead of 0·8 g./day, and Vitamin C at 25 instead of 75 mg./day. Waterlow puts requirements of *first-class* protein, all in g./kg. body weight/day, for an infant under 6 months at 1·5 (7 g./day in all), falling to 0·5 at puberty, and 0·35 for adults. For pregnancy he adds 0·4 and for lactation 0·2.

As for the supposed requirement that half the protein intake be in the form of protein from animal products (meat, fish, eggs and dairy products), it should have occurred to those who made this statement that there have been and are very large numbers of people in Europe as well as in Asia who, for religious or customary reasons, have been vegetarians throughout their lives, and who have consumed little or no dairy produce either. Several doctors[1] have been able to study some members of a European religious group, the Vegans, whose vegetarianism is so strict that they do not allow themselves to consume dairy products or eggs (or even honey), which are consumed by some vegetarians. Sinclair persuaded a number of members of this group to come to the Radcliffe Hospital in Oxford for a thorough physiological examination, and was unable to find any defects, except for a possibility of a qualification regarding supplies of Vitamin B_{12} which perhaps can be obtained only from animal sources. In treating patients (mainly children) known to be suffering from serious protein deficiency (called *kwashiorkor* in Africa) Brock finds it desirable to feed a diet containing 10 per cent fish meal or 18 per cent dried milk: though the possibility of a purely vegetable diet, even in these cases, is upheld by Scrimshaw in Guatemala, who has fed a diet based on cottonseed (*Incaparina*). Both human and animal tests indicate however that leaf protein is to be preferred to seed protein.

It will be shown below that a community at the lowest level of agricultural productivity, living predominantly on cereals, even on coarse cereals such as barley, maize, sorghum or millet, if they have enough calories, will also receive enough protein; though this is not the case with peoples living predominantly on root crops such as cassava, sweet potatoes, yams, or taro.

An attempt to state baldly the average calorie requirements of a population may lead to serious error. Requirements of calories are

[1] Dr. Hugh Sinclair, Magdalen College, Oxford, and others; results privately communicated.

functionally related (though not directly proportional) to the weight of the body. They are also influenced by environmental factors — less food is required to maintain body temperature in a warm climate than in a cold one. Active physical work increases calorie requirements, as also do pregnancy and lactation in women.

A population with a high proportion of children (as is the case with most of the populations of Asia and Africa) will simply for that reason require less calories *per head* than a population with a greater percentage of adults. The calculations which follow are based on Table 7, page 45, in the 1957 FAO Report on Calorie Requirements, which relates to such a population, with both birth and death rates fairly high, and a high proportion of children, and of pregnant and lactating women in the population.[1]

Before we proceed to allow for the effects of varying body weights however, we should meet the objection sometimes raised, that these varying body weights themselves are the consequence of varying levels of nutrition. Some make this statement in the extreme form that all differences in body weights throughout the world, from a British policeman down to a central African pygmy, have been so caused, and could be removed by a uniform level of good nutrition — though whether this could be done in a single lifetime, or would require several generations, they do not say; and if they have the latter in mind, they are implying the inheritance of acquired characteristics, which most geneticists regard as a scientifically objectionable proposition.

TABLE I.   FOOD CONSUMPTION AND BODY WEIGHTS OF DIFFERENT CASTES IN AN INDIAN VILLAGE

	Average Income Rs./Person/ Month	Food Consumption Calories/ Person/Day	Average Body Weights of Adults (kg.)	
			Male	Female
Fishermen	6½	1580	48	41
Harijans (low caste)	7½	1940	46	40
Miscellaneous castes	10	1960	48	41
Agricultural castes	8	2440	49	42
Brahmins and Vaisyas	18	2720	51	45

[1] This table as printed however shows a weighted average requirement for the whole population of 1954 calories, whereas the components add up to 1953 — presumably a misprint.

A very interesting study of a village near the Mysore coast shows the differences which prevail within an Indian community.[1]

We are dealing here with people who have been living, probably for many generations, at violently contrasted levels of income and of nutrition. Between castes the differences in body weight, though discernible, are small in comparison with the differences in weight which prevail between the regions of the world.

In view of the importance of the subject, it is surprising how little information has been collected (that is to say, statistically reliable information, as opposed to impressions based on a few cases) of average heights and weights, even in advanced countries. Information is available regarding the average heights of army recruits in some countries which have *universal* military service (where selective military service prevails, the figures will clearly be biased above the national average). Thus Italian official figures[2] show a steady rise in the average height of 20-year-old conscripts from 162·4 cm (64 ins.) for men born in 1854 to 167·4 cm. for men born in 1929. The contention that this rise can be explained by improved nutrition does not appear very probable in view of the steadiness of the rise, while substantial improvements in the Italian diet did not occur until comparatively recently. Sir Ronald Fisher held that the rise was due to obscure genetic factors slowly working themselves out. Some doctors have contended that this increase only shows that physical maturity is coming earlier, not that the *final* height of Italian men has changed.

Bennett[3] 'has tried, without much success' to assemble what appears to be reliable information on this subject. His list is headed by Montenegrin tribesmen, who are said to have an average height of 182·5 cm. (6 ft.). United States soldiers going to war in 1941–5 had an average weight of 70 kg. and height of 176·5 cm. — these figures should have been only slightly biased by the exclusion of a small number of rejected men. European men appear to average about 65 kg.: the only figure given for Africans (Sudanese) is 57 kg. Latin Americans appear to average 56 kg. Statistics for admissions to prisons in Canton, which should be accurate, though perhaps slightly biased below the average level of the population, give a weight of 49 kg.; most of eastern Asia appears to be within the range 50–55 kg. The African pygmies, at 40 kg.

[1] Swaminathan and others, *Indian Journal of Medical Research*, November 1960.
[2] *Italian Statistical Abstract* (English version), 1954, p. 111.
[3] In *The World's Food*, p. 209.

weight and 140 cm. (55 ins.) height, are separated by a wide margin from all other peoples.

An early Indian study in 1868[1] showed differences between castes comparable with those given above — though the main object of the study was to draw attention to the small size of the Mulchers, a primitive tribe living in the hill forests of Cochin, and subsisting on jungle products.

For men in their twenties, heights and weights were as follows:

	Average Height (cm.)	Average Weight (kg.)
Brahmins	164	53
Other caste Hindus	165	53
Pariahs (untouchables)	165	50
Tank diggers (menial caste)	165	48
Mulchers	152	43

Burgess and Musa (Malayan Institute for Medical Research 1950) found heights of 161 and 148 cm., weights of 51 and 43 kg. respectively, for adult males and females.

A still earlier study[2] of 'some rude tribes' of southern India, primitive hunting communities in the jungle, however, gave 48 kg. as the average weight of men, 38 kg. of women.

Likewise the Khyeng, a primitive agricultural community in Burma,[3] showed men of an average weight of 50 kg., women of 43 kg.

The Hanunóo, primitive pagan cultivators in the Philippines, classified by ethnologists as 'early Asiatic', show[4] for men an average weight of 48 kg., as with the African pygmies, and height of 153 cm.

Africans on the average appear to be much larger than Asians. McFie in 1956[5] surveyed six villages in Uganda. One village, which shared its country with bands of pygmies, and may have intermarried with them to some extent, had men averaging 52 kg.

[1] G. E. Fryer, 'A Few Words concerning the Hill People inhabiting the Forests of the Cochin State', *Journal of the Royal Asiatic Society*, Vol. 3, 1868.

[2] J. Shortt, 'An Account of some Rude Tribes, the supposed Aborigines of Southern India', *Transactions of the Ethnological Society*, Vol. III, 1865.

[3] G. E. Fryer, 'On the Khyeng People of the Sandoway District', *Journal of the Asiatic Society of Bengal*, Vol. XVIV, Part I, 1875, p. 40.

[4] H. C. Conklin, *Hanunóo Agriculture*, a report on an integral system of shifting cultivation in the Philippines, FAO Forestry Development Paper No. 12, Rome, 1957, p. 10.

[5] J. McFie, Uganda Protectorate Nutrition Surveys, *A Comparison of the Health of Six Villages consuming different types of food*, 1956, p. 23.

(160 cm. height) and women 48 kg. But the other five villages, with widely different food habits, showed men of weight 58–64 kg. (165–175 cm. height) and women 51–59 kg.

We now return to the FAO tables of calorie requirements in different types of community. The adjustments for body weight, and for temperature, have been carefully made, and cannot be improved upon. But the basis from which all the figures are originally calculated is a 'reference man', who appears to be a European weighing 65 kg. and who spends most of his day in a manner rather ambiguously defined, but not apparently working very hard.

As we have some direct information of calorie requirements of Africans in Nigeria working at various tasks[1] it appears preferable to use these as our basis, and also to compute Asian figures from them by adjustments for body weight and temperature; making our own estimates of the proportions of the day devoted to various activities.

It may seem surprising to those not acquainted with Africa, but it appears from all the evidence available (which is discussed in more detail in a later chapter) that the average African at present, subject to periods of intense activity at certain seasons of the year, nevertheless on the average over the year devotes only about four hours per working day to field work. A somewhat higher figure appears to prevail in India, much higher figures in China and the Caribbean. Alternative sets of calculations are given in the table for men doing four hours' field work a day, and for men doing eight hours' field work a day.

The apportionment of time for the rest of the day is admittedly highly conjectural.

Phillips's experiments were carried out on seven subjects, aged 24 to 33, with weights ranging from 43 to 63 kg., averaging 55 kg. His results for calorie requirements while walking, and in sedentary activities, are used direct in the table below. The sleeping figures are deduced from FAO's 'reference man', with adjustment for body weight and temperature.

For field work, Phillips's figures, adjusted by Trowell,[2] range

[1] P. G. Phillips, 'The Metabolic Cost of Common West African Agricultural Activities', *Journal of Tropical Medicine and Hygiene*, London, 1954, Vol. 57, No. 12. Phillips computed calorie requirements per hour from the rate of oxygen consumption as measured by the Douglas bag.
[2] H. C. Trowell, 'Calorie and Protein Requirements of Adult Male Africans', *East African Medical Journal*, May 1955, Vol. 32, No. 5, p. 156.

from 213 calories/hour for carrying a log of 20 kg., to 269 for grass cutting, 274 for hoeing, the principal agricultural activity of Africans, 360 for sawing, 372 for bush clearing, and 504 for tree felling. It is well known, however, that men engaged in extremely arduous tasks such as the latter cannot work continuously. The FAO calorie report quotes (page 59) an estimate by Lehmann to the effect that men engaged in such work, if they are to preserve their health, must be allowed rest pauses, which bring their overall average for calorie consumption down to 300 per hour. Converting to African body weight, and reducing slightly, we take a figure of 250 calories/hour for requirements while working.

Experiments in India[1] showed that men in their 20's doing hard labouring work in a Southern Indian textile mill, of average body weight 47 kilograms, used energy at the rate of 203 calories/hour, averaged over an 8-hour shift. This is considerably harder work than is presumed for the F.A.O. 'Reference Man'. The total requirements of these Indian labourers, including basic metabolism and non-work activities, were put at 3050 calories/day. As against this, a Japanese farmer[2] weighing 52 kilos, and doing 7½ hours farm work per day, has his needs put at only 2500. This figure, for a larger-bodied man in a colder climate, is so much lower than Banerjea's that one may conclude that it has been taken from the F.A.O. Reference Scale — which is based on a European Reference Man of somewhat sedentary habits, and is inadequate for men doing prolonged hard work. Results obtained by Fox[3] in 1950 show only 165 calories/man hour equivalent for farm work (including the walk to and from the plots).

Walking was found to require 145 calories/hour for men, 126 for women. Various farm tasks were analysed, and found to call for energy expenditure at rates between 95 and 315 calories/hour for men (less for women, in the body weight proportion).

Phillips's and Trowell's results give higher figures, for men

[1] Banerjea and others, *Indian Journal of Medical Research*, 1959, Vol. 47, p. 657.
[2] Watanabe, *Shikoku Acta Medica*, Vol. 15 (in Japanese — quoted by MacArthur).
[3] *A Study of Energy Expenditure of Africans Engaged in Various Rural Activities*, London University Ph.D. Thesis. Averaged over the year, per head of the whole village population, 222 calories/day (plus 46 calories/day for remunerative work other than on their own farms). Expressed per head of the adult male equivalent of the working population (taking women as 55/63 of men, in accordance with their relative weights) this becomes 365 calories/day/man equivalent. The farm work done by the men, including the walk to and from the plots, was only 1·6 hours per day, averaged over the year; by the women 2·95 hours.

averaging 55 kilograms weight, of 184 calories/hour for walking, and 213–504 for various farm tasks. Fox however points out that the performance of heavy farm tasks was interspersed by considerable periods of rest, or performance of light tasks.

Very much higher figures have been estimated for the rate of calorie utilization in very short periods, by men doing heavy logging.[1] The rate of calorie consumption *per minute* is given at 16·5 for Swedish and 9·8–11·7 for Indian loggers. Presumably these rates can only be maintained for short periods. It is interesting to notice, however, that the energy output was almost exactly proportionate to the relative body weights, of 72 kilograms for the Swedes and 45–50 for the Indians. (Heights were 175 centimetres and 154–7 centimetres respectively.)

The adjustment of FAO's European 'reference man' to African conditions gives a requirement of 2707 calories/day; whereas our own calculations direct from African data raise this figure to 2820, even at the present rate of working, or 3402 if an eight-hour day is to be worked. These latter figures form the basis for the calculations for the other regions shown in the table.

An attempt was made also to estimate the way in which the average African woman spent her day, and consequently her calorie requirements. Even after allowing however for the amount of field work, and heavy housework such as pounding grain and carrying water, done by the African woman, the result came out very little different from that obtained by starting with the European 'reference woman', and converting for African body weight

TABLE II. CALORIE REQUIREMENTS OF MEN AGED 20–29, CENTRAL AFRICA

	Hrs/day	Cal./hour	Cal./day	Hrs/day	Cal./hour	Cal./day
[a]Field work	4	250	1000	8	250	2000
Other active work and recreation (e.g. housebuilding, dancing)	1	250	250	1	250	250
Walking	2	184	368	1	184	184
Sedentary activities	9	78	702	6	78	468
Sleeping	8	62½	500	8	62½	500
Total			2820			3402

[a] Based on Trowell-Phillips results.

[1] Hansson, Lindholm and Birath, *Men and Tools in Indian Logging Operations*, Skogshögskolan, Stockholm, 1966.

and temperature. Apparently the FAO physiologists credited the
European woman with a good deal of heavy housework; at any
rate she cleans and manages a much larger house than the African
woman.

The estimate of only five hours *active* work per day in the first
column of Table II may be considered low. But it is high in comparison with one detailed estimate available.[1] In the region of
Adamaoua in Cameroun, a good rainfall area with some livestock
and apparently enjoying a good mixed diet, men worked on the
average 4·75 hours/day, of which 2·1 were in agriculture, varying
with the season. Working hours for women totalled 6·1 for the
Adamaoua District and 3·75 for the town of N'Gaoundéré, the
former including 0·7 and the latter 0·25 for water carrying.

Burgess and Musa,[2] studying Malay and Southern Indian
immigrant groups in peasant farming, fishing, and wage earning
on a rubber estate, show in the following table the fundamental
difference in the pattern of physical activity of both men and
women in the wage economy.

Included in the recorded hours of physical activity for women
are the tasks of pounding rice and of carrying water, which have
been classified as moderate work. Transplanting of seedlings from
the nursery to the rice field was done by women, and constituted
their main activity in farming. Women played a more important

TABLE III. RECORDED HOURS OF PHYSICAL ACTIVITY OF ADULTS IN DIFFERENT MALAY COMMUNITIES

Group	Heavy (Hrs.) M	F	Moderate (Hrs.) M	F	Light (Hrs.) M	F	Total Hours M	F
Smallholders	1·3	0·5	1·2	2·5	0·8	0·1	3·3	3·0
Fishing Community	3·2	—	0·3	2·6	0·5	2·6	4·0	5·2
Labour Group	3·8	3·0	1·3	3·7	2·3	0·3	7·5	7·1

M = Males   F = Females

[1] Winter, *Le Niveau de Vie des Populations de l'Adamaoua*, République
Fédérale de Cameroun, Ministère de l'Économie Nationale.

[2] R. C. Burgess and Laidin Bin Alang Musa, *A Report on the State of Health,
the Diet and the Economic Conditions of Groups of People in the Lower Income
Levels in Malaya*, Institute for Medical Research Report No. 13, Federation of
Malaya, 1950.

part in the wage earning group than in either of the other two groups earning over a third of the total income. The recorded hours show that they assisted the men tapping rubber on a hilly estate which was classified as heavy work.

Both in the smallholding and fishing groups, the men were much less active than in the wage earning group. The main farming activity was the preparation of the rice fields, and for fishermen the very heavy work of rowing and handling large nets which Burgess and Musa classified simply as heavy because frequent intervals of short rest were required.

In some of the remoter parts of Africa we hear of men devoting less than 1000 hours/year to agricultural work. Baldwin[1] sampled two cocoa-farming villages in northwest Nigeria and found that the average number of working hours per adult working male per year were 997 and 1327 respectively. These represented 660 and 800 man-hours/ha./year, a level of labour input which for marginal productivity is still high. Anne Martin[2] found that in the comparatively economically advanced region of Calabar in Southern Nigeria men averaged throughout the year only 4 hours/day agricultural work. Platt[3] found in Nyasaland in 1938 that the average amount of land cultivated in three villages was only 1·1 ha./family. Hours/year ranged from 400–900 for men, 580–760 for women, and 67–80 for children.

One of the authors found[4] in Gambia in 1949 that adult men and women engaged in agriculture averaged only 855 hours/year (133 days) in agricultural work. In the village of Warwar in the Cameroun in 1953, a subsistence economy into which cash cropping was just being introduced, Refisch found[5] that for most of the year the men averaged 4, the women 5 hours/day agricultural work; but for some three months each year both sexes averaged 10 hours/day.

For the Toupourri tribe in North Cameroun, Guillard[6] gives labour days per year spent on other work as well as work in the fields.

[1] K. D. S. Baldwin, *The Niger Agricultural Project*, Blackwell, Oxford, 1957.
[2] A. Martin, *The Oil Palm Economy of the Ibibio Farmer*, Ibadan University Press, 1956.
[3] B. S. Platt, *Nutrition Survey*, Colonial Office Library (Mimeographed).
[4] M. R. Haswell, *Economics of Agriculture in a Savannah Village*, Colonial Research Studies No. 8, 1953; and privately communicated.
[5] University of London M.A. thesis in Anthropology (available in Colonial Office library).
[6] J. Guillard, 'Essai de mesure de l'activité du paysan africain: le Toupourri', *Agronomie Tropicale*, Vol. XIII, No. 4, Paris, July–August 1958.

Average Number of Days Spent

	Men	Women
Work in the fields	106	82
Other work	88	107
Free time	161	165
Sickness	10	11

Gourou[1] also gives higher figures for the Zandé, in the north-east of Congo (Kinshasa), of 6·1 hours/day (including 2·4 agriculture) for the married men, 8·5 (including 3·8 agriculture) for the married women.

While our estimate of the calorie requirements of an able-bodied man under African conditions comes out somewhat higher than the result based on the FAO scale, we have to conclude that the FAO scale requirements for children, and in consequence their estimates for the whole population, have been placed considerably too high. Fox's estimate in Africa is very much lower.

TABLE IV. CHILDREN'S CALORIE REQUIREMENTS PER DAY

FAO Reference Scale			Fox (Africa)		
Age	Male	Female	Age	Male	Female
0–1	1120		0–2	700	600
1–3	1300		3–5	808	751
4–6	1700		6–10	1072	918
7–9	2100		11–15	1262	1249
10–12	2500	2400	16–20	1526	1296
13–15	3100	2600			
16–19	3600	2400			

The principal reason for concluding that the lower scale must be preferred is a recent study by MacArthur[2] which showed, amongst other things, that the application of the FAO scales to Japan, a comparatively high income country, would indicate that about a third of the Japanese were hungry (in the full sense of the word, receiving inadequate calories). FAO have based some of their principal conclusions on work done by Cullumbine in Ceylon; MacArthur pointed out, what had not been generally understood before, that a number of his results were from high income families, who were consuming of their own choice, and living healthy and active lives on diets considerably below the FAO scale.

[1] *Annuaire du College de France*, 1968–9.
[2] *Journal of the Royal Statistical Society* Pt. 3, 1964.

TABLE V. CALORIE REQUIREMENTS PER DAY

	Assumed body weights of adults kg.	Average temperature C°	Requirements per man aged 20-29		Requirements[b] per head of whole population					Total	
			Sedentary	Net[a] addition each hour/day worked	Children[c]	Women	Men			Men working 4 hour day	Men working 8 hour day
							Sedentary	Net addition each hour/day worked			
Central Africa	57½	25	2026	172	400	526	646	55		1792	2012
India, S.E. Asia	50	25	1829	155	400	447	582	49		1625	1821
Southern China	50	20	1880	159	411	459	599	51		1673	1877
Northern China	55	10	1967	167	433	528	626	53		1799	2011

[a] i.e. 250 cals/hr working, less 78 cals/hr which would have been consumed in sedentary occupation.

[b] Different sections of the population weighted according to their relative numbers, so that the figures can be summed directly to give average requirements per head of whole population.

[c] FAO 'Reference Scale' reduced by 45 per cent. Requirements adjusted for temperature, not body weight.

We can also draw some conclusions from the evidence for China. On the FAO scale, assuming that most of the men are actively engaged in physical work, with Chinese climates and body weights, calorie requirements for the whole population will range from 2200 calories/person/day in the south to nearly 2400 in the north. A series of careful estimates[1] indicate that average calorie intakes in China have been below 2000 ever since 1959, and in the worst period, about 1961–2, were well below 1800. These are very unsatisfactory diets, even on the reduced scale proposed below; if the FAO scales are correct, there must have been a heavy fall in the Chinese population since 1959.

Estimates of calorie requirements were also made, as shown in the table, for India and south-east Asia — regions which include a large proportion of all the world's subsistence cultivators. The average body weights however had to be fairly arbitrarily assumed. The average temperatures also were only approximately estimated from examination of the maps of isotherms.

We have considerable details about food consumption in pre-Communist China. Buck[2] paid over 1,000 trained men each to spend a year in his native village, where he understood the dialect and customs, compiling full information on all agricultural operations. In addition, detailed surveys of food consumption were made in 136 representative villages, showing an average of 2533 calories/person/day. This was subject to considerable regional differences, falling to 2240 in the winter wheat-millet growing area. There were also very marked differences between villages, even in the more prosperous areas. Some 30 per cent of the villages in Northern China, and 7 per cent in Southern China, were below minimum requirements, while some villages on the other hand were consuming food at a rate more than twice minimum requirements. These marked differences between villages indicate, amongst other things, the lack of transport, and also the great variability of harvests. One can only hope that it is not the same villages which are hungry year by year.

For Communist China, the best available information indicates that, except for the single year 1958, when the harvest was unusually good, food consumption per head has been substantially below the level of the 1930s.

In the *Yearbook of Food and Agricultural Statistics* published by

[1] *China Quarterly*, various dates 1961–3.
[2] *Land Utilization in China*, Nanking, 1937.

FAO a table is given showing the protein and calorie content of the average diets of certain countries. Contrary to the usual trend, the countries for which information is now published constitute a much shorter list than that which was published a few years ago; this is a tacit admission that much of the previous information was highly inaccurate. It is necessary to mention this, because many readers may still have some of the earlier published figures, now abandoned, in their minds. For instance, in the early 1950s some very low figures were quoted of Indian grain output and calorie supply per head, and many people still think in terms of these figures. During this period, however, when there was a widespread prevalence, or at any rate threat, of compulsory state purchase of grain, there was every inducement for the cultivator to understate his grain output, so as to avoid compulsory purchase, to leave himself some grain for sale on the black market, or possibly even to qualify for a ration himself. The official estimates were almost certainly understated. In 1947 one of the writers had a most illuminating conversation on this subject with Gandhi, who was very interested in economics. He pointed out what was happening, and strongly criticized Nehru's policy. Drop rationing and price control, he said, and every Indian would have to work harder, which he could well do. Nobody but Gandhi would have been so frank on this subject.

On the other hand, the willingness of the Indian Government over this period to devote foreign exchange, which was badly needed for other purposes, to the purchase of grain, shows that it considered the situation dangerous.

Most of the countries for which information is now published by FAO are economically advanced countries in which there is no question of a lack of calories. Among the low figures entered is one of 2210 calories for Japanese consumption, which might at first sight appear to be barely adequate. In Japan, however, people willingly devote a substantial proportion of their food expenditure to fish, fruit, vegetables and other products whose calorific return is comparatively low per unit of money spent; they would not do this if they were hungry. The average Japanese body weight is still low (though now found among school children to be rising rapidly)[1]

---

[1] The Japanese Education Ministry, after checking 5 million students, reported that 12-year-old boys and girls were ½ in. taller and 2 lb. heavier than those of the same age in 1936. The average Japanese of 12 is now 4 ft. 8 in. tall and weighs 75 lb. The Ministry attributed the growth to improved diet (*New York Times*, 24 June 1957).

B

and, for a temperature which can be taken as intermediate between that of northern China and southern China, a diet of this calorific value would appear to be adequate. A figure for Japan of 2310 was found in a study by the United States Department of Agriculture (see below).

The figure now given by FAO for India is 1950 calories per head (2050 in the U.S. Department of Agriculture study). Though Indian agricultural statistics are improving, no one well acquainted with the subject could say that they are yet precise. Good field studies in India are still scarce. Recently an enquiry was started, under international auspices, with a view to making fully detailed records of food production and consumption in certain selected villages.[1] Surveys were made in twelve villages, spread over areas of four different soil types, which showed the following average consumption of calories per head per day:

Well-drained loam with irrigation	2141
Stiff black clay	2018
Poorly drained clay	2005
Poor sandy soil	1853

On the basis of a four-hour working day, these all left some margin to spare: in the poorest village however supplies were barely adequate for an eight-hour working day.

Another study on average calorie intake throughout Asia, Africa and Latin America was recently completed by the United States Department of Agriculture.[2] In a number of cases they come out with figures significantly higher than those of FAO. In one calculation they find a large number of countries below what they state to be the minimum level of calorie requirements: but this was after allowing, not only for milling and storage losses of grain, but also for an assumed further 15 per cent wastage in consumption. It does not seem reasonable to assume that really hungry people would waste so much food.

Their results may be classified as follows (omitting countries which are clearly nowhere near the bread line):

---

[1] L. D. Stamp, *Geographical Review*, New York, January 1958, quoting work by Shafi, referring to villages in the eastern part of the state of Uttar Pradesh, in the years 1953 to 1956.

[2] U.S.D.A., FAS-M 101, 104, 108, Parts II, III and IV. *Food Balances in Foreign Countries*, Washington, 1960–61.

TABLE VI. AVERAGE CALORIE INTAKE — AFRICA, ASIA, LATIN AMERICA

AFRICA (standard 1792 on basis of 4-hour day)

Tunisia	2170	Rest of former French West Africa	2450
Tanzania	2175	Cameroun	2470
Libya	2180	Morocco	2480
Angola	2215	Rhodesia-Nyasaland	2500
Algeria	2230	Liberia	2540
Kenya	2240	Former French Equatorial Africa	2575
Ethiopia	2295	Ghana	2605
Sudan	2295	Togo	2645
Egypt	2340	Congo	2650
Guinea	2400	Nigeria	2680

ASIA (standard 1625 on basis of 4-hour day)

Pakistan	2030	Jordan	2085
South Korea	2040	Indonesia	2125
Iran	2040	Philippines	2145
India	2050	Burma	2150
Ceylon	2060	Thailand	2185

(standard 1821 on basis of 8-hour day)

Syria	2225	Japan	2310
Iraq	2255	Lebanon	2415
Malaya	2290	Taiwan	2430

LATIN AMERICA (assumed standard 1850)

Haiti	1875	Guatemala	2175
Bolivia	1880	Honduras	2190
Ecuador	1935	Colombia	2225
Dominican Republic	1950	Venezuela	2255
El Salvador	1975	Paraguay	2355
Nicaragua	1985	Panama	2370
Peru	2040	Costa Rica	2555

The African (except for Tunisia) and Asian figures look probable; but the Latin American figures look improbably low.

If people's food falls short of their calorie requirements it does not follow that they die. They may indeed live for years on end on an inadequate diet. Resistance to many kinds of illness however is indubitably weakened, and both sickness and mortality are much greater than they would be if the community were better fed. The FAO experts describe what happens in such a community — 'The whole manner of life is adapted to an insufficient supply of calories, with results that are socially undesirable: lack of drive and initiative; avoidance of physical and mental effort; excessive rest.'

We can recognize these symptoms in some present and past communities. Quite a widespread phenomenon is 'pre-harvest hunger'. The variations of food intake, and of the changes in body weight which accompany them, were measured by Culwick[1] in a dietary survey among the Zande of the south-western Sudan. Calorie intake curves and weight trends were high after the main harvest, declining towards the end of the dry season, and falling sharply at the beginning of the new agricultural season.

TABLE VII.   ZANDE CALORIE INTAKE CURVES AND
WEIGHT TRENDS

	Average Body Weight		Average Calorie Intake	Average Protein Intake
	men kg.	women kg.	cals./head/day	g./head/day
First harvest	54·5	49·5	2,275	41
Main harvest	56·5	49·0	2,775	60
Dry season	57·5	50·5	2,400	56
Beginning of new agricultural season	56·0	50·5	1,925	33
Mean heights cm.	167·5	157·5		

The community were obviously eating above requirements at certain seasons, though at lowest levels of intake they appear to have received an inadequate supply of calories. On the other hand, the extensive system of axe and hoe agriculture practised by this peasant group left them access to a wide range of wild products. It is well known that nutritional surveys have not taken account of snacks and nibblings apart from main meals. Children penetrate far into the bush in search of wild fruits, and men and women certainly consume wild products while at work clearing food farms. Time spent foraging may in fact constitute part of the reason for the low number of hours actually spent on clearing.

In general people were gaining weight during the latter half of the rainy season, from the maize harvest onwards, and losing during the dry season, when qualitative observations showed that their feeding was ragged and haphazard. Culwick emphasizes that the overall pattern hides a great deal of individual variation, and that individual circumstances readily overrode the general seasonal trend. She saw people 'put on years in age or go haggard in a few

[1] G. M. Culwick, *A Dietary Survey among the Zande of the South-western Sudan*, Ministry of Agriculture, Sudan Government, 1950.

weeks, and some months later they would hardly be recognizable as they shed their apparent years, rounded out again in body and restored their usual manner of living'. Signs of stress were reflected in not bothering, or not being able, to prepare and cook proper meals, and the general impression was one of a precariously maintained balance between a state of relative wellbeing and states of stress, complex in both origin and manifestation. Abbott, who carried out a clinical survey of Culwick's group, draws attention to the dearth of knowledge of African dietary requirements, and states that due cognizance must be taken of the parasites which the African supports.

Arising out of a study of growth and mortality in children in an African village, McGregor[1] came to the conclusion that infectious disease and inadequate maternal care are probably the major factors contributing to high mortality and impaired growth in young children, and that malnutrition seems to be more often secondary to disease than primary.

A survey made in 1950 showed that malaria was hyperendemic, the crude parasite rate for all ages being 54·7 per cent; that approximately 36 per cent and 33 per cent of villagers were carriers of microfilariae of *wuchereria bancrofti* and *anopheles perstans* respectively; that 2·5 per cent of the population were suffering from trypanosomiasis; and that hookworm and ascaris infections abounded. Against this background of varied and heavy parasitization there was a recurrent shortage of harvested cereals, although inadequate supplies were reinforced by extensive collection of bush fruits, nuts, berries, and green leaves.

In India, faecal-borne illnesses are the most formidable problems, now that the incidence of malaria has been greatly reduced by eradication programmes. Intestinal infestation by worms is widespread, of which hookworm is the most important. Intestinal parasites offer a strong competition to the human body in metabolizing food. The economic loss from deaths occuring from faecal-borne diseases, as well as from the illnesses with attendant disability and lowered productivity, continues to be serious in rural India.

Preoccupation of women with their crops was given as the reason for a fall in calorie intake at certain times of the year in Northern Rhodesia by Thomson,[2] who studied a group of cultivating families.

[1] I. A. McGregor, 'Growth and Mortality in Children in an African Village', *British Medical Journal*, 23 December 1961.
[2] B. P. Thomson, *Two Studies in African Nutrition*, Rhodes-Livingstone Paper No. 24, Manchester University Press, 1954, pp. 49, 51.

Although grain may be plentiful, when they were engaged on certain agricultural operations the women only returned to the village in the evening to cook. She observed, however, that the men were probably getting a fairly adequate diet, and that the group that suffered most was the women, though she admits that 'cook's titbits' taken from the pot may have been considerable. Typical of such communities is the heavy dependence on a starchy staple. She states a strong case for higher intakes of animal foods, since they contain a better ratio of essential amino acids than those derived from vegetable sources. Even in Japan however the weight of meat, eggs and milk in the diet of farm families is small, amounting to only 4 per cent of their total protein intake. Japanese farmers are heavy eaters with 80 per cent of their total calorie intake coming from cereals, mainly rice. Intake of proteins averages about 63 g./day, almost entirely from vegetable sources.

In Africa, maldistribution may arise with younger members of the family, and lactating women, who are eating the same low-protein high-calorie food, but are unable to do so in sufficient quantity to meet their protein requirements.

Greater dangers arise when primitive cultivators change from one staple to another. Gourou[1] warns that protein shortages increase with the spread of manioc cultivation (also known as cassava, or tapioca, and which is poorer in protein than yam or millet). Pulses can however be grown on relatively dry and infertile soils, which not only increase the fertility of the soil, but have a high protein content and are good sources of minerals and vitamins of the B group. Their proteins supplement rice proteins, and a greater intake of pulses is easier to bring about than an increase in the consumption of meat, milk or eggs.

One supposed consequence of inadequate feeding can be denied categorically, namely the fantastic claim by De Castro that it increases fertility. The evidence for underfeeding increasing fertility in animals which De Castro adduces is uncertain enough: his supposed evidence for this happening among humans is ridiculous. Such evidence as we have[2] indicates that the natural fertility (when not artificially impeded) of Europeans is higher than that of Asians and Africans.

De Castro finds a good deal of hunger in his own country, Brazil,

---

[1] P. Gourou, *The Tropical World*, 3rd ed. 1961, p.74.
[2] See Sauvy, *Population*, October-December 1953, on Japanese fertility; and W. Brass, *The estimation of total fertility rates from data for primitive communities*, World Population Conference 1954, on African fertility.

which has now been responsible for running its own affairs for a very long time; nevertheless, he tries to prove that anything wrong in Brazil is still the result of 'colonialism'. He makes no proposals for agricultural reforms, apart from the adoption of Lysenko's ideas on genetics, which he greatly favours; so far as he proposes anything, it seems to be greater reliance upon primitive rather than on commercial agriculture.

In any plans for remedying the considerable actual hunger, and widespread low diets with threat of hunger, which prevail in the world, it must be the improvement of agriculture in the poorer communities (representing a preponderant proportion of the earth's inhabitants) which principally receives attention.

Some readers may be disappointed. Are there no plans, they may ask, for producing even more food in the countries which already find their abundant productivity embarrassing — United States, Canada, Australasia, possibly Western Europe — and distributing it among the poorer communities?

Such plans have indeed been discussed. The difficulties which they will encounter will not be predominantly economic, however, but of a diplomatic and political nature. The present government of China, for instance, when approached by the International Red Cross — the most non-political approach possible — with an offer of gifts of food, promptly denied that anyone was short of food in China. India has accepted some food from the United States — but has almost made a favour of doing so. With Asia and Africa as they are now, full of newly-formed countries neurotically pre-occupied with the concept of 'independence', we must expect that most governments will be unwilling to admit that there is anything wrong with their food supply, or to accept gifts of food.

And, moreover, an economic problem arises too, in respect of the really poor and backward communities, who live a great distance away from railways, roads, shops, government offices and the like. These people live perforce almost entirely on food which they can produce in their own villages; and will have to continue to do so until methods of transport and distribution are greatly improved. An attempt to feed them on imported food, generously donated by governments at the other end of the world, would raise very serious transport and distribution problems. Lacking other means of transport, loads of food would have to be carried for long distances on men's heads.

In any case, prudent statesmen, both in the giving and in the receiving countries, recognize that such gifts of food, even when they can be organized, should be regarded only as a strictly temporary measure. They must not be allowed in any way to delay the urgent task of helping the peoples of the poorer countries to produce more food for themselves (or, in a few cases, other products which they can exchange for food in the world market). A state of dermanent dependence is not desired by either party.

CHAPTER II

Pre-Agricultural Man

Biologists used to tell us that the human race has been in existence on this earth for half a million years. More recently, they have been telling us that remains of what were obviously genuine humans can be dated a million years back — though how the dating is done is not precisely explained, and indeed biologists seem so casual over the whole matter that one sometimes wonders whether they have even got the right number of zeroes.

Whether its duration has been a million or half a million years, it remains true that by far the greatest part of the whole time which the human race has spent on this earth — though the number of people living in those distant aeons was far, far smaller than the number living now — has been passed in communities living solely by hunting, fishing and the gathering of wild products, without any knowledge of, or need for agriculture: and a few such communities survive to this day.

We should not idealize primitive life, the life of the 'noble savage', which made such an appeal to jaded eighteenth-century aristocrats and literary men (making up most of their facts to please themselves, because they were almost entirely lacking in knowledge about the actual life of such peoples). But we need not go to the other extreme, and commiserate unduly with our ancestors for the life which they lived — least of all should we believe the wild fictions about cave men, which are still written up as scientific knowledge for children's textbooks. Conditions of primitive hunting peoples must not be judged, wrote Carl Sauer,[1] 'from their modern survivors, now restricted to the most meagre regions of the earth, such as the interior of Australia, the American Great Basin, and the Arctic tundra and taiga. The areas of early occupation were abounding in food.'

We should therefore imagine our ancestors living in warm forest and grasslands where game, fuel and water were abundant. It was perhaps only in comparatively recent times that they found such

[1] *Geographical Review*, January 1947, Vol. IV, p. 263.

land pre-empted, by agricultural communities or by other hunters, and were compelled to make their homes in the colder and more arid regions of the world. It is true that their lives were not long — the evidence of the burial grounds shows that a man of forty was a rarity in the palaeolithic world — but a life in the open air, subsisting entirely on game and fish caught by oneself, must have been very attractive to able-bodied young men — at any rate if we judge from the large sums which wealthy men are willing to spend in order to enjoy a few days' fishing or shooting in remote surroundings, in the nearest replica of primitive conditions which it is possible to create at the present time.

With high mortality rates, however, due to accidents in the hunting field, and the inability of such communities to give any support to ill or infirm people, the rate of population growth was almost negligibly slow — had it not been, the world would have passed through the hunting and fishing stage, and reached the agricultural stage, far quicker than it in fact did.

Not long ago, archaeologists were unable to reach, within very wide limits, any valid conclusions about the places and times of the origin of agriculture. The discovery of the method of radio-carbon dating for archaeological remains however has thrown a flood of light on this problem during recent years. The evidence, conveniently summarized by Cipolla,[1] shows that the oldest known agricultural settlement was where some springs of water provide natural irrigation for the hot dry land at Jericho, dated about 7000 B.C. Although no doubt there are many further discoveries yet in store, nevertheless judging from the way in which subsequent sites appear to spread outwards from it, it is quite possible that there is something in the traditional belief that the Middle East was the original cradle of civilization. Within 500 years of the original known agricultural settlement in Jericho, agriculture was being practised in Kurdistan. Within a little more than another 500 years pastoralists were grazing domestic animals on the southern shore of the Caspian Sea. The oldest agriculture in the Nile valley appears to have been about 4500 B.C. By 3300 B.C. agriculture had spread to what is now the extremely arid area of Baluchistan (Western Pakistan). But as early as 3650 B.C. agriculture had reached the western hemisphere, and maize was being grown in New Mexico. Whether this knowledge was brought by sea travellers across the Pacific, or by nomads crossing the Bering Strait, or was indepen-

[1] C. M. Cipolla, *The Economic History of World Population*, Penguin, 1962.

dently discovered, is not known. By 2200 B.C. maize growing was being practised in Peru. By 3000 B.C. agriculture had penetrated Africa as far south as Kenya.

The requirements of living space of pre-agricultural man may be considerable. For a community living entirely by hunting, fishing, and the gathering of any wild fruits or roots which may be going, we must expect to record population densities, not in persons per sq. km., but in sq. km. per person. Nougier[1] estimated that the inhabitants of Australia before the coming of white settlers had about 30 sq. km. per head to hunt over,[2] and it was generally agreed that they did not have much to spare.

In Tasmania, with good rainfall and abundant fishing, in comparison with the Australian mainland, the native population (still at the palaeolithic stage of culture at the arrival of the white man) was estimated[3] at 4000, i.e. 17 sq. km./person. A most interesting account[4] of the South Island of New Zealand shows that about the thirteenth century, when the country was inhabited by the Moriori, and the moa (large flightless birds) were there for them to hunt, population density was 10–15 sq. km./person: but by the eighteenth century, after the moa had been exterminated by the hunters, and the Moriori had been exterminated by the Maori invaders, density was down to a figure of over 30 sq. km./person.

In a cold climate the Eskimos and Indians of north-western Canada now require 140 sq. km. per head. Grahame Clark[5] thinks that space requirements per man range from 80 to 500 sq. km. per head in sub-arctic lands. Rätzel[6] quotes a figure between 40 and 90 sq. km. for temperate climates. Childe[7] gave a figure distinctly higher than Nougier's (over 40 sq. km.) for land requirements per head of the Australian aborigines; but points out that this figure may fall in better provided regions, to 20–25 on the American prairies and as low as 10 in the warm humid climate of the Pacific coast of North America. Under particularly favourable conditions, as on the shores of rivers which enjoy a regular run of salmon, the

---

[1] *Population*, Paris, April–June 1954.

[2] It is a mistake to imagine, as is commonly supposed, that the whole interior of Australia is desert. The area of true desert is very limited. A very large part of the country is semi-arid, which is quite a different thing. Such country will support fairly abundant game.

[3] Krzywicki, *Primitive Society and its Vital Statistics*, p. 59.

[4] Cumberland, *Geographical Review*, April 1962.

[5] Grahame Clark, *Archaeology and Society*, 2nd ed., London, 1947.

[6] Quoted by Taylor, *Canadian Journal of Economics and Political Science*, August 1950.

[7] G. Childe, *What Happened in History*, Penguin, 1954.

figure may fall to 1·5. Sauer also estimates less than 2½ sq. km./ person as the potentiality of the best lands occupied by primitive peoples. Under these conditions, he thinks, they are likely to combine in groups of 6 to 12 families to hunt and collect over an area of 80 to 100 sq. km. (i.e. a radius of about 5 km.) with a permanent central camp site; and so we have the beginnings of civilization. This estimate of 5 km. radius is only for the best hunting and fishing land; if we assume a community of 50 people and an average space requirement of 10 sq. km./person, the radius of the settlement becomes 12½ km. The formation of a settlement has to be, Sauer pointed out, a careful economic decision; to try to organize hunting over too great an area involves an uneconomic amount of travelling to and from the camp site.

It was under such conditions, Childe thought, that the people of the Magdalenian period were living in Europe, originally in the open air: they took to caves when the climate suddenly became colder. It appears that they were able to organize quite an active social life; at any rate they left us some magnificent paintings.

Primitive agriculture (which may have come before the domestication of animals) reduces space requirements to something between 1 and 5 sq. km./person, according to Rätzel. With the domestication of animals this figure falls to ½. Allan[1] estimates the areas required, in sq. km./person, by various pastoral tribes in East Africa at 1·3 for the Masai in Tanganyika, 1·1 for the Fulani, 0·8 for the Turkana, 0·6 for the Masai in Kenya, and 0·5 for the Somalis. He also quotes a mixed economy, the Baggara, who are occupying 1 sq. km. per person. However by the time people are living in settled villages, and really taking agriculture seriously, the figure may go on falling down to 0·15. Gourou[2] gives a striking illustration of this in the case of two tribes living side by side, in land of similar climate, in South Eastern Angola. The Chokwe, growing cassava, occupy 0·05–0·08 sq. km./person (although only 1/25th of their land is actually harvested in any one year, plots being rotated on a three-year cycle). The neighbouring Handa occupy ten times as much land, grazing 10 cattle to the sq. km., and requiring 50 cattle to provide for the average family of 6–10 persons. A little millet is also grown by the women. But there is a moral to this tale. Pastoral life was regarded as more prestigious,

---

[1] *The African Husbandman*, p. 309.
[2] *Impact*, 1964, No. 1.

and the Chokwe began copying the Handa, and occupying much larger areas of land.

Domestication of animals — in this case the reindeer — greatly improves the population-carrying capacity of the Arctic too. Soviet scientists[1] have estimated that one reindeer can live on the grazing from 0·6 to 1 sq. km., so that a tribe living on the milk and meat of reindeer, and on fish, should only require a few sq. km. per person.

The largest Neolithic village found anywhere, Cipolla points out, had only three to four hundred inhabitants. Assuming 10 km. as the radius over which people are able to travel for food-producing activities (and this is a high assumption), this gives the community an area of 314 sq. km. for this purpose, a little below 1 sq. km./person. We can see therefore that communities even of this size, which seems very small to us, are only possible when the agricultural arts have advanced beyond the most primitive stage, and probably include the domestication of animals.

Nougier drew his conclusions from burial grounds, and from the ratio between palaeolithic and neolithic remains. The palaeolithic inhabitants of France were quite comfortably off with 55 sq. km. of space per head (i.e. only 10,000 population for the whole of France). Neolithic France however, as early as 2000 B.C., still using stone implements, though more skilfully shaped than those of the palaeolithic men, without any bronze or iron, was living according to Nougier at a density of 0·1 sq. km. per head, i.e. the whole country was carrying a population of 5 million. Many French writers however hold that this was the population of Gaul at the time it was invaded by Julius Caesar; if this is so, there must have been a long preceding period of population stagnation. But even if the population in 2000 B.C. was half or less of Nougier's estimate, it still follows that it must have been, by the standards of that time, a dense population, already dependent upon comparatively advanced agricultural techniques.

Palaeolithic Britain, according to Nougier, was inhabited only by 'some hundreds or thousands'. Only the Thames valley was fully occupied. Grahame Clark is more specific. Early palaeolithic Britain, he considers, had a permanent population of only about 250, but may have had some summer visitors from Europe. By the mesolithic period he gives Britain a population of three to four

[1] V. N. Andreev and Z. P. Savkina, *International Grassland Conference*, Reading, 1960, p. 166.

thousand[1] with an average of 65 sq. km. per head, or fairly com-
fortable living room. Neolithic Britain had a population of 20
thousand (12 sq. km. per head) and Middle Bronze Age Britain 30
to 40 thousand. Most of these were in England, where they had
less than 5 sq. km. of hunting ground per head, and really had to
begin to think about agriculture. In Scotland, according to Childe,
there were still only 2,500 people in the Early Bronze Age, with an
average of 30 sq. km. per head, still able to live by hunting.

At some time between 3000 B.C. and 2000 B.C., even if the amount
of land were still 12 sq. km. per head when Scotland was taken into
account, higher densities of population were prevailing in the
south, and it became necessary to practise agriculture, the art of
which was probably acquired from Gaul.

With neolithic agriculture, the population of England continued
to grow, though its density was still much less than in Gaul. The
invasion of the Belgae (though there is some dispute about this) is
said to have introduced the heavy wheeled plough, which made
possible the cultivation of the clay soils in which Britain abounds
(the first British agriculturists had to confine themselves to the
cultivation of light sandy soils). By this time, Grahame Clark
estimates that population had risen to 400 thousand, mostly in
England and Wales rather than in Scotland, i.e. a density of ½ sq.
km. or less per person.

The land which now constitutes the United States and Canada has
a total area of 17 million sq. km., or 14 million if we deduct the
tundra; perhaps a further small deduction should be made for
completely arid land. In the sixteenth century, at the time of the
arrival of the white man, this area had a population of one million.[2]
The North American Indians too about that time were facing
their 'population crisis', and were beginning to find it necessary to
change over to agriculture. Agriculture in Mexico and Peru, as we
have seen above, had been in existence for thousands of years, and
had made great civilizations possible. Geographers believe that it is
possible to trace the spread, about this time, of maize growing up
the valleys from Mexico, while the higher ground remained
occupied by hunting peoples.

By the latter part of the seventeenth century, travellers and
settlers in New England had acquired considerable knowledge of

---

[1] This estimate is confirmed by Professor H. J. Fleure, *Geographical Review*,
October 1945.

[2] A. Landry, *Traité de Démographie*, Paris, 1949; Vanzetti, Società Italiana di
Sociologia Rurale, *Land and Man in Latin America*, 1961.

the means of livelihood of the American Indians there. A careful survey makes possible an interesting estimate of the sources of food supply of a people who were in transition from hunting to an agricultural economy. The transition towards agriculture by this time, however, judging from the proportion of their calories which it supplied, was two-thirds completed.

The following table gives M. K. Bennett's compilation[1] of the diet of American Indians in New England in the first three-quarters of the seventeenth century, as recorded by a large number of contemporaries.

While population growth appears to have been the motive force compelling our ancestors, and others (possibly with great reluctance at the time) to abandon the hunting life for the agricultural, there is an interesting possibility that this process may occasionally go into reverse. The disappearance of the Norse community in Greenland about the fourteenth century is an event which undoubtedly took place, though its causes are much debated. Some hold that wars, or epidemics, aggravated by a worsening of the climate, are sufficient explanation; but Stefansson, who knows the country well, holds that the Greenlanders, cut off from contact with Europe by the King of Norway's commercial monopoly, found a hunting and fishing life more congenial than working on their agricultural settlements, and after a short time intermarried with

TABLE VIII. AVERAGE DIET OF AMERICAN INDIANS
MEASURED IN CALORIES PER HEAD PER DAY

	U.S. 1952	American Indians (New England) 1605–1675
Grain	740	1625 –
Meat and poultry	700	250 +
Milk and milk products	512	
Sugar	500	
Vegetable fats and oils	274	25 –
Vegetables and fruits	210	100
Tubers	94	50 –
Nuts and legume seeds	94	200 +
Eggs	90	25 –
Fish and shellfish	13	225
Cocoa and chocolate	13	
	3240	2500

[1] *Journal of Political Economy*, October 1955.

and became indistinguishable from Eskimos. In the substantial depopulation of Britain which appears to have occurred in the fifth and sixth centuries A.D. the inhabitants of some areas also probably reverted to a hunting life.

To this day it is still possible to find truly nomadic peoples living on meat, fish, and wild seeds and roots, though anthropologists will have to hurry: they have not many more years in which to make their records and measurements, before such communities become sophisticated, and begin to obtain their food supplies from elsewhere.

In 1941 Holmberg[1] successfully measured the quantities of meat consumed daily by the Siriono — a group of semi-nomadic hunters and food gatherers inhabiting an extensive tropical area of eastern Bolivia. No clothing of any kind is manufactured or worn by the Siriono; they hunt wild game with bows and arrows. Unlike many of their South American Indian contemporaries, who have developed or adopted methods of trapping fish, they also do all their fishing with the bow and arrow, a factor which limits their fishing activities to the dry season, when rivers and lakes are low and the waters are clear.

Meat is the most desired item in the diet of these Indians. Holmberg attached himself to a band of about 50 adults, and kept records of the amount of game hunted and consumed for a period of three months. No meat was being introduced from outside. Per head of the total population of the tribe meat consumption appeared to be at the rate of only 0·22 kg./day. Even allowing for a large margin of error, the average Siriono eats at the most 125 kg./year of meat obtained from hunting with bows and arrows, equivalent to about 850 calories/person/day.

In the Siriono economy, collecting ranks next to hunting in importance, particularly of wild fruits and wild honey. Small plots of mixed garden crops are invariably planted during the semi-sedentary rainy season when the waters of the numerous lakes and rivers of the area are still too high to allow extensive migration, and meat supplies are reduced; they seldom sow plots of any size as they are often not at hand to reap the harvest. Eating habits depend largely upon quantities of food available for consumption at the moment. Holmberg records that when food is plentiful people eat to excess and do little else. It is not uncommon for four people to eat a peccary weighing 27 kg. at a sitting. When meat is plentiful, a man

[1] Smithsonian Institution of Social Anthropology, Publication No. 10, 1950.

has been known to consume 13 kg. within 24 hours. But when food is scarce they go hungry while looking for something more to eat. He emphasizes, however, that though the supply of food is rarely abundant and always insecure, starvation does not occur.

Still more primitive — and voracious — are the Bushmen of South West Africa. 'The Bushmen,[1] a remnant of the original inhabitants of Africa, may still be found — the last of primitive man. They do not cultivate the soil; the men hunt with bows and poisoned arrows; the women and children wander far afield in search of roots, leaves and berries. Hunger compels them to eat everything that is edible — buck, hyena, leopard, snakes, birds, frogs, locusts, grasshoppers, flying ants; they have an intimate knowledge of wild products, and know exactly where and at what time of the year they will find particular foods. They are prodigious eaters when they are fortunate enough to kill a large animal. Men weighing no more than 45 kg. (7 stone) will consume at one sitting up to twenty times the quantity of food which would normally be eaten by a settled cultivator; they have a remarkable elasticity of stomach. Thrust back by frontier contacts to live under the harsh climatic conditions of the Kalahari Desert where temperatures can change overnight from quite severe frosts to 35° C during the day, their numbers have dwindled to a mere 15–16,000. Communities living by hunting and food gathering require very large areas of land per person merely to subsist, and under the near-arid conditions of the Kalahari where there is nothing but damp sand from which to procure water — skilfully sucked through a hollow reed and transferred for storage to ostrich egg-shells — density of population is as low as 300 sq. km. (approximately 120 sq.m.)/person.'

Further ideas on the food supply of pre-agricultural man are given by Pirie.[2] On an area of 20 sq. km. (which we have taken above as about the area required to support one person in grass-land country), and taking the median of the four separate estimates which Pirie quotes, we must conclude that the stock of game animals is about 130 tons liveweight. Small game may reproduce itself very rapidly; let us however make the unfavourable assumption that this game consists only of large, slow-breeding animals, reproducing themselves on the average only every three years.

---

[1] M. R. Haswell, 'Economics and Population in Africa', *The Month*, November 1960.

[2] *Journal of the Royal Statistical Society*, Series A, Vol. 125, Part 3, 1962.

This area then still yields 40 tons liveweight of meat per year. An active population, requiring 2500 calories per person per day, and living entirely on meat (they would have an excessive intake of protein, which would be excreted without harming them), and assuming that they are not so fastidious as we are about consuming tripes and heads, etc., would require, however, only one ton of game, measured liveweight, per head per year.

A higher estimate[1] makes the stock of indigenous game animals in Africa 12·2 liveweight tons/sq. km., as against 3·5 which can be obtained with European cattle, and 1·75 with African cattle. Moreover, the indigenous meat is good; and many African pastoralists are beginning to think that it would suit them better to shoot out the predatory animals and preserve the wild game, rather than keeping cattle.

Does the primitive hunter really require a forty-fold margin over his requirements? It appears that he does. Most of the game, in fact, is eaten by wild predatory animals; man cannot hope to extirpate them, or even keep them in check, until his own numbers have substantially increased. Skilful though primitive hunters have been in devising bows and arrows, boomerangs, etc., and in tracking large animals, they often have to work hard actually to kill them. Finally, there is the important point that when they do catch a large animal they have no means of preserving it and, in spite of the feats of trenchermanship which they perform, a large proportion of the meat is bound to be wasted.

The reader who wishes to study more closely the possibility of obtaining meat supplies from the indigenous game in Africa should read the admirably thorough study by Sachs and Glees.[2] The authors estimate the stock of nine wild potential meat animals in an area of 30,000 sq. km. in the Serengeti (including some peripheral grazing which is shared with the neighbouring cattle herds). The Serengeti area itself is described as semi-arid, not capable of being grazed by cattle because of tsetse-fly infestation. The principal meat animals are wildebeest, Thompson gazelle and zebra. The liveweight stock of meat animals (of which the above three species constitute more than 80 per cent) is estimated at 4·3 tons/sq. km. — substantially lower than the estimates of Pirie and Russell. The ratio of meat and edible offals to live weight is put at

---

[1] Professor Walter Russell, private communication.
[2] *Preservation of Wild Life, Utilization of Wild Mammals and Processing of Game Meat*, Government of Federal Republic of Germany, Tanzania Project FE. 428 (in English).

only 43 per cent (the offal of the zebra, and of the lesser species, is inedible). The authors estimate the possible annual rate of slaughter at only 10 per cent of the stock. It appears (though it is not stated) that they are leaving a substantial proportion of the potential output to be consumed by predatory animals, or shot by tourists, as the case may be. The authors also organized a series of taste-tests to judge the acceptability of the meat. Buffalo, wildebeest, topi and zebra were rated excellent, indeed to the point where they could well be canned for export, but elephant somewhat unsatis-factory. Yields of dressed meat were carefully estimated (from 8 kg. for a Thompson's gazelle to 400 kg. for a buffalo, 700 for a hippopotamus and 1500 for an elephant). The authors then pro-ceeded to make an economic estimate of the cost of hunting, trans-port, slaughtering, dressing (but excluding overhead costs), indicating a cost of game meat of only 0·38 shillings/kg. — as compared with the present Tanzania price of 2·2 shillings/kg. for beef.

CHAPTER III

Shifting Agriculture[1]

That care and feeling for the distant past, which have shown themselves in many striking results obtained by Danish archaeologists, led Jørgensen[2] to try an experiment reproducing, so far as possible, the conditions under which the pioneers of agriculture in Denmark worked. A group of students volunteered to clear and burn, with primitive tools, the sort of scrubland (lacking heavy tree growth) which is believed to have prevailed in large parts of Denmark at that time. They were forcibly reminded of one drawback with which pioneers of agriculture in hitherto uncultivated areas to-day in Africa and Australia are all too familiar, namely that every bird for miles around considers that these new edible seeds were planted for his benefit. The Danish volunteers put in much time bird-scaring, but nevertheless still obtained a very poor harvest. For clearing the land, with primitive iron tools, it was found that they worked at the rate of 245 man-hours/ha. cleared. Clearing which still leaves the big stumps in the ground[3] calls for 37 man-days/ha. cleared (probably only about 200 man-hours, as the working day is short). Beckett[4] from experience in Ghana estimates that the clearing of heavy forest calls for 50–75 man-days/ha., even when the big trees are left (in any case, cocoa farmers may find them useful for shade); for re-clearing secondary bush, 25–37 man-days/ha.; but clearing the open savannah in the drier climates, rather than the thick rain forest, requires 10–20 man-days/ha. only. An estimate for the labour required for forest clearing by hand in the United States in 1860[5] indicates a labour requirement of 80 man-days/hectare.

Present-day Africans presumably have sharper axes than iron-

---

[1] Grateful acknowledgement is made to the Leverhulme Trustees for awarding a research grant to one of the authors for a study of the transition from subsistence to cash economies in underdeveloped countries. Much of the resulting information is given in Chapters III and IV.

[2] *National Museets Arbejdsmark*, 1953, p. 43.

[3] Galletti, Baldwin and Dina, *Nigerian Cocoa Farmers*, London, 1956.

[4] Private communication. See also W. H. Beckett, *Akosoaso*, London School of Economics Monograph in Social Anthropology, No. 10.

[5] Primack, *Journal of Economic History*, September 1966.

age cultivators in Denmark; at the same time, they have more abundant scrub growth to clear. For bronze-age cultivators the task would have been heavier, and for the first agriculturists, using flint axes, heavier still. There is a present-day professor of archaeology who gives demonstrations, slow but sure, of cutting down a small tree with a shaped flint which he holds in his hand; he has not measured the labour which the first agriculturists would have put into clearing a hectare of land, but it must have been considerable.

Shifting cultivation is the most primitive type of agriculture. It has been defined by Pelzer[1] as 'an economy of which the main characteristics are rotation of fields rather than crops; clearing by means of fire; absence of draught animals and of manuring; use of human labour only; employment of the dibble stick or hoe; short periods of soil occupancy alternating with long fallow periods'. But, as he points out, just as advanced agriculture does not depend upon the animal-drawn plough, primitive agriculture does not depend upon the hoe; a more fundamental distinction may be made in terms of land use. Shifting cultivators clear with axes and hand knives preferably virgin forest (leaving the stumps of large trees scattered over the area), burn the brushwood, and raise a crop generally for one, two or three years in succession, after which the land is rested for periods up to twenty years or more to allow time for soil fertility to be restored by recovery of the natural vegetation.

This system of 'cut and burn', or shifting agriculture, has been not merely (as it had to be) the practice of pioneer agriculturists anywhere in the world; it has persisted over very long periods of time as the regular system of agriculture for most of the inhabitants of 'Black Africa', for many inhabitants of Latin America, and in some less densely populated regions in Asia. It persisted in remote parts of Sweden until 1920.

Agriculture, the actual cultivation of plants, as opposed to the collection of naturally growing produce, probably using very simple tools, began about 7000 B.C. (The earliest known traces of agriculture, dated by the radio-carbon method, have been found in the neighbourhood of Jericho, and there are signs of its having spread progressively from its middle Eastern origin.)[2] The early Egyptians and Babylonians, with their rich irrigated alluvial lands, appear to have been hand-cultivators. Ploughing with draught

---

[1] K. J. Pelzer, *Pioneer Settlement in the Asiatic Tropics*, New York, 1954.
[2] Cipolla, *Economic History of World Population*.

animals was introduced in more difficult soils and climates. There is evidence of it having occurred in Denmark about 1500 B.C., and in India about the same date, at the time of the Aryan invasions; there is no sign of it in China until about 350 B.C.[1]

The fertility of the soil, it is said, is restored by the practice of abandoning clearings after a few years and resting the land for long periods. The word 'fertility' here is very ambiguous; and the questions of plant chemistry and soil science involved should be set out in a little more detail. Those familiar with the subject must excuse an elementary exposition.

The growth of a plant, besides its obvious requirements of air, sunlight and water, calls also for certain substances in the soil, to be taken in through its roots. Of the whole known range of elements, plants seem to require a great number, including such unlikely elements as zinc, manganese and boron, though only in minute traces. There is a great deal of further research still to be done in this field. Some areas of land are poor infertile heathlands because of deficiencies of certain trace elements; but this is not the question at issue for the shifting cultivator, who is no worse placed than many modern farmers in his inability to remedy such deficiencies.

Apart from trace elements, the plant finds absolutely necessary for growth, and has to draw from the soil by its roots in substantial quantities, nitrogen, phosphorus, potassium, calcium, sulphur, magnesium, and iron. The three latter appear to be present in adequate quantities in almost every soil. Of all the other four, natural supplies are supplemented by modern farmers with their fertilizers.

But does not the soil also require to be adequately supplied with 'organic matter' or 'humus'? These two terms are somewhat indefinite, and in addition, unfortunately, have come to have emotional values attached to them. It is necessary therefore to describe the situation precisely. The literal meaning of the word 'organic', in this sense, is a compound containing the element carbon (generally excluding, however, the inorganic carbonates, and one or two other compounds). On this definition, certain artificial fertilizers, such as cyanamide and urea, are 'organic' because they contain carbon, while others such as sulphate of ammonia are not. (This distinction may appear far-fetched, but it is

[1] W. H. McNeill, *The Rise of the West*, University of Chicago Press, 1963, pp. 26-7.

already of importance in India, where urea is favoured as a more 'natural' fertilizer.) In communities lacking artificial fertilizers (including the whole world until a hundred years ago and, by definition, all shifting cultivators now), fertilization of the soil with additional supplies of nitrogen, phosphorus and potash can only be done through 'organic' means, i.e. manuring with the residues of plants and animals (though most of the calcium required for manuring soil was obtained from inorganic sources). This fact alone may account for the great and sometimes excessive concern for organic manures which many people feel.

The excreta of livestock make a most valuable form of manure available for people who cannot buy chemical fertilizers, since they concentrate in a limited area nitrogen, phosphorus and potash which may have been obtained by grazing over a wide area. The ashes of a tree have lost all their nitrogen in the process of burning, but yield considerable supplies of calcium, phosphorus and potash, particularly the latter, in much greater abundance than could be obtained in any other manner, because the deep roots of the trees bring back from the subsoil much of what had been leached (i.e. washed downwards by the action of water) from the top soil. Leaching is particularly rapid in high rainfall tropical areas, and so the top soil tends quickly to lose fertility which (for a cultivator who cannot buy artificial fertilizers, or keep livestock) can only be restored by periodically cutting and burning the trees.

'Humus' is a somewhat indefinite term for that part of the soil formed from decomposing plant and animal remains. The litter of fallen leaves, bark, etc., from a forest is an important source of humus. Its chemical structure is indefinite, including a great variety of organic compounds; it is also a very important source of nitrogen. There is still a great deal which is not known about the chemistry of nitrogen in soils, particularly in tropical soils; the amount of nitrogen available for plant growth fluctuates in a remarkable manner. It has long been known that certain leguminous plants will bring down nitrogen from the atmosphere to enrich the soil; but it has only recently been discovered that certain blue-green algae, found in a great variety of soils, also have the same capacity.

But humus must not be regarded solely as a source of nitrogen, which might eventually be replaced by artificial fertilizers, or cultivating algae, or some other device. The other organic compounds in the humus appear to be very important not so much for the chemistry as for the physics of the soil, helping it to preserve its 'crumb structure', by methods only partially understood. This 'structure' of the soil enables it to hold more water, which is very important in hot climates; and without it also a large part of the valuable top soil is liable to be eroded away by wind or rain. In any case, an abundant supply of organic matter in the soil probably helps the beneficial algae.

Most fertilizing just consists of reconcentrating, in the cultivated field, those chemical elements which had been scattered, in the grassland or the subsoil. Artificial fertilizing with potash or phosphorus draws upon the resources of certain mines in other parts of the world, whose supply, however, is limited. The artificial nitrogen fertilizers, on the other hand, draw on the nitrogen from the atmosphere, and there is no limit to their supply.

The burning of the fallen scrub by the shifting cultivator destroys the humus in the uppermost layers of the soil. Lower in the soil, the humus remains, and is the principal source — and probably not an adequate one — of nitrogen for the subsequent crop. As population increases, the shifting cultivator has to work on a rather shorter cycle of cutting and burning. The soil research work now in progress indicates that repeated burning at fairly short intervals, with the consequent destruction of humus, may have a very serious effect on the soil, leading eventually to a regrowth, in place of the previous thick scrub, of a thin savannah-type woodland, which when cleared yields a very infertile soil for cropping.

The burning however also completely destroys all weeds and weed seeds over the whole area. This constitutes one of its principal attractions for the tropical cultivator. For the first year at any rate, not only is the soil rich in phosphorus and potash (if not in nitrogen) but it is also weed-free. Weeds grow very fast in the tropics, and the difficulty of getting the weeding done during the growing season is the principal limiting factor on the amount of ground which a family can cultivate. In subsequent years, productivity rapidly falls off, and weed infestation becomes unmanageable, till the land has to be abandoned.

Peters[1] found the Lala shifting cultivators, growing finger millet on poor soils in Zambia, operating an average cycle of 17 years. Attempts to reduce the cycle to 9–12 years resulted in a loss of yield of 25 per cent, which brought the community below sub-

[1] D. U. Peters, *Land Usage in Serenje District*, Rhodes-Livingstone Paper No. 19, 1950.

sistence level. One of the writers has observed that shifting cultivation (now abandoned) in a region of Gambia could only be operated on a 20-year cycle — on soils exceptionally poor, even by African standards.

Conklin, on the other hand,[1] in a detailed study of the pygmy Hanunóo in the Philippines, on good volcanic soil with abundant rainfall, observed that the average cycle of what he called a *swidden* (this is not a Filipino word, but an old English dialect word meaning 'burnt clearing') lasted 12 years, of which 2–4 were cultivated, the remainder fallow. In Sarawak, with good rainfall but comparatively poor soil, Freeman[2] observed the Iban practising on the average a 15-year cycle (ranging from 20 years on the poorer to 10 or less on the better), with two years' crops taken when virgin jungle was cleared, but only one crop from secondary jungle. In a somewhat similar climate in Yucatan, the tropical southern part of Mexico, in the village of Chankom, Redfield and Villa[3] observed a nine-year cycle (two years' cultivation and seven years' fallow). They pointed out, however, that this was beyond the capacity of the soil. The village of Chankom, established only fifty years previously, was already showing signs of disintegration — people were tending to leave the village, and to clear and cultivate individual plots for themselves in the more distant forest, which was expected to be more fertile. This was in spite of the fact that the poorer soils, constituting about half the area of the village's land, had not been cultivated at all.

De la Pena, one of the leading officials of the Mexican Department of Agriculture, estimated[4] that as much as three million hectares in Mexico were still cultivated by 'shifting' methods, on a ten-year cycle on the average, and yielding $1\frac{1}{2}$ tons maize/ha. — a considerably better yield than that obtained by many sedentary cultivators. However, certain primitive maize cultivators, namely the North American Indians[5] of the seventeenth century, who had probably only acquired the art of maize growing a few centuries earlier, from further south — but who could practise rotational cultivation on fertile forest soils hitherto uncultivated — obtained

[1] H. C. Conklin, *Hanunóo Agriculture*, a report on an integral system of shifting cultivation in the Philippines, FAO Forestry Development Paper No. 12, Rome, 1957.
[2] J. D. Freeman, *Iban Agriculture*, Colonial Office Research Study No. 18, 1955.
[3] P. Gourou, *The Tropical World*, 3rd edition, 1961.
[4] World Population Conference, 1954, Rome.
[5] M. K. Bennett, *Journal of Political Economy*, October 1955.

yields of 2½ tons/ha. Redfield and Villa found average yields of maize of only 1 ton/ha. Allan[1] has assembled sufficient data to make possible a very interesting comparative study of the rates at which yields fall off in 'cut and burn' agriculture, shown in Chart I.

CHART I

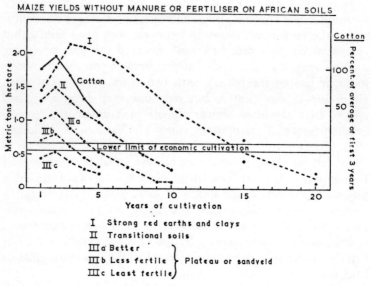

MAIZE YIELDS WITHOUT MANURE OR FERTILISER ON AFRICAN SOILS

I   Strong red earths and clays
II   Transitional soils
IIIa Better   ⎫
IIIb Less fertile ⎬ Plateau or sandveld
IIIc Least fertile⎭

Redfield and Villa also found in Yucatan that second-year yields were 25–50 per cent below those of the first year. Peters observed the Lala working at or below what Allan regarded as the lower limit of economic cultivation.

The Hanunóo had a highly sophisticated system of shifting cultivation, growing as many as 280 different crops, of which several dozen are regularly cropped together with rice, thus avoiding the dearth in the pre-harvest months. Rice, the most valued crop, is planted from the first year on newly-cleared *swiddens*. It is followed by other grain and root crops, whose growth appears to be compatible with that of the gradually re-encroaching forest trees. Yields of rice are fairly high, averaging 2·3 tons/ha. rough rice. The rice harvest is generally followed by a maize crop in the same year.

[1] *The African Husbandman.*

Freeman quotes some Malayan data showing that the first crop of rice on newly cleared jungle land may be over 2 tons (rough weight)/ha.; but the second crop about 1·5, the third crop below 1 ton/ha. The Iban however obtained an average of only 0·73 tons — but the year of investigation was admittedly a poor one. Freeman adds:

A special feature of Iban agriculture is the cultivation of a wide range of catch crops, interspersed on the same land as the padi (rice). A few, such as ensabi (a kind of mustard plant, the leaves of which are eaten) are sown separately, immediately after the burn. Others are planted simultaneously with the padi, the seeds being mixed up in the same sowing basket and sown into the same dibble holes. The most important of these are cucumber, pumpkin, luffa, and gourd. All of these are ready to eat before the padi has ripened . . . . Cucumber and pumpkin leaves are cooked as vegetables as soon as they have formed . . . . Around the edges of the farm clearing, and in the immediate vicinity of the hut (farm hut or watch-house), which stands at its centre, various other plants are grown, such as cassava, maize and pineapples . . . .

Among the Land Dayak, also in Sarawak, who practise both shifting and sedentary agriculture, Geddes[1] observed yields of rough rice of 1·9 tons/ha. on swamp land, and 1·6 for upland rice. Similarly Leach[2] in Sabah also found a yield of 1·9 tons/ha. of rough rice under the best conditions of shifting agriculture. Izikowitz[3] found only 1·15 tons/ha. among the Hill Lamet in Vietnam.

Even taking account of the heavy initial labour requirements for forest clearing, labour input per worker for shifting agriculture is low and discontinuous. So long as land is available, the shifting cultivator finds this method of production, per kilogram of grain produced, less demanding of labour than is sedentary agriculture. Geddes pointed out that the Land Dayak, whose economy is on the borderline between shifting and sedentary agriculture, are nevertheless well aware of labour requirements as well as of yields. Yields of rough rice per man-hour worked proved to be 0·87 kg. for swamp rice and 0·9 kg. for upland rice, in spite of the lower yield per hectare of the latter (quoted above: the labour inputs were 2165 hours/ha. on the swamp and 1663 on the upland rice). Conklin gives a very detailed account of labour requirements in Hanunóo farming.

[1] W. R. Geddes, *The Land Dayaks of Sarawak*. Colonial Research Study No. 14, H.M.S.O., 1954.
[2] E. R. Leach, 'Some Aspects of Dry Rice Cultivation in North Burma and British Borneo', *The Advancement of Science*, Vol. VI, No. 21, 1949, p. 28.
[3] K. G. Izikowitz, *Lamet: Hill Peasants in French Indo-China*, 1951.

TABLE IX. MAN-HOUR COSTS IN HANUNÓO SWIDDEN FARMING

(estimated annual minimum average labour requirement)
Based on available case data

| | | Man-Hours/ha. of New Swidden in | | |
| | | climax forest | second growth woody | bamboo |
Stage	Activity			
1	Site selecting	6*	3*	3*
2	Slashing	60	100*	150
3	Felling*	350*	150	40*
4	Firebreaking	10	40*	40*
	Firing	4*	2*	2*
	Reburning*	175	100*	50
5	Planting maize	10	10	10
	Planting rice	150	130	130
	Interplanting	300	300	300
	Replanting	5	5	5
	Fencing	150	150	150*
	Protecting	150*	75*	75*
	Guarding	400*	200*	200
	1st weeding	}100	150	150
	2nd weeding		200	200
	Thinning and last weeding	200	250	250
6	Harvesting maize	80	80	80
	Harvesting rice	300	300	300
	Storing rice	30	30	30
	Cleaning	200	200	200*
7–8	Non-grain cultivation and harvesting	500*	500*	500*
	Total man-hours	3,180*	2,975*	2,865*

* closely related tasks included.

Freeman's study is also valuable in giving us a detailed account of labour requirements for cultivating both virgin jungle and secondary jungle. Based on their average day worked of 6·6 hours, we have the following:

TABLE X. TIME EXPENDED BY THE IBAN IN MAN-HOURS PER HECTARE

	Kampong (or virgin jungle)	Danum (or secondary jungle)
Slashing	98	82–98
Felling	195–228	65–82
Secondary clearing	32–82	32–82
Dibbling	65	65
Sowing	82	82
Weeding	195–260	244–326
Reaping	228–326	228–326
Transporting	17	17
Minimum total	913	815
Maximum total	1158	1076

Cultivation appears to have been much less intensive than among the Hanunóo. Figures do not include however certain kinds of work such as constructing fences, erecting traps, and the crucially important job of standing guard over the ripening paddy. Weeding, here as in Africa, is seen to be a limiting factor. The time within which it has to be completed is short, if the crop is not to be spoiled; and the work is considered too degrading for men to do, although sometimes the older men will help if the amount of land to be weeded exceeds 0·8 ha./woman available.

If a family do not have sufficient labour to complete their harvesting, they will hire a neighbour, paying him a gantang (2·4 kg.) of rough rice/day together with a mid-day meal or, in effect, the value of about 3 kg. rough rice/day. As will be seen later, this is the order of magnitude of the real wage which has prevailed among near-subsistence cultivators in different parts of the world, at different times.

The Iban appear to enjoy a similar climate to but poorer soil than the Hanunóo. From their lower labour input, they obtain a yield of about 0·75 kg./man-hour rough rice. The Hanunóo, with the higher labour input, appear to obtain about the same yield of rice per man-hour, together, however, with all their subsidiary crops; and in total appear to be considerably better off.

The question is raised whether we could not do a good service to African cultivators by redesigning their tools for them. But they have advanced a long way from the simple wooden digging sticks which were used by their remote ancestors (and by ours: and which can still be seen in some of the most isolated regions of New Guinea). Some Africans had discovered how to work iron before their contacts with Europe began in the fifteenth century. Iron has always been an expensive commodity for primitive peoples, and they use it as sparingly as they can. Nevertheless, they have discovered how to make large-bladed hoes, which can move as much earth as the large iron spade of the European gardener. Separate hoes have been designed for men and for women, carefully adapted to their strength and stature. Many of those familiar with the problem believe that African empiricism has already discovered as much as any European designer could when faced with this problem, although Allard[1] concluded that redesigned hoes for hand weeding could give a productivity 10–20 per cent higher than traditional hoes.

We may now consider the densities of population which are possible with shifting agriculture. The reader must beware of becoming confused between the sq. km./person, which are the units in which we measured population densities for hunting people, and the persons/sq. km. which we are using now.

We should remind ourselves that the primitive pastoral communities, found where the land is not forested, and may indeed be semi-arid, live at a density of about 2 persons/sq. km.[2] Though not so wasteful of the land and its resources as are the primitive hunting peoples, they nevertheless fall far short of fully exploiting the potential mean output of the land, which Pirie estimates at 50 kg. liveweight gain/ha./year (5 tons liveweight gain/sq. km.). Even if we halve this figure, as some would do, it seems clear that primitive pastoral peoples, lacking fences, haymaking implements, etc., are unable to exploit the full growth of grass in the favourable seasons of the year; and also they probably lose many livestock to predatory animals.

In the highly productive agriculture of the Hanunóo, a cycle of 12 years is required, and about 20 per cent of the land is deemed uncultivable for 'ritual, geographical or vegetational reasons'. Nevertheless, Conklin computes the maximum population capacity of the land at as high as 39 persons/sq. km. Van Beukering[3] reached very similar conclusions about maximum possible popu-

[1] *Bulletin Agricole du Congo Belge*, 1960, pp. 603–15.
[2] Rätzel, quoted by Taylor, *Canadian Journal of Economics and Political Science*, August 1950.
[3] J. A. van Beukering, *Het Ladagvraagstuk, een Bedrijfs — en sociaal econo-misch probleem*, Mededeelingen van het Department van Economische Zaken in Nederlandsch-Indie, No. 9, 1947.

lation density in studying primitive peoples in Indonesia with a culture similar to that of the Hanunóo.

On the other hand, for the Iban in Sarawak, Freeman calculated that there was a danger of land degradation when the ratio rose above 20 persons/sq. km.; he drew his own sample in the Baleh region, where the figure stood at 5–6 only.

In Zambia Allan[1] has estimated this maximum density at only 8 persons/sq. km. Grove[2] calculates a *minimum* density of 125 persons/sq. km. of land actually cultivated — any attempt to cultivate at lower densities, i.e. to occupy plots exceeding 0·8 hectares/person, would be going beyond the limit capable of being cultivated by hand, with the shortness of the African rainy season, and also the abundant weed growth which it brings. But if we assume an average cycle of 20 years between cultivations, two years cultivation in each cycle, and one-third of the land incultivable, then Allen's and Grove's figures are reconciled. At the same time Grove points out that, under conditions of African hand-tool agriculture, a population density of 27 persons/sq. km. or more is necessary if driving away of wild animals and recutting of scrub are to be sufficient to keep the tsetse fly in check. L. H. Brown[3] of the Kenya Department of Agriculture put the labour requirements for scrub-cutting to keep the fly in check at 1500–2000 man-days/sq. km./year. This had been neglected in Kenya and fly infestation was reoccurring, with the following consequences in the grazing areas:

	Cattle/sq. km.	
	Originally	Present-day
Land of 900–1000 mm/year rainfall	55	12
Land of 500–650 mm/year rainfall	25	7

Besides the fly reinfestation, over-grazing and shifting cultivation had replaced the original good grass by the inedible bush *Dodonaea viscosa*.

Gourou[4] also quotes a great range of figures, from 10 persons/sq. km. as the maximum satisfactory density for the primitive growers of upland (i.e. unirrigated) rice in the Ivory Coast of West Africa, to 120 for the Sacatepequez province of Guatemala. This is the only malaria-free province in Guatemala, which helps to explain

[1] *Rhodes-Livingstone Journal*, 1945.
[2] Contribution to Symposium *Essays on African Population*.
[3] Quoted by de Wilde, *Agricultural Development in Tropical Africa*, pp. 110, 175.
[4] P. Gourou, *The Tropical World*, 3rd edition, 1961.

the high density. Owners of coffee plantations in this province, at any rate until recently, persuaded the Guatemalan government to impose forced labour to enable them to obtain their labour requirements; this at any rate is a good indication that there was among the subsistence cultivators no serious underoccupation below the level of employment to which they were accustomed. In some regions in Sumatra, Gourou found maximum population densities ranging from 15 to 40 persons/sq. km., with a seven-year cycle of cultivation, and with about half the land too rough or too swampy to be cultivated at all.

Peters's estimate for the poor soil cultivated by the Lala was that deterioration might begin when population density rose to no higher than 2 persons/sq. km. He found the whole territory in an advanced stage of degradation in 1945, when the mean density population of the whole plateau was only 3 persons/sq.km.

Much higher figures are given by de Wilde,[1] who estimates maximum persons/sq. km for 'bush fallow' as follows:

Fertile soil, abundant and well-distributed rainfall	40–50
Average for forest zone	20
Poor soil, scanty rainfall	10–15

It may be noted, however, that the village studied by Redfield and Villa in Yucatan, with good rainfall but apparently poor soil (half the soil was left permanently uncultivated), was proving economically unstable with a density of only 10 persons/sq. km.

Even at these low levels of productivity there is a certain amount of trade in agricultural produce; and with a comparatively productive system of shifting agriculture, as among the Hanunóo, it becomes substantial and regular. Redfield and Villa observed that cultivation of a little under 0·5 ha./person/year gave an average yield of maize of 480 kg./person/year, 215 kg. of which were consumed and the remainder sold. Among the Hanunóo some 10–15 per cent of the agricultural product is traded, some of it for other foods, some for manufactures, including salt, beans, pottery, medicine, scented hair-oil, and flash-lamps.

The Iban, cultivating on the average only 0·32 ha./person/year, do not on the whole produce much trading surplus (they leave 30 per cent of their land uncultivated, and rotate the remainder over a 30-year cycle; the average labour input is only of the order of magnitude of 750 hours/ha. cultivated). Consumption of rice (rough

[1] *Agricultural Development in Tropical Africa*, Vol. I, p. 21.

TABLE XI. NUMERICAL DATA ON SHIFTING CULTIVATORS

Name of tribe	Country	Date	Ha./person/year Felled	Ha./person/year Cultivated	Production in grain equivalents kg/person/year	Average persons/family	Percentage of family available for agricultural work	Average hours/year worked	Principal crop
Iban	Sarawak	1949–51	0·32	0·24	176[a]	5·7	60	508[b]	Hill rice
Land Dayaks	Sarawak	1949–51		0·28	219[a]	7·0	60[c]	640[d]	Hill and swamp rice
Dusun	Borneo	1944–5		1·52[f]	319–525[h]	4·2	60[g]	588[d]	Rice and rubber[e]
Lala, Serenje Plateau	N. Rhodesia								
Cycle over 20 years			0·097	0·069	298	4·5			Finger millet
Cycle 17–20 years			0·105	0·073	250	5·9			do.
Cycle 13–16 years			0·069[i]	0·049	265	7·5			do.
Cycle 9–12 years			0·057[i]	0·036	169	6·1			do.
North Mamprusi[j]	Ghana	1932–6		0·27	171	12·0		548	Millet and sorghum

[a] Rough rice.

[b] 77 days of 6·6 hours.

[c] Assumed. Precise figure cannot be ascertained as the villagers prefer to exchange labour with each other and to work in groups.

[d] Assumed 6·6 hours/day.

[e] Described as 'in a state of transition from primitive culture'. Rubber converted at 2·1 kg. = 1 kg. rough rice (ratio prevailing before the 1950 boom). Draught animals are used to the extent of 25 buffalo days/ha. cultivated.

[f] Of which 1·20 under rubber (57 per cent of all families had rubber plantations).

[g] Assumed.

[h] For rice and rubber respectively.

[i] Cultivators who clear the forest on a long rotation leave the large trees standing. On a short rotation they clear the scrub more thoroughly, and hence are only able to undertake a smaller area.

[j] C. W. Lynn, *Agriculture in North Mamprusi*, Gold Coast Dept. of Agriculture, Bulletin No. 34, 1937. The primitive, pagan North Mamprusi people were (at the time of Lynn's survey) purely subsistence cultivators, growing no cash crop and paying no taxes.

c

weight) was 220 kg./person/year (i.e. some two-thirds of their total calorie requirements); another 15 kg./person/year of rice were used for seed, and 50 kg. used to feed poultry and hunting dogs, for religious sacrifices, and for brewing beer. The cultivable land available averaged 11 ha./person (70 per cent of the total area). The average worker worked for 508 hours a year. Statistical information for some communities practising shifting cultivation has been assembled in Table XI.

Freeman has an interesting account of commercial relations within the village:

> Each season, some families succeed in producing a surplus, while others find themselves with a deficit; and so, year by year, scores of different families exchange gongs for padi or padi for gongs . . . . Brass gongs are the principal form of property in which the Iban invest their savings. These gongs have the great advantage of being untouched by the Borneo climate and are virtually indestructible; further, they have a marked prestige value and can be displayed and used on ceremonial occasions . . . . It frequently happens however that a family is not prepared to part with any of its gongs or other property. In these circumstances recourse is had to the traditional scarcity food of the Iban — sago. Most Bilek families possess small plantations of sago palms, specially planted as a scarcity crop, for no Iban relishes *mulong* (as prepared sago is called), and it is only eaten under duress when padi cannot easily be procured. When planted sago is not available, the men set off to scour the jungle for the wild palms, from which the nomadic tribes of Borneo — such as the Punans — habitually obtain the sago which is the main item of their diet.

Naturally the economist is particularly interested in the process of transition from shifting to sedentary agriculture. The Lala, in the difficult situation in which Peters described them, are in a process of transition to a more settled type of agriculture, with subsidiary but permanent hoed gardens which did not share in the degenerative process of 'cut and burn' agriculture; the gardens were maintained in one spot as long as the village remained in existence. Sedentary or permanent cultivation in which peasant cultivators till the same piece of land year after year, in combination with irrigation on flooded plains or in delta regions, will support considerably higher population densities. Employing buffaloes for the heavy labour of ploughing and carrying home the grain, the Dusun, settled cultivators of the Penampang plains in North Borneo,[1]

---

[1] M. Glyn-Jones, *The Dusun of the Penampang Plains in North Borneo*, Report to the Colonial Office (unpublished).

obtain an average of 325 kg. of paddy/head/year from the cultivation of wet rice, which compares closely with the estimated minimum requirement. Combining the output of rice and rubber, the economic grain equivalent produced averaged 537 kg./head/year. Perhaps more important to the peasant than the labour of draught animals in terms of crop yields is the manure applied to his fields. In Glyn-Jones's sample, a small amount of grazing was available; in addition, they graze rice fields which are thus manured. No systematic feeding of livestock is practised.

One of the writers has been able to observe a later stage of the process among the Mandingo tribe in Gambia. In 1950, the shifting cultivation of plateau lands was supplemented by rice grown continuously on annually flooded river flats. It was estimated that these plateau lands had all been cleared over periods ranging from 15 to 50 years. The more favoured sandy loams fringing the river valley were no longer cropped under shifting cultivation, but were cultivated continuously. 'Cut and burn' cultivations further afield, under these conditions of population pressure, were sometimes cultivated for three or five years continuously, as against the three which seem to be the safe maximum for 'cut and burn' cultivators; in such cases (growing millet) the crops of the later years were often total failures. Twelve years after, in 1962, it was found that breakdown of the extended family to form nuclear family units had left most households short of men to work at shifting cultivation, men being willing to join the women in the more intensive cultivation of rice swamp lands in the river valley.

Uganda now has about 0.5 ha./person of *cultivated* land. As population density has increased, the proportion of land that could be left to rest has naturally declined. In one small area in Teso which was subject to intensive agricultural surveys in 1937 and 1953 the ratio of resting to cropped land dropped between these two dates from 1·5 to 1·2. These figures may be typical of the densely populated districts. For the country as a whole, the annual reports of the Agricultural Department give a ratio of available to cultivated land of 7·0 in 1952 and 6·8 in 1960.

Lack of adequate female labour in the weeding season limits the amount of food which can be grown, and it may be that one of the best services which well-wishers could render to primitive cultivators is to supply them with herbicides, together with sufficient technical staff to supervise their application (if wrongly mixed, they may kill the crop as well as the weeds). But anything which can persuade them that weeding is not necessarily degrading work for a man, and that the men should help the women at this task, will do much good. There are signs that the change is taking place. 'Within the peasant family itself there are signs that the old distinction of work between the sexes is beginning to break down. In the Eastern Province of Uganda women can be found ploughing and men weeding.'[1]

While interesting examples of an economy in transition from shifting to settled agriculture can be found, a great deal of Africa still subsists by shifting cultivation.[2] Gourou[3] estimates that in the whole of 'Black Africa' (Africa excluding the Sahara and north thereof, and the Republic of South Africa) the amount of land cultivated, in any one year, is about one-thirtieth of the potential cultivable land. It is not that Africans are ignorant of, or incapable of, settled intensive agriculture. The island of Ukara in Lake Victoria (Tanzania) maintains an agrucultural population at a density of 225 persons/sq. km.; or an even higher density if we take into account the hills of bare rock, which constitute a large part of the area of the island. On this island is found some of the most intensive agriculture in the world, with every field cropped twice a year, cattle fed on cultivated fodder crops and kept in sheds, and the manure carefully spread. Similar though less striking examples of intensive agriculture are found in a few other isolated parts of Africa, including the mountains of Madagascar. It appears that there are historical reasons for these settlements, where the people have been hemmed in by enemies, and compelled to subsist on much smaller areas than they would like. These communities living 'under siege' in inaccessible mountains include the Naudemba, Lamba and Cabrais of Togo (the latter living at 211 persons/sq. km.), the Toura of Ivory Coast, the Lomba of Dahomey, the Mitsogo of Gabon, the Nuba of Kordofan, the Sidamo of Ethiopia, the Agoro of Uganda, and the Kamba of Kenya. In a few cases densities over 600 persons/sq. km. were found. There are several instances of this intensive agriculture being abandoned

---

[1] G. B. Masefield, *Agricultural Change in Uganda*, Food Research Institute Studies, Vol. III, No. 2, 1962.

[2] In growing cereals on poor pasture land, so as to increase the yield, the African cuts the grass and heaps it into little piles, which are then burned. The whole field is then prepared and sown. At harvest time the treated areas bear vigorous clumps of grain, while the rest of the field has a poverty-stricken aspect. See P. P. Leurquin, *Agricultural Change in Ruanda-Urundi, 1945-60*, Stanford, Food Research Institute, 1963.

[3] P. Gourou, private communication.

when the country becomes peaceful and the siege is lifted. The system of shifting cultivation must be judged to be a definite preference on the African's part. So long as abundant land is available, as it is in most of Africa, it yields him better returns, in kg. grain/man-hour of labour input, than does settled agriculture.

A recent book by Ester Boserup[1] makes a most interesting review of the interaction between population growth and changes in agricultural methods, both in the countries practising various forms of subsistence agriculture now, and in Europe in the past. Economists, to give themselves opportunity to practise their analytical methods, tend to assume both agricultural methods and property relationships as given, whereas historians know that they are both subject to continuous change. It is in this way that they come to accept the highly simplified theorem of Malthus, whereby population grows up to the limit of subsistence, after which it is kept in check by 'vice and misery'; or, at any rate, while admitting that changes in agricultural technology have taken place, treat them as exogenous events. The truth is that the changes in agricultural methods are not exogenous, but are themselves the consequence of population growth. To demonstrate that this proposition is true, rather than the converse, namely that new agricultural methods are discovered, and that population growth is the consequence of these discoveries (Malthus's theorem) we have the convincing case that nearly all these changes call for much greater effort on the part of the cultivator, who therefore is most unlikely to adopt them until he is compelled to by rising population.

The repetition of the process of 'cut and burn', with gradually increasing frequency, affects not only the fertility of the soil, as measured by its chemical components, but also its physical condition. In the first phase, described as 'forest fallow', burning a mature forest growth, it leaves a soil which is loose and friable and also weed-free, which can be planted and cultivated with little effort. Repeated burning of less mature growth brings us to the stage described as 'bush fallow', where the soil has become less friable and more compact, requiring much greater effort to cultivate it with hoes; while at the same time weed infestation has become more serious. In the final stage, described as 'short fallow', the soil has become infested with perennial rooted weeds, which cannot be

---

[1] *The Conditions of Agricultural Growth.*

controlled by hoeing without exceptional effort.[1] At this stage the cultivator may advance to plough agriculture, if he can keep draught animals; or, as may have happened in some cases, relapse into nomadism, using extensive areas of low-rainfall land for grazing, and living predominantly or solely on livestock products.

To Gourou, a man of fertile ideas, we owe another very interesting proposition concerning the Maya civilization, which flourished in Central America about the sixth century A.D., in Yucatan, a hot humid area of dense forest growth. One geographer, with a preconception that civilizations can never flourish in such areas, has hypothecated that the climate in the sixth century must have been very different from what it is now. In support of this theory not a single fragment of direct evidence is available. From the large stone buildings which the Maya left, only recently uncovered from thick jungle, we must conclude that they had an advanced civilization, also some knowledge of astronomy and mathematics. From counts of the numbers of their houses it has been estimated that their population density averaged 60 persons/sq. km. Their agricultural methods, however, were the same 'cut and burn' method of maize cultivation which is used by their successors in the same area today. Gourou points out that so dense a population, using these methods, must inevitably have been confronted before long by exhaustion of soil fertility; and the population which supported the cities and temples must have been compelled to scatter again. In this factor alone he can see the cause of the disappearance of the Maya civilization.

The Inca and Aztec civilizations also depended upon maize grown by similar methods. The Incas, however, lived in a low rainfall area where the soil does not lose fertility so rapidly through leaching, and irrigated their crops, thereby probably obtaining high yields. The Aztecs inhabited country of intermediate climatic type. It is interesting to notice however that they built their capital city on a lake, thereby making possible for themselves a system of transport tapping a more extensive area than was possible for the Maya with their loads carried on men's heads along jungle paths.

[1] De Wilde (*Agricultural Development in Tropical Africa*, Vol. II, p. 51) considers, however, that Kikuyu grassland, with its strongly matted roots, cannot be economically broken by ox-plough or tractor, and requires hand cultivation at over 100 man-days/ha.

CHAPTER IV

Agricultural Progress Measured in Grain Equivalents

The wheat which supplies our bread undergoes various milling processes, removing the outer layers of the grain, which are sold for animal feeding, until (except for the minority who like wholemeal bread) only about two-thirds of the weight of the original grain is left. The demand, on the part of most consumers, for highly milled white flour is a matter of taste and choice; the fact that people can consume 'wholemeal' bread indicates that such a high degree of milling is not a physiological necessity. But on the other hand, it appears that we are not entitled to say that the whole wheat grain (after crushing and cooking, but without milling away any of the bran, etc.) is edible and digestible by human beings, as it is by animals. There appears to be some difference of medical opinion on this point. 'Bran is used industrially for polishing steel', said one medical upholder of the view against eating it, 'but why use it on your intestines?'

The same conclusion is upheld when we examine the information obtained by those who study African life, in various parts of the continent. African tribesmen's knowledge of medicine is very limited; but they are often short of food, and have to economize their supplies carefully, and not allow any avoidable waste. The consensus of opinion among those who have examined this matter appears to be that Africans, even when threatened by hunger, still consider it necessary to mill off something like 10 per cent of the wheat or other grain which they may be consuming. Long experience may have taught them that this portion of the grain is indigestible by the human interior, even for a hungry man.

Further medical study is necessary before this question is settled. But for the present, to be safe, we will assume that it is necessary[1] to mill off 10 per cent by weight of any wheat, maize, millet,

---

[1] Platt however implies only 2 per cent inedible. See *Tables of Representative Values of Food Commonly Used in Tropical Countries*, Medical Research Council Special Report No. 302, 1962.

sorghum, etc., consumed. The millings, of course, are available to feed livestock.

In the case of rice, the problem is different. The husk is clearly inedible by humans. Its removal leaves 'brown rice', weighing about 80 per cent of the original rough rice. But even the most austere consumers find a certain amount of further milling necessary. The milled rice eaten in Japan is $73\frac{1}{2}$ per cent of the original weight, and an even higher figure appears to prevail in Formosa. Most rice-eating countries, on the other hand, mill the grain down further to a weight averaging some 67 per cent of the original rough rice, as low as 60 per cent in some cases.

A kg. of wheat or similar grain, therefore, in the hands of a cultivator who has to exercise strict economy, will be milled down to 900 g., which will yield 3150 calories. The table in Chapter I showed that calorie requirements per day, averaged over the whole population, men, women and children, might be as low as 1625 for the smallest-bodied people, in the warmest climate, with the men averaging only 4 hours' work per day, to 2011 for a larger-bodied people, in a colder climate, with the men working 8 hours per day.

It follows that a community living entirely on grain (with a few wild plants, or other source to supply vitamins and minerals) will require, at this rate, anything from 520 to 640 g./person/day, according to the varying circumstances described above, or 190 to 235 kg./person/year of *unmilled* grain. These figures might be reduced a little for people consuming the grains (certain millets) which have higher calorie values than other grains, but only by about 5 per cent. An interesting contemporary confirmation of this[1] is seen in the scale of taxation levied by the Vietcong on the areas controlled by them in Vietnam. In the upper Delta area an income of 240 kg. paddy/person/year is taken as the untaxable minimum, above which taxation is collected on a progressive scale. In the more prosperous (or perhaps more politically sensitive?) Lower Delta area, however, the untaxable minimum is placed at 400 kg.

The protein content of grain is very variable, but it averages over 11 per cent. People consuming grain at this rate therefore would obtain sufficient protein, even on the higher scales formerly thought necessary; certainly on Waterlow's scale of only 35 g./person/day.

[1] Sansom, D.Phil. thesis, Oxford University, 1969.

Some 210 kg. of grain/person/year can therefore be called the subsistence minimum.

But this is still rather an abstract figure. Even the poorest community will want some break in the endless monotony of a cereal diet, something which adds flavour without being always the most economical source of calories and proteins, some meat or fish or fruit, which may make a call upon agricultural resources which would otherwise be devoted to growing cereals. Moreover, in most parts of the world, clothes are necessary for warmth as well as for decency. Poor agricultural communities now no longer have the abundant supply of animal skins which were available to their ancestors in hunting communities, and they cannot afford to buy artificial fibres, so they must devote some of their agricultural resources to producing cotton, flax, or other fibre to make their clothes. Studies by FAO show that even the poorest communities require about 1·5 kg./person/year of fibre.

Is there any convenient way of relating these requirements of fibre, and of other non-cereal products which poor communities may produce in small quantities, to their main crop of cereals?

It is clear that the conversion of other products on calories alone, as is sometimes proposed, would not be satisfactory. Were we to do this, we should have to reckon a ton of meat as approximately equivalent to a ton of grain — whereas we know that the meat contains valuable proteins, and that almost everywhere in the world it would be readily exchangeable for six or seven tons of grain. Furthermore, a calorie basis for comparison would mean that we would have to put no value at all upon numerous agricultural products which people are glad to have for various purposes — cotton, tobacco, jute, coffee, tea, and so on.

This issue was met for the first time, it appears, by Buck in his book, *Land Utilization in China*. In comparing productivity, income and so on between farms in an advanced country, we bring into account the different products, and the different costs, by expressing them all in money as a common unit. This procedure comes so naturally to us that it seems pedantic even to describe it. It appeared to Buck, quite rightly, that this was not the way to measure output in a subsistence agricultural community such as China. Even where we can put a price on a crop, which is by no means always the case, there are doubts as to how far it really represents its value under these circumstances. Most of the crop may be grown for subsistence consumption, and only a small and unrepresentative part of it traded for money. The natural unit for measuring production in such a community is the kg. of grain. Buck therefore took as his unit one kg. of whatever type of grain was predominantly consumed in the neighbourhood (measuring rice with the husks removed, other grains raw). Potatoes and similar root crops he valued at 15 per cent of the corresponding weight of grain — their relative calorie content is about 20 per cent, but as they contain very little protein, 15 per cent is quite a fair value. All other products were converted to grain equivalents in accordance with the rates at which they exchanged against grain (sometimes the exchanges were in fact actual barters of various commodities, rather than money transactions) in the local markets — not necessarily using the same exchange rates throughout China. Buck also converted oilseeds and legumes into grain equivalents on the basis of their calorie value. He omitted livestock products altogether; but as in any case these are produced in such small quantities in China, the omission did no serious harm.

To apply this method of reckoning to the productivity of farmers in America or western Europe, expressing all their output as tons of 'grain equivalents', would be pedantic and misleading. The critic will rightly point out that the results would vary very greatly according to the exchange ratios of other products against grain, which vary greatly between country and country, and indeed between year and year. But in a subsistence economy, by definition, the greater part of the output must in any case consist of grain (or root crops). The amount of other products is comparatively small; and uncertainties about their valuation will therefore affect the result much less. But the application of this method even to a medium-income economy is in danger of leading to serious statistical distortions, as soon as there is any substantial proportion of the agricultural economy in which productivity and prices are likely to be influenced by factors other than those which determine productivity and prices in the production of cereals.

For preparing totals for international comparison, later in this chapter, a set of weights are used (given in Appendix) on wheat as a base obtained by averaging F.A.O. weights[1] for the four medium- and low-income areas, Latin America, Near East, Far East and Africa. Comparisons of these relative prices with those prevailing in U.S.A. on the one hand, and those prevailing in subsistence-

[1] *F.A.O. Monthly Bulletin of Agricultural Economics and Statistics*, March 1960, p. 13.

agriculture countries on the other hand, reveal a great number of differences, some of which appear to be of a chance or local nature in the subsistence country, but many of which are systematic. The systematic differences are rather surprising. Fruit, vegetables, meat and dairy products in nearly all cases seem to be very much *cheaper*, relative to grain, in the low income countries. Part of this will be explained by the fact that fruit and vegetables, and to a less extent milk, are labour-intensive commodities, which might therefore be expected to be cheaper in the low-income countries. It is probably also the case that there is a comparatively low long-run supply elasticity for animal products, requiring a substantial rise in their relative price in order to secure the much larger supplies demanded in high-income countries.

These differences are brought out in a striking manner in a paper by the Russian scientist, Malin, at the World Population Conference,[1] in which he itemized what he considered a desirable diet, which he then converted to grain equivalents at Russian relative prices, obtaining a total of 578 kg./person/year. At United States relative prices, on the other hand, this same diet would have been valued at 1544 kg./person/year. (Both calculations exclude agricultural products consumed in the form of stimulants, i.e. alcohol, tea, tobacco, coffee, etc., and textile fibres.) Likewise Patel[2] showed that agricultural production per head in the United States, measured at Indian prices, was only 2·3 times Indian production; measured at American prices, which put a much greater relative value on meat, fruit, etc., the ratio would be approximately 7.

While the generalization can be sustained, it will be seen how variable are the figures (see Appendix).

A most interesting confirmation of this principle comes, however, from quite a different source, namely a historical rather than a geographical comparison. Bowden[3] points out that the period 1630–49, concerning which most historians are preoccupied with the great political changes taking place, was an extremely bad period economically, with real wages in both agriculture and building at less than half their value in the base period 1450–99. This was a period of greatly rising prices and declining real income. However, the factors by which the different commodity group index numbers rose between 1450–99 and 1630–49 were striking.

[1] Belgrade 1965.
[2] *Economic Journal*, March 1964.
[3] In the *Agrarian History of England and Wales* (edited by Finberg), Vol. IV, p. 673 and Appendix.

Grains	7·88
Other arable products	6·62
Livestock	6·48
Animal products	4·57
including dairy products	4·14

Animal products had become relatively much cheaper during this period of distress. The price of milk in 1618 is given at $2\frac{1}{2}$ pence/ gallon, or a price by weight exactly one-third of the on-farm price of wheat, whereas the present price by weight is about 1·2 times the price of wheat.

Converted into grain equivalents, the minimum allowance of $1\frac{1}{2}$ kg./person/year for textile fibres becomes 14 kg. We must also make some allowance, though we cannot put a precise figure to it, for other agricultural products besides grains and roots required, even under the most austere conditions. Our final conclusion is that subsistence requirements, expressed in our units of grain equivalents, are somewhere between 250 and 300 kg./person/year, varying substantially, as we have seen, with climate and average body weight.

It should be added that a community producing precisely the minimum requirements, calculated as above, unless their harvests year by year are strictly uniform, or unless they keep reserves, will be intermittently hungry in bad seasons.

An important question, on which remarkably little is known, is the extent of storage losses among low-income cultivators. Very high figures are sometimes quoted, up to 35–50 per cent, and it is undoubtedly the case that this sometimes occurs. The situation is at its worst for people who have to grow the entire year's food requirements in the short rainy season, and then store them in their own huts.

Storage in properly constructed huts, sealed pits, or earthenware jars reduces losses. An efficient commercial or co-operative organization, with rat-proof concrete-floored buildings, can reduce storage losses (through beetles, midges, etc.) to the order of magnitude of 5 per cent.

Observations made in a number of low-income countries generally indicate that prices immediately before the harvest are appreciably higher than immediately after the harvest. An example of this is given in Chart II showing seasonal fluctuations in the price of maize in Accra.[1] This price difference should represent

[1] Werner Lamadé, 'Möglichkeiten einer Maismarktpolitik in Ghana', Zeitschrift für ausländische Landwirtschaft, Aug. 1966.

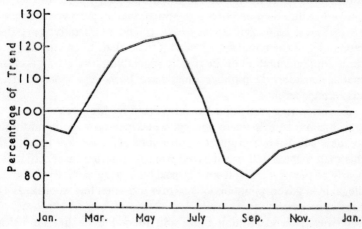

SEASONAL FLUCTUATIONS OF WHOLESALE PRICES OF MAIZE IN ACCRA, 1956–1963

the estimated rate of storage loss, plus handling costs, plus interest, depreciation, maintenance and profit on the capital invested in storage buildings by a merchant. The expected rates of return on investment are high in such cases; this serves to confirm the estimate that physical storage losses are of a comparatively low order of magnitude. This does not prove, of course, that the rate of storage loss is low when the farmer does his own storage. He may indeed be well advised to sell his crop immediately after the harvest, at a comparatively unfavourable price, even if he has to buy some back at a substantially higher price later, rather than attempt his own storage.

Grain equivalents as a measuring device were also used very successfully by de Vries, at that time Agricultural Adviser to the International Bank in Washington.[1] De Vries expressed all output in Asian countries in terms of milled rice per head of total population (not only of population engaged in agriculture). His method differs somewhat from Buck's, in that another grain, say millet, which has almost the same calorific value as milled rice, but which sells at a lower price in local markets, because it is much less palatable, is converted into rice equivalents in accordance with this price — unlike Buck's procedure, where all grains count equally.

[1] For some years Rector of the School of Social Studies, The Hague; previously he had worked for many years in Indonesia.

In Vietnam in 1939,[1] where population densities are extraordinarily high, the more prosperous 40–50 per cent of the population, representing the families of those who own more than 1 ha. of land and more than one draught animal, had an average income of 1810 francs, equivalent to 2070 kg. milled rice/family/year; the remainder of the population just about half that. Even allowing for some supplementation of the rice by vegetables, fish, etc., it is clear that a considerable number must have been very close to true subsistence level.

An interesting study of a Libyan village by Meliczek[2] showed a cash income equivalent to 770 kg. wheat/person/year, in addition to their subsistence crops, or approximately 1000 kg. in all. Of this cash income half was derived from non-agricultural activities, nearly 20 per cent being from charcoal burning, an activity declared illegal by a government anxious to preserve such few woodlands as Libya possesses.

It was from examining these and related data that de Vries ventured on a bold and extremely fruitful generalization about the stages of agricultural progress, all measurements being made in kg. of unmilled grain equivalent/total population/year. The true subsistence minimum stands a little below 300 kg. grain equivalent/person/year. As production increases, perhaps to a level of 350, most of the increased product, not unexpectedly, is used to improve the diet. Even under these circumstances however a certain proportion of the crop has to be set aside for the purchase of a few necessary non-food commodities, payment of taxes, etc.

By the time a production per head of 400 units has been reached, however, the community is selling a substantial part of its agricultural product — this indicates, in effect, the urgency of other needs besides food, for clothing, building materials, medicine, and so forth. In the very poorest subsistence communities practically every family has to work on the land, and anything which they have in the way of non-agricultural goods or services, i.e. minimum requirements of clothing, shelter, etc., has to be provided by their own part-time efforts. As production rises, it is possible to sell some of the agricultural output in exchange for imports from a distance, or to employ a certain number of full-time craftsmen.

Not until 500 units have been reached is it worth while employing animal rather than human labour. Up to 750 units, draught and

[1] P. Gourou, Institute of Pacific Relations, Ninth Conference, 1945.
[2] *Socio-Economic Conditions of a Libyan Village*, Technical University of Berlin, 1964.

meat animals alike have to live on straw, bran and other by-products, together with a little grazing (de Vries suggests that 600 units may be about the point at which communities find it possible to set aside some land for pasture) — and the animals do not thrive on it. Possibly a little grain is spared for the work animals at the busiest season of the year when they most need encouragement. It is only beyond the productivity figure of 750 units that there is enough grain to spare for regular feeding to livestock, particularly to pigs and poultry, who cannot digest cellulose as cattle do, but require concentrated food in the form of grain or roots, as do we. It is at this stage that the cultivator should decide that the feeding of grain to livestock is worth while. The characteristic economy of western European and North American agriculture has now begun.

Agricultural and Livestock Production

Expressed in grain equivalents, kg./person/year

Under 300	Subsistence hand-tool agriculture or grazing.
300–500	Subsistence hand-tool agriculture or grazing with some trade.
500–750	Agriculture with draught animals and grazing herds.
Over 750	Mixed farming including the feeding of grains and concentrates to pigs, poultry and other animals.

An illustration of a case where cereals are abundant, and poultry can be kept, comes from Thailand. Janlekha[1] estimates that in the Minburi village area, a chicken of an average farm family helps itself to up to 40 kg. of rice (4 tangs of paddy) annually. The cost of raising chickens for the farmer is entirely in paddy. The average hen lays about 143 eggs a year or 36 eggs (say 1·5 kg.) for every tang (10 kg.) of paddy she eats. Most of the eggs are sold for approximately 4 baht per dozen, and since a tang of paddy costs about 7 baht the gross profit is nominally 70 per cent. This means a steady cosy little income for the Thai peasant, even if he has to spend it at once on other foods.

Economic grain equivalent in kg./bird/year can be computed as follows:

Production	67·21
Consumption (3·25 oz/bird/day)	39·92

[1] J. E. de Young, *Village Life in Modern Thailand*, 1955, p. 100.

We get a good illustration of de Vries's principle from Naylor's classification[1] of groups of farms in Iraq.

Kg. Grain Equivalent/Person/Year

Net farm product after meeting animal feeding, seed and irrigation charges	Cash sales of farm products	Grain fed to livestock (deducted before computing net income)
500	13	163
737	203	226
1089	446	424
1820	1042	327

A supply of grain for feeding animals of 163 kg./person/year would hardly enable a family of five to keep one small working horse, at any rate in a country where hay is scarce. At the higher income levels, on the other hand, in a country where the keeping of pigs is forbidden, and poultry are probably greatly subject to disease, grain supply to animals seems to level out at about 400 kg/person/year, leaving more to be sold for cash on the higher productivity farms.

Now that our agriculture has entered the tractor age, we tend to think of that as having been preceded by a 'horse age' of immemorial antiquity. In fact, the horse cultivation of the nineteenth and early twentieth centuries represented an important technical advance on what had gone before. In many parts of Europe ox ploughs are still to be found; they were predominant in this country until the late eighteenth century, and survived into the nineteenth century in Scotland. In Yugoslavia, to take an interesting modern example, horse cultivation is only general in Voivodina, the wealthiest and most developed part of the country, and ox cultivation prevails elsewhere. It is true that the technique of ploughing with oxen was much the same for an eighteenth-century peasant in England, for an Asian at the present day, as described by Virgil in the Georgics, or even as used by Homer's contemporaries. But even the ox plough represents an important technical advance on the most basic form of agriculture, namely cultivating the soil by hand hoes. This primitive and laborious form of agriculture is still the practice of the majority of African cultivators, of a substantial number in Asia, and of many in Latin America.

There is an economic equilibrium between the ox plough and

[1] Privately communicated.

the hand hoe. De Vries[1] stated that, under current conditions in Indonesia, the cost of keeping a buffalo only doubtfully balanced the additional output obtained through his labours; and that there were, in fact, signs of the economy slipping back to hand cultivation. Two buffaloes with a plough will cultivate three times as fast as hand cultivation on a large plot, but only $1\frac{1}{2}$ times as fast on a small plot.[2] In those regions with a very short wet season, however (discussed below), it may be necessary for the cultivator to use draught animals, whatever the cost, in order to get his cultivation done in time.

A similar regression appears to have been taking place in the community of which the grandfather of one of the authors was a member, namely the Scottish highlands[3] in the early nineteenth century. Increasing population density, higher rents, and lower prices for their produce, meant that crofters in some of the poorer districts were unable to afford even ox ploughs, and reverted to hand cultivation. In the months January to April it was estimated that a man could dig 2 ha.

It is true that there is an important exception which proves the rule. Japan, although a technically advanced country in other directions, is still largely using hand cultivation. India, at a lower level of productivity, keeps milch cattle (though they yield very little milk) and uses ox ploughs, and apparently has been using them for a very long time. Maybe they descend from an age when productivity was higher, and cattle were easier to feed. Also perhaps without them the cultivation of the lands of central India, with their very short wet season, would probably not have been possible. But in any case, as the slaughter of cattle is forbidden in India, farmers prefer to use at any rate the stronger cattle as draught animals.

It is also true that, over large areas of Africa, the use of both cattle and horses has been prevented by the tsetse fly, which carries trypanosomiasis. It has been shown in some areas that this destructive pest can be eliminated though the problem still remains as to how to keep the fly out once this has been done. It does *not*, however, follow that draught animals will soon be introduced into these areas — the level of productivity is still too low in many cases.

[1] E. de Vries, World Population Conference, Rome, 1954.
[2] Van der Koppel, *Die Landbouw in den Indischen Archipel.*
[3] M. Gray, *The Highland Economy, 1750–1850*, Edinburgh, 1957.

An illustration of this was recently found in Gambia by one of the writers[1] in which an attempt had been made unsuccessfully to introduce draught oxen into a hand-hoe economy; the cultivators insisted that they could not feed both themselves and the oxen. Measurement of agricultural output in *milled* rice equivalents showed that the level of productivity did not exceed 438 kg./person/year, and averaged only 270 kg. The ration recommended for draught oxen included 1 kg. grain/beast/day. Though the local type of ox is a mixture of Ndama and Zebu breeds, with a noticeable predominance of Ndama blood which accounts for its relatively high degree of resistance to trypanosomiasis, there is grave risk of over-worked and under-fed draught oxen going down with this disease.

The use of draught animals leads to a further substantial increase in production, *if* sufficient land is available, as it is generally in Africa. In many regions in the Middle East and Asia, however, there is not sufficient land to keep all the cultivating families occupied if they use draught oxen; there ensues, therefore, 'disguised unemployment' until (and this may take a very long time) new labour-intensive types of farming can be introduced (silk, tobacco, fruit, etc.); or until more urban employment becomes available.

India reports some 0·4 cattle per head of total population, 0·1 sheep, a somewhat larger number of goats, and an insignificant number of pigs (which are regarded as unclean by most caste Indians). Buck's figures for China show only 0·17 draught animals/head of rural population, 0·16 pigs, 0·12 sheep and goats, 0·7 poultry, and an inappreciable number of dairy cows.

Gilbert Slater[2] pioneered detailed surveys of some southern Indian villages in 1916, and the University of Madras resurveyed the same villages in 1936–7. Agricultural production per head had fallen over this period, and with it the number of livestock carried.

A comparable account of the stages of agricultural development, from the point of view of an administrator imposing taxation, is given with some precision by Winter.[3] The first stage which Winter describes as 'pure subsistence' includes what we have defined as

[1] M. R. Haswell, *The changing patterns of economic activity in a Gambia village*, Department of Technical Co-operation Overseas Research Publication No. 2, 1963.
[2] G. Slater (editor), *Some South Indian Villages*, University of Madras Economic Series 1, 1918.
[3] E. H. Winter, *Bwamba Economy*, East African Institute of Social Research, 1956.

Name of Village:	Vadamalaipuram		Guruvayur	
Grain used as basis for 'grain equivalents':	Millet		Paddy	
	1916–17	1936–7	1916–17	1936–7
Kg. grain equivalent/ person/year	—	394	398	304
Livestock/person				
Cattle and buffaloes	0·60	0·61	0·42	0·18
of which milk animals	0·14	0·07	0·06	0·03
Sheep and goats	1·71	0·72	0·15	0·05
Pigs	0·06	—	a	a
Poultry	—	0·62	—	—
Kg. milk/milking animal				
Cows				345
Buffaloes				487
Kg. milk/person				
Cows				4·1
Buffaloes				6·8

a Included with sheep and goats.

'pre-agricultural' (e.g. the Pygmies and Bushmen), and also the earliest stages of subsistence agriculture, which he tersely defines as 'no cash crops; no tax; no import or export of labour'.

Winter's second stage is defined as 'subsistence with taxes'. Here we have some cash crops grown, and a certain amount of labour going to seek employment elsewhere, for the principal purpose of paying the tax. Administrators have imposed taxes in Africa, not only because they need revenue, but also with the deliberate object of provoking a transition from pure subsistence to a cash economy. It is not for us now to debate the very large question of whether this has been a desirable policy; we may perhaps now be entitled to say that, if there are grounds for applying it, it should nevertheless be applied with great caution and moderation. Winter gives numerous examples of African communities in this stage, such as the peoples of Ruanda Urundi, the Karamoju, the Masai, and the Bukonjo of former French West Africa.

Winter's next stage is defined as 'subsistence plus cash crops', the stage by which taxes have now become a comparatively minor part of total cash outlay, and cash crops are grown with the object of making money for the purchase of a variety of commodities. Such communities seldom have to send men to work away from the district; and at the same time seldom receive labour from other districts. Examples in Africa are the Teso, the Basoga, the Lango, the people of Sekumaland and of Gambia.

The next stage, which Winter defines as 'subsistence plus cash' is, somewhat paradoxically, one in which quite a large proportion of the men do seek work outside the district. The desire for cash expenditure is greater, and the men travel a considerable distance to get fairly high-paid work. Malawi, Togo, and the Kikuyu are examples of this stage.

Winter's fifth and sixth stages are those in which most of the agricultural labour is working for wages, firstly on agricultural plantations (e.g. the Nigerian oil-palm area, or parts of Uganda); later in a fully industrial economy, such as the Rand in South Africa. It must be pointed out that, while certain communities have passed through these stages, they are by no means universal; agricultural development may lead to an economy still mainly dependent on individual and family farmers, as in the United States.

A definite exception to de Vries's generalization, however, appears to be provided by the Hausa of Northern Nigeria. A survey of six villages in the Zaria province[1] showed agricultural production, in kg. grain equivalent/person/year, ranging from 148 to 396 only and a substantial *import* of food from outside the region to bring consumption up to minimum standards. This, however, is a good case of *exceptio probat regulum* — the exception 'proves' the rule in the old sense of the word 'prove', testing its limits and underlying assumptions. The land inhabited by the Hausa is dry savannah, with a short wet season, the only time of the year at which agriculture is possible. Even this is unreliable, and the distribution of the rainfall within the wet season erratic. Millet, a hardy crop, is best able to stand these conditions; but even so the agriculturist cannot be at all sure of his return. Under these circumstances, the Hausa, who are believed in any case to have been the descendants of immigrant nomads from the north, have become considerable practitioners of trades and handicrafts.

The village whose agriculture had been most productive (or perhaps had had the best luck with rainfall in this particular year) produced 396 kg. grain equivalent/person (190 grain and 206 cotton, of which latter 181 were sold). In addition, the men earned

[1] M. G. Smith, *The Economy of Hausa Communities in Zaria*, Colonial Research Study No. 16.

an average of 90 units by handicraft and 39 by trade; the women, trading on their own account, as is the West African custom, another 98; the sale of forest products brought in fifteen, and men working outside the village six, or a total of 644 kg. grain equivalent/person in all. Of this, 143 was used to purchase food from outside the village, bringing consumption of farm products up to 358.

The following table gives interesting further details of these six villages (including the one described above) arranged in ascending order of food consumption:

TABLE XII.   HAUSA CONSUMPTION OF FARM PRODUCTS

Kg. Grain Equivalent/Person/Year

Consumption of						
agricultural products	245	252	293	296	333	538
Non-cereal consumption included above	108	116	113	128	171	163
Agricultural production	188	148	229	362	190	396
Agricultural products sold	51	26	75	136	73	181
Agricultural products purchased	108	130	139	70	216	143
Grain	724	375	551	702	668	690
Other crops	2670	700	1095	2020	1135	1820
Principal export crop	Ground nuts	None	Cotton	Cotton	Ground nuts and sugar	Cotton
Access to road	No	No	Yes — recent	Near	Yes — old trade route	Yes — all season

The importance of access to transport in facilitating economic development could hardly be shown more clearly.

A study of the economic position of women in Bamenda in the Cameroons[1] shows that population density has risen from 13 persons/sq. km. in 1933 to 15·5 in 1948 and 26 in 1958, i.e. they now have 4 ha./person. However, the amount of land actually cultivated is only 0·18 ha./person (the same in 1948, and 0·15 in 1933), only about one-tenth of the farm land being cultivated in any given year; 16 per cent is used for grazing — but only the roughest grazing 'under range conditions' by cattle belonging to the nomadic Fulani, *not to the local inhabitants*. Responsibility for food production is left to the women who practise a system of rotational

[1] P. Kaberry, *Women of the Grassfields*: A study of the economic position of women in Bamenda, British Cameroons; Colonial Research Publication No. 14, 1952. Also W. M. Bridges, MS, 1934.

grass fallowing; the period varying from two to ten years, depending on availability and accessibility of land. The women (who work about 1200 hours/year on farm crops) obtained a yield of 1566 kg. grain equivalent/ha./year in 1933 (238 kg./person/year); an additional 150 kg./person/year was contributed by a few other men growing coffee for cash. In subsequent years, the area under food crops and coffee was increased; but yield per ha. appears not to have changed. Meanwhile, Fulani cattle trespass had become a major problem, causing widespread destruction of crops (the more numerous the cattle, the greater the income of the Fulani); by 1958 many outlying farms had been abandoned and women were beginning to fence in their crops.[1] In Kaberry's view, the present farming system could be symbiotic with a separate grazing system if it were possible to resolve farmer-grazier relations.

Bamenda, 4,500 feet above sea level, has frequently been cited as one of the most fertile areas of West Africa, with a soil and climate favourable to the production of coffee, pyrethrum, linseed and quinine, apart from numerous local food crops. To subsistence cultivators living under such generous conditions of soil and climate the raising of draught oxen must appear a superfluity.

Studies of Uganda villages much more densely populated show the transition to draught animal cultivation nearly completed (Table XIII).

The ploughs in Moruita appeared to be underpowered, and more oxen (and more grain to feed to them) necessary.

The situation in India and Pakistan is illustrated by data for the hill and submontane regions of the Punjab.[2] On farms averaging 1·11 ha./person (8·0 persons/family), after providing for the feeding of livestock, they produce 439 kg. grain equivalent/person/year, of which as much as 225 is milk. Livestock holdings per family average 3·4 draught oxen, 2·6 milch cattle, and 1·7 young stock. The average farm feeds to livestock 2280 kg./year of grain and similar foods, together with 1170 kg./year of grain equivalent of fodder crops and roughages, or 4050 kg./year in all, of which 1368 is to 2·6 milch cattle (who together yield 1519 kg./year milk).

The Punjab, however, is one of the most agriculturally advanced regions of the whole sub-continent, with holdings of livestock much higher than the average.

---

[1] P. Kaberry, *Report on Farmer-Grazier Relations*, London University, mimeographed, April 1959.
[2] *Family Budgets of Nineteen Cultivators in the Punjab, 1953–54*, Punjab Board of Economic Enquiry, Publication No. 39.

TABLE XIII. TRANSITION TO DRAUGHT ANIMAL CULTIVATION IN UGANDA VILLAGES

	Moruita[1] 1955	Kasilang[2] 1953	Ajuluka[3] 1937	Opami[3] 1937	Kasilang[2] 1937
Percentage of land hand-cultivated	1	5	5	28	29
Ha./person:					
Total land area	1·12	1·73	1·82	3·19	2·10
Cultivable land	0·85	1·17	1·49	3·15	1·33
Cultivated	0·68	0·52	0·52	0·52	0·52
Production kg. grain equivalent/person/year					
Food crops	360	298	303	331	293
Cash crops	296	195	320	204	278
Total	656	493	623	535	571
Production do., net of grain fed to draught oxen	621	447	580	504	525
Draught oxen/person	0·21	0·28	0·26	0·79	0·28
Ha. grazing/person	0	0	0·40	0·34	0

[1] P. N. Wilson, 'An Agricultural Survey of Moruita Erony, Teso', *Uganda Journal*, Vol. 22, No. 1, March 1958.

[2] P. N. Wilson and J. M. Watson, 'Two Surveys of Kasilang Erony, Teso', *Uganda Journal*, Vol. 20, No. 2, September 1956.

[3] M. G. de Courcey-Ireland, H. R. Hosking and L. J. A. Loewenthal, *An Investigation into Health and Agriculture in Teso, Uganda*, Entebbe, 1937.

CHAPTER V

National Totals of Agricultural Production

A valuable generalization made by de Vries is that in a subsistence agriculture country we must expect agricultural
output to rise at about the same rate as population. It is
constrained upwards as well as downwards. As there is little
margin to spare, if agricultural output rises slower than population,
there will soon be a famine. But conversely, if it rises more rapidly
than population, and if we maintain the assumption that the country
is to remain a subsistence agriculture society, without fundamental
transformation into a commercial and industrial country, then it
will find itself with a surplus of agricultural produce which would
overwhelm the frail structure of local marketing. This generalization is supported by evidence from our own past.

Eighteenth-century France,[1] though somewhat chivvied by
Britain, was nevertheless the greatest military and commercial
power of the time, and the world's scientific and cultural
centre. However, it was still essentially a peasant economy, and
from the beginning of the eighteenth century to 1790 the
average rate of growth of agricultural product was only 0·5 per cent
a year, as compared with the population growth of 0·2 per cent a
year.[2] If we covered the whole period from the beginning of the
eighteenth century to the end of the Napoleonic Wars we would
get a still lower figure; but it might be contended that this was
including an unduly large proportion of war years per century.

Goldsmith[3] found for Russia for the period 1860–1913, i.e. even

[1] J. C. Toutain, *Le Produit de l'Agriculture Française de 1700 à 1958*, Vol. II,
Cahiers de l'Institut de Science Economique Appliqué, Supplement No. 115,
July 1961.
[2] The higher figures for both production and population given by Toutain on
p. 204 of his report appear to be for an area which was territorially enlarging.
The figures quoted above are estimated for a constant area. Territorial enlarge-
ments during the eighteenth century (Lorraine and Corsica) are quoted by
Toutain on p. 24 of the first volume of his report, and they added 7·4 per cent to
the area of France. It is assumed that the population change was in the same
proportion.
[3] International Association for Research in Income and Wealth, Hindsgavl
Conference, 1955.

during the period of railway construction and the first steps of industrialization, agricultural production growing at 2 per cent a year, as against population growing $1\frac{1}{2}$ per cent a year.

Even in eighteenth-century England, the supposed classical case of an economic 'take-off', total real product per head of population[1] was estimated to be increasing at only 0·3 per cent per year between 1700 and 1770, 0·6 per cent from 1770 to 1800; and during these periods productive manufacturing industries and commerce were playing a rapidly increasing part in national output, so that the rate of growth of agricultural productivity per head must have been substantially less than these.

Germany between 1800 and 1883[2] provides an example of the next stage of development. During this period the rate of population growth averaged 0·8 per cent per year, higher than in the eighteenth century. Agricultural production increased at the rate of 1·1 per cent per year, still only a small lead over population. Between 1883 and 1900 the rate of growth of agricultural production accelerated to 2·1 per cent per year, while the rate of population growth had risen to 1·2 per cent per year. This increased agricultural production, relative to population, not only enabled everyone to eat rather better, but also set free resources to enable an increased proportion of the population to work in industry and other non-agricultural employments, which occupied only a quarter of the population in 1800, 59 per cent in 1883, and 68 per cent in 1900.

For Indonesia[3] we have an estimate of milled-rice consumption per head at 115 kg. for 1836. During the nineteenth century cassava was introduced into Indonesia. On the FAO scale one kg. cassava is worth 0·194 kg. milled rice, which appears to give an adequate representation of its value as a food. This coefficient is used in the following table for rice and cassava consumption in Indonesia.

	Rice	Cassava	Combined consumption rice equivalents[4]	Protein from these sources
	kg./person/year			*g./person/day*
1836	115	0	115	31
1913	102	71	116	29
1936–40	86	159	117	27

[1] P. Deane and W. A. Cole, 'The Long Term Growth of the United Kingdom', International Association for Research in Income and Wealth Conference, 1959.
[2] Bitterman, *Die Landwirtschaftliche Produktion in Deutschland, 1800–1950.*
[3] Van der Koppel, *De Landbouw in den Indischen Archipel.*
[4] Boeke, *Economics and Economic Policy of Dual Societies,* p. 278, gives consumption data for Java indicating 156 kilograms milled rice equivalent/person in 1936–40, including 24 maize, 7 sweet potatoes, 6 soya bean and 2 groundnuts.

During this period however a substantial production of sugar, tea, rubber and other commercial crops was introduced. The protein supply obtained from rice and cassava was not adequate, even on Professor Waterlow's standards; a certain amount of protein may have been obtained from other sources. Additional production in Indonesia in the latter period, of crops grown little or not at all in 1836, in kg. of milled rice equivalent per head of population (information from Java only) was 34 of other staples (maize and sweet potatoes) and 64 of 'commercial' crops (principally sugar and rubber, with some soya beans, groundnuts, copra, coffee, tea and tobacco).

When we look for an example of a country breaking out of subsistence agriculture into commercialization and industrial development, the most dramatic case is undoubtedly that of Japan, especially as the country started from a very low level. The modernization of the Japanese economy began with a single dramatic event in 1868, the counter-revolution against the nobility and samurai and the resumption of power by the Emperor Meiji. For the better part of the previous two centuries, the Tokugawa period, the emperors had been ciphers in a country entirely ruled by the nobility, a country[1] of 'virtually stationary population of 28 to 30 millions, pressed close to the limits of subsistence afforded by the simple rice economy of the coastal plains and mountain valleys, with its restricted commerce and handicrafts and burdensome exactions of feudal aristocracy'.

After the Meiji restoration a population growth at the rate of about 1 per cent per annum began. Japanese historians point out that much of this change should be explained by the cessation of the practice of infanticide. But Japan showed a capacity for increasing agricultural production at a very much greater rate. Lockwood has assembled sufficient information[2] (the Japanese have always been very good at keeping statistics) to construct index numbers of agricultural and fishery output back to the period 1885-9. For most of the period the data can be reweighted to FAO units to make them fully comparable with all our other information. In the decade beginning 1885-9 Japanese agricultural production was growing at the rate of 2·3 per cent a year. From 1905 onwards it was growing at the rate of 3·5 per cent per year, which appears to

[1] W. W. Lockwood, *The Economic Development of Japan*, O.U.P., 1955.
[2] See also E. F. Penrose, *Food Supply and Raw Materials in Japan*, Chicago, 1930.

have been the highest rate of growth of agricultural product of any country in the world at that time. This high rate of growth was continued into the 1920s, after which it was checked, primarily by the collapse in the market for silk, then one of Japan's most important agricultural products.[1]

Before we proceed further in studying rates of change of agricultural product, it is desirable to know something about its absolute level in different countries. We wish to define it 'net of agricultural inputs', that is to say, we wish to avoid double counting of produce used for seed, animal feed or manure. This is possible from figures produced by FAO and the United States Department of Agriculture (Table XIV).

TABLE XIV. TOTAL PRODUCT FROM AGRICULTURE EXPRESSED IN KG. ECONOMIC WHEAT EQUIVALENT/PERSON/YEAR

	Food	Non-food	Total
NORTH AFRICA			
Algeria	498	137	635
Egypt	410	119	529
Ethiopia	466	23	489
Libya	298	39	337
Morocco	549	44	593
Sudan	556	76	632
Tunisia	489	50	539
REST OF AFRICA			
Angola	358	150	508
Cameroun	387	208	595
Congo and Ruanda-Urundi	364	48	412
Former French Equatorial Africa	351	61	412
Former French West Africa (excl. Guinea)	356	72	428
Ghana	393	244	637
Guinea	344	7	351
Kenya	405	58	463
Liberia	325	177	502

[1] A study by a Japanese-American writer, J. I. Nakamura (*Agricultural Production and the Economic Development of Japan, 1873-1922*, 1967), attempts to prove that throughout the period specified, Japanese agricultural production was increasing at the rate of only about 1 per cent per year. His conclusion is quite untenable — see detailed review by one of the authors in *Journal of Agricultural Economics*, Sept. 1967. Japanese critics have treated this book even more harshly.

Nigeria and British Cameroons	476	31	507
Rhodesia and Nyasaland	390	124	514
South Africa	871	150	1021
Tanzania	334	92	426
Togo	370	96	466

NEAR EAST

Iran	529	45	574
Iraq	653	47	700
Israel	794	32	826
Jordan	431	4	435
Lebanon	315	17	332
Syria	491	195	686
Turkey	680	108	788

FAR EAST

Burma	567	22	589
Ceylon	377	241	618
India	346	36	382
Indonesia	465	60	525
Japan	504	36	540
Malaya	410	543	953
Pakistan	372	60	432
Philippines	678	32	710
South Korea	418	17	435
Taiwan	619	33	652
Thailand	587	65	652

LATIN AMERICA

Bolivia	397	24	421
Brazil	656	239	895
Chile	761	92	853
Colombia	641	235	876
Costa Rica	782	325	1107
Cuba	1508	96	1604
Dominican Republic	755	180	935
Ecuador	524	91	615
El Salvador	356	315	671
Guatemala	368	162	530
Haiti	341	73	414
Honduras	455	98	553
Mexico	572	149	721
Nicaragua	577	314	891
Panama	641	33	674
Paraguay	856	98	954
Peru	510	105	615
Venezuela	403	82	485

Sources: *Food Balances in Foreign Countries*, U.S.D.A. FAS-M-101, 104, 108, 1960/1, Part II, III, IV.
FAO Production Yearbook, 1960.

Buck's device of converting all agricultural products to a common unit by using prices prevailing in local markets has much to commend it, especially when dealing with information from Chinese villages and other remote places. These advantages, however, appear to be overshadowed by the advantages of having a uniform scale for all countries, if we wish to make international comparisons. Furthermore, it is desirable to choose a scale which will accord with the weighting system now used by FAO for the construction of their index numbers of agricultural production, which are based upon regional wheat relative price weights for different parts of the world. For the purposes of this book, a median has been taken of the three FAO regions — the Near East, the Far East, and Africa.

FAO weights for cattle, pigs, sheep and poultry have been converted to meat on the basis of available information on slaughter rates, average carcase weights, and meat production under tropical conditions. Cattle for beef are killed older and leaner than in temperate climates, when the meat is said to have more flavour. Sheep are less well finished, and have less wool, in the tropics; pigs are smaller and are apt to mature at lighter weights.

Apart from grains referred to above, conversion coefficients for one or two principal crops may be noted: the shelled equivalent of unshelled groundnuts does not vary unduly, averaging about 67 per cent. The ginned yield of unginned cotton may range from 25 to 33 per cent, however, whilst the conversion coefficient for wool is much higher in the tropics than in Britain where fleeces are rain washed; the average clean yield of greasy wool is 67 per cent in Britain compared with 52–56 per cent in the tropics. (See Appendix for data on relative prices.)

It must be remembered that the figures in Table XIV are expressed per head of the whole population, and in countries with a substantial proportion of non-agricultural population, the productivity of the agricultural population is to that extent higher than indicated by these figures. This is not the case, however, with the poorer countries; here we may approximately apply de Vries's categories to the figures shown. The low figures for some West African countries, particularly Guinea, Tanganyika, Jordan, India, Pakistan, South Korea, Bolivia and Haiti, all give serious cause for concern. Libya and Lebanon on the other hand have substantial alternative sources of revenue (oil and commercial development respectively) enabling them to purchase food.

Now that we have before us food consumption data in a number of countries which can be restated in wheat equivalents, we can test our theory about the nature of diets. The poorest communities, we have estimated, will probably make their diets as economical as possible or, in other words, will aim at getting near to three calories for every gram of wheat equivalent consumed. (Theoretically, they might do even better; if they lived entirely on millet, sorghum or buckwheat, which most people find unpalatable, they would be getting as many calories from each gram as they do from a gram of wheat, while only having consumed two-thirds of a gram of 'wheat equivalent', according to the measures which we are now using.)

As has already been stated, even the poorest subsistence community finds wheat bran indigestible, at any rate in large quantities, and so they mill off about 10 per cent of the weight of wheat, being left with a residue which yields about 3·4 calories/g., or 3·06 calories/g. raw wheat (if they had eaten the wheat unmilled they might have obtained, according to the reference books, 3·16 calories/g.).

This theory is seen to be approximately borne out. Even the poorest community, however, cannot get higher than 2·85 calories per g. of economic wheat equivalent consumed (Table XV). At higher levels of consumption, this ratio falls off rapidly, as an increasing proportion of fruit, meat, dairy products, etc., palatable but costly in terms of wheat equivalent, are included in the diet.

There are a few unexpected jumps in the series. The low figures for Bolivia and Nicaragua indicate a high proportion of meat in the diet — though the total calorie intake appears inadequate. The comparatively high figures for the Cameroun and Nigeria, are related to a high proportion of sweet potatoes, yams and cassava in the diet, indicating a possible protein shortage. In Tanzania, the poorest country, the effect of a certain amount of meat consumption in the pastoral regions is offset by millet consumption elsewhere.

Buck gave detailed data for consumption in 136 separate Chinese villages in the early 1930s. These were likewise ranged in ascending order of calorie consumption, and each tenth village selected for analysis on the same lines, all food consumed being expressed in wheat equivalents by the same international scale as used above (not on Buck's original scale, based on Chinese prices, etc.).

In this case, however, the results did not indicate a declining ratio as the nutrition of a village improved (the range covered was

TABLE XV.   ECONOMIC AND CALORIE VALUE OF DIETS

Country	Food consumption expressed in kg. economic wheat equivalent per person per year	Calories Per capita per day (actual)	Per gramme of economic wheat equivalent consumed
Former Fr. West Africa (excluding Guinea)	314	2450	2·85
Angola	330	2215	2·45
Tanzania	334	2175	2·38
Guinea	335	2400	2·61
Liberia	341	2540	2·72
Togo	344	2645	2·81
Former Fr. Equatorial Africa	354	2575	2·66
India	354	2050	2·11
Congo and Ruanda-Urundi	363	2650	2·66
Kenya	366	2240	2·23
Haiti	377	1875	1·81
Guatemala	379	2175	2·09
Pakistan	383	2030	1·93
Honduras	389	2190	2·05
Cameroun	397	2470	2·27
Libya	398	2180	2·00
El Salvador	400	1975	1·80
Fed. of Rhodesia and Nyasaland	416	2500	2·19
Nigeria and the British Cameroons	435	2680	2·25
Ecuador	444	1935	1·59
South Korea	448	2040	1·66
Ethiopia	464	2295	1·81
Indonesia	471	2125	1·65
Ghana	477	2605	1·99
Egypt	480	2340	1·78
Dominican Republic	480	1950	1·48
Burma	485	2150	1·62
Syria	491	2225	1·65
Bolivia	492	1880	1·39
Tunisia	502	2170	1·58
Ceylon	514	2060	1·46
Thailand	518	2185	1·54
Peru	527	2040	1·41
Malaya	528	2290	1·58
Iraq	536	2255	1·54

Country	Food consumption expressed in kg. economic wheat equivalent per person per year	Calories Per capita per day (actual)	Per gramme of economic wheat equivalent consumed
Iran	537	2040	1·38
Japan	549	2310	1·54
Taiwan	551	2430	1·55
Lebanon	553	2415	1·59
Morocco	556	2480	1·63
Sudan	561	2295	1·49
Mexico	573	2725	1·74
Jordan	573	2085	1·33
Nicaragua	586	1985	1·24
Algeria	587	2230	1·39
Venezuela	608	2255	1·35
Philippines	631	2145	1·24
Panama	634	2370	1·36
Turkey	656	2650	1·47
Brazil	657	2818	1·57
Colombia	657	2225	1·23
Costa Rica	701	2555	1·33
South Africa	741	2620	1·29
Cuba	776	2870	1·35
Paraguay	817	2355	1·05
Chile	823	2610	1·16
Israel	998	2715	0·99

Sources: *Food Balances in Foreign Countries*, U.S.D.A. FAS-M-101, 104, 108, 1960/61 Parts II, III, IV.

Food consumption per head is not the same as in the previous table because of exports, imports and changes to stocks of food.

from 1000 to 4000 calories/person/day). The distinction was rather regional. The average for all the villages surveyed was 2·67 calories/g. wheat equivalent, which was about what was to be expected in relation to the figures for other countries given in the previous table. But for the rice-eating villages the average was only 2·20. A gram of wheat equivalent corresponds to 1·25 g. of rough rice, or 0·92 g. of milled rice, giving 3.32 calories, if we assume milling at the minimum Japanese rate. So it is not rice eating as such, but some other features in the diets of the rice-eating villages — they are in the richer part of China, and consume more meat and fruit — which account for this low figure. There were, however, several villages whose diet consisted predominantly of millet, sorghum and other coarse grains, which appeared to be satisfactory in that it did not include excessively high proportions of root crops, or a low proportion of vegetables. In these villages the calories obtained per g. of wheat equivalent consumed were about equivalent to the full theoretical figure of 3·16 — the calories lost in the consumption of meat, vegetables, etc., were fully made up by the greater cheapness of millet in relation to wheat.

These coarse grains, particularly millet, are dry and difficult to eat. Africans mix leafy vegetables with them to make them more palatable. In many parts of Asia it is regarded as a degradation to have to consume millet instead of rice.

Nevertheless, if we set out to state the physiological minimum requirements of mankind, we must assume that people threatened with an actual shortage of food will be willing to eat millets, etc., and in this way obtain 3·16 calories per g. wheat equivalent consumed. This means that each calorie consumed per day calls for 0·1155 kg. wheat equivalent to be consumed per year.

The above analysis enables us to restate more precisely our provisional conclusions on minimum requirements in terms of kg. wheat equivalent per head per year, at 230 for small-bodied people in a hot climate, rising to 275 for fairly large-bodied people (adult males 60 kg.) in a cold climate. Including a minimum requirement of textile fibres, therefore, we can state the minimum agricultural requirements of mankind as ranging from 245 to 290 kg. wheat equivalent/person/year, according to varying climates and body weights: in round figures, a little over a quarter of a ton.

We may now examine in more detail the nature of agricultural growth beyond subsistence level. In the normal course of events, we should expect it to be in livestock products or crops other than the subsistence crops (cereals and roots). This is however not always the case — a country may continue to expand its production of subsistence crops beyond its own requirements, and export some of them.

The method used in the following table is to record the output of all these non-subsistence products, converted into wheat equivalents, in kg. per head of population. A conventional allowance of 250 kg. wheat equivalent for subsistence is made at the end of the table. Exports of subsistence products are added and, in some cases, imports debited. This method is not merely for the purpose of saving a certain amount of arithmetic, in compiling the data for the subsistence crops; it is also because of the fact that in many of

D

these countries information on the output of the subsistence crops, and still more, of the quantities used for seed and animal feeding, which should be excluded from estimates of final agricultural output, are much less accurately known than we might wish. The subsistence figure is meant to include the wheat equivalent of fruits and vegetables, which may be consumed in fairly large quantities by subsistence populations, and of whose output we have very little accurate information.

Considerable diversities in the pattern are noticeable. Milk, for instance, is completely absent in China and the Philippines, virtually absent in Japan. It is almost as important a product in India as it is in Brazil. It plays a larger part in the cooler climates, particularly Sweden and Russia. Supplies of meat seem to go up as the economy advances, subject to the important qualification that Japan and the Philippines, with their comparatively large supplies of fish, need less meat on that account. Eggs never form a large part of output in such countries. The other crops, apart from tobacco which is widely grown round the world, tend to be specialized to the countries which are climatically suited to them, except for silk, which could have been grown in a variety of climates, but which flourished in Japan due to the long experience of the people, and their low wages.

The supply of information about the rates of growth of agricultural production in the low-income countries is gradually improving, although there are still many gaps in our knowledge. FAO began compiling the index numbers of food production and of total agricultural production, using as uniform as possible a system of weights, and first taking 1934–8 as their base. They now use an improved weighting system and 1952–6 base, and information is available for a substantially increased number of countries. FAO set out to make these index numbers net of seed and animal feeding stuffs.

An alternative set of results has been provided by O.E.C.D.[1] These are obtained from countries' own national accounts statistics, and are based on national systems of weighting, which may differ substantially from the international system used by FAO. They are measured at given prices throughout. They set out to measure 'value added by agriculture', which means that they make debits not only for seed, feeding stuffs, etc., but also for the 'industrial inputs' — equipment, chemical fertilizer, transport and other

[1] *National Accounts of Less Developed Countries, 1950–66*, Table G.

TABLE XVI. PRODUCTION OTHER THAN CEREALS, ROOTS, FRUITS AND VEGETABLES FOR LOCAL SUBSISTENCE, IN KG. WHEAT EQUIVALENT/HEAD OF POPULATION/YEAR

Country	Year	Meat	Milk	Wool	Eggs	Silk	Fish	Sugar	Tea	Coffee	Cocoa	Jute	Cotton	Tobacco	Other crops	Net imports (−) or exports (+) of cereals and roots	Total	Add 250 (assumed) for subsistence	Population m.	Total Product (m. metric tons wheat equivalent)	Do. in present day boundaries
China[1]	1933	31			6		8						11	4	8	−2	68	318	500	159	
"	1955-6	21			4		15	1	1				15	4	6	+4	71	321	628	202	
India[2]	1931-2[a]	8	75	1	1		8	1	1			9	12	9	24	+7	158	408	271		
Philippines[3]	1960	10	63	1	1		5	13	5					5	26	−12	142	392	27.4		
"	1935-7	29			1		5	16	7	1		6	13		63	−12	228	478	12.8		
Iraq[4]	1934-5	84	37	21	4		45						1		16	+35	242	492	3.55		
Japan[5]	1895-9	5	0.7		3	20	43		6						4	+1	83	333	42.7	14.2	
"	1900-4	6	0.9		4	23	46		5							−1	89	339	45.2	15.3	
"	1905-9	7	1		6	26	51		5							−3	97	347	48.1	16.7	
"	1910-14	7	1		7	32	88		6							−12	133	383	51.3	19.6	
"	1915-19	8	1		7	43	123		5							−6	189	439	54.9	24.1	
"	1920-4	8	2		7	44	173		6							−20	229	479	58.8	28.2	
"	1925-7	8	2		16	75	219		6							−33	293	543	61.7	33.5	
"	1934-8	12	6		16	56	215		6						8	−28	291	541	69.0	37.3	
Syria[4]	1934-5	57	92	22	8		(10)						8	6	122	−13	315	565	3.4		
Egypt[4]	1934-5	78	39	1	7		(10)	9					153	16		+1	318	568	15.3		
Palestine[4]	1934-5	23	106	5	17		(10)	9							307	−89	385	635	1.23		
Sweden[6]	1861-5	100	261	5	5		(20)									+30	406	656	4.0		
Turkey[4]	1934-5	88	157	15	11		(20)						18	18	101	+11	445	695	16.0		
Cyprus	1934-5	76	46	14	18		(5)	6					11	11	270	−22	450	700	0.366		
Yugoslavia[7]	1939	172	180	9	18		6	6						7	11	+33	441	691	15.8		
"[b]		48	138		15		1	1													
"[c]		375	315		51			21													
Brazil[3]	1924-5	127	79	4	5		(10)	49		144	8		25	14	36	−17	484	734	34	25.0	
"	1934-5	145	77	5	7		(10)	60		225	14		48	20	43	−23	631	881	41	36.1	
"	1938-9	149	76	5	9		(10)	63		168	14		63	18	35	−20	590	840	44	37.0	
U.S.S.R.[8]	1913	188	230	12	18			26					10	5	11	+69	572	822	139.3	114.5	129
"	1928	179	262	13	7			18					11	8	22	+7	545	795	151.1	120.4	135
"	1932	177	170	5	13			9					16	12	28	+20	468	718	158.1	113.5	128
"	1937	106	205	7	16			30					31	13	33	+19	472	722	165.1	119.2	133
"	1940[d]	173	177	8	18			25					21	13	36	+71	549	799	198.0	158.2	
"	1950	144	188	10	24			33					43	14	64	+57	557	807	186.3	150.3	
"	1955	182	223	13				48					39		61	+30	656	906	199.0	180.3	
"	1959	241	318	17	32			55					41	19	61	+24	838	1088	210.5	229.0	

[a] Excluding Princely States and Burma. [b] Kosmet (most densely populated area). [c] Voivodina (least densely populated area). [d] Boundary change.

[1] For 1933: J. L. Buck, *Land Utilization in China*. For 1955-6: *An Economic Profile of Mainland China*, U.S. Joint Economic Committee, 1967.
[2] V. K. V. Rao, *The National Income of British India, 1931–32*, London, 1940.
[3] *International Institute of Agriculture Yearbook*.
[4] Bonné, *Economic Development of the Middle East*, 1943.
[5] W. W. Lockwood, *The Economic Development of Japan*, O.U.P., 1955.
[6] Myrdal and others, *The National Income of Sweden, 1861 to 1930*.
[7] Mihailović, *World Population Conference*, 1954.
[8] *The Real Product of Soviet Russia*, U.S. Senate Committee on the Judiciary, 1961.

TABLE XVII. GROWTH-RATES PER CENT PER YEAR — AGRICULTURE AND POPULATION

	Agricultural production (FAO)		Value added in agriculture (O.E.C.D.)	Population	
	1934–8 to 1952–6	1952–6 to 1965–7	1950–2 to 1964–6	1934–8 to 1952–6	1952–6 to 1965–7
LATIN AMERICA					
Brazil	1·8	4·1	4.6	2·3	3·1
Colombia	3·3	3·0	3·1[a]	2·2	3·5
Cuba	2·2	1·0		1·9	2·3
Dominican Republic			3·4[b]		3·6
Guatemala		5·2	3·9[a]	2·5	3·1
Honduras		4·0	2·4[a]	2·3	3·2
Jamaica			3·5[a]		1·6
Mexico	3·6	5·3	4·3	2·5	3·6
Nicaragua			3·2		3·0
Panama		4·3	4·4	2·6	3·1
Paraguay			2·4		2·7
Peru	2·3	2·4		1·9	2·2
Venezuela		6·1	5·6	2·9	4·0
FAR EAST					
Burma	−0·5	2·1		1·3	2·2
Ceylon	2·3	3·0		2·3	2·5
India	0·9	2·0	2·1	1·3	2·3
Indonesia	0·9	1·5		1·1	2·4
Malaysia	1·6	3·9		2·1[h]	3·0
Pakistan	0·6	2·3	2·2	1·1[i]	2·2
Philippines	1·9	3·2	3·1	2·1	3·6
South Korea	0·2	4·7	3·9[c]	2·1[g]	2·5[o]
Taiwan	1·3	4·3		2·7	3·4
Thailand	3·0	5·0	4·8[d]	2·0	4·0
AFRICA AND NEAR EAST					
Algeria	0·7	−1·8		1·5[j]	2·1
Ethiopia		3·2			
Iran		3·5		0·6[k]	2·9
Iraq		2·4		2·6[l]	2·8
Libya		5·9			3·6[p]
Morocco	2·1	1·4	1·4[d]	1·6[m]	3·1[q]
Nigeria			3·2[b]		
Syria		2·7	4·6[e]	2·6[n]	3·2
Tunisia	1·3	0·2	3·0		1·6
Turkey	3·0	3·6		2·0	2·6
Uganda			3·7[f]		2·5
U.A.R. (Egypt)	1·4	3·0		2·0	2·4

[a] 1950–2 to 1963–5
[b] 1950–2 to 1962–4
[c] 1953–5 to 1964–6
[d] 1951–3 to 1964–6
[e] 1953–5 to 1963–5
[f] 1954–6 to 1964–6
[g] All Korea, 1934–8 to 1953
[h] 1936–8 to 1952–6
[i] 1941 to 1952–6

[j] 1936 to 1952–6
[k] 1937 to 1952–6
[l] 1934 to 1952–6
[m] 1939 to 1952–5
[n] 1937–9 to 1952–6
[o] 1953 to 1965–7
[p] 1954 to 1965–7
[q] 1956 to 1965–7

purchases which play so large a part in the agriculture of the advanced countries. Even in the poorest countries, however, there must be a small debit for the depreciation of tools and buildings. By this reckoning the O.E.C.D. rate of growth should always appear a little lower than the FAO index. This is usually but not always the case. Where the difference is in the other direction, we should probably put this down to a difference in the weighting system, or, in some cases, to the period of years covered.

During the war years, some of the subsistence agriculture countries were themselves battlefields; and in the others, production was seriously disturbed by disorganization of markets. Between the 1930s and the mid-1950s, as is seen from the table, production in many cases had failed to rise at a rate sufficient to keep pace with population growth. During the subsequent decade the situation has improved. Attention should be drawn, however, to the countries where agricultural production is rising less rapidly than population. In Latin America these include the Dominican Republic and Colombia by a small margin, and Cuba by a very wide margin. Paradoxically, Venezuela, which could afford to let agriculture slip in view of its very large oil revenues, has in fact expanded agricultural production at a high rate — perhaps wealthy business-men are investing in agricultural estates, and running them efficiently.

The available figures for Africa reveal a very bad situation in Algeria, and fairly bad in Morocco and Tunisia. In Algeria at any rate this can be blamed upon political disturbance. Egypt, in spite of her high rate of population growth in a rigidly constrained land area, nevertheless shows a substantial increase in agricultural production per head. For Ethiopia and Nigeria, no population figures are available (in one case due to the lack of, in the other case to the falsification of the census). But it is unlikely that population growth exceeds the recorded rate of agricultural growth of 3·2 per cent in either country. Libya, like Venezuela, is another example of an oil-rich country which is clearly investing in agri-culture, hitherto of a very low productivity. But Iraq, another oil-rich country, is showing only a moderate increase in agricul-tural production; Iran, also with oil, is doing better.

Burma suffered heavily in the war and subsequent political disorder, but is now just about keeping pace with population growth. Ceylon, in spite of some political disturbances, has increased agricultural production faster than population. In the

Philippines, agricultural production is gradually falling behind the high rate of population growth; but this is not the situation in Thailand, a country of similar land and climate and a substantial exporter of agricultural produce. Pakistan has had a better rate of agricultural growth than India. (This is almost entirely due to improved irrigation and fertilizing in West Pakistan, while impoverished East Pakistan stagnates.) In India, after good development in the 1950s, production fell behind population growth again in the 1960s. The situation was made worse by two succeeding exceptionally bad seasons in 1965 and 1966.

The situation in India was analysed more thoroughly by Sen.[1]

TABLE XVIII. AGRICULTURAL AND POPULATION RATES OF GROWTH, INDIA

	Per cent per year			
	Area cultivated	*Yield*	*Agricultural product*	*Population*
1900–19	0·29	0·24	0·53	0·25
1920–39	0·24	− 0·44	0·20	0·83
1940–49	0·66	− 1·63	− 0·97	1·32
1950–60	1·18	2·34	3·52	1·98

We also have similar information[2] for Taiwan, where cultivable area cannot be expanded, and double cropping prevails to an increasing degree.

	Increase per cent per year	
	Agricultural output	*Population*
1910–20	1·7	1·3
1930–39	4·2	2·4
1939–45	−12·3	0·5
1945–52	12·9	4·9
1952–60	4·0	3·6

Lockwood points to the most spectacular feature of Japanese economic growth — the very rapid growth of industry after the turn of the century. With large numbers moving into industry, incentives to the cultivator were sustained by the supplies of textiles, hardware, building materials, etc., available to him at low prices. More significant than the aggregate growth in the Japanese economy, however, was the sustained rise in the efficiency of labour. In farming, most of the efficiency gain was the result of

[1] World Population Conference 1965.
[2] Hsieh and Lee, Chinese-American Joint Committee on Rural Reconstruction, Economics Digest Service 17, 1960.

simple scientific improvements, plant breeding, increased irrigation and use of fertilizers; in industry the productivity of labour
advanced more rapidly with the harnessing of mechanical energy
to industrial pursuits. But the gain in transport efficiency, measured
in human effort, Lockwood regards as the outstanding case of
saving labour on a massive scale — and the availability of transport
enabled labour and capital to be combined and concentrated in
various specialized ways, resulting in the exchange of surpluses in
widely organized markets.

The Mexican revolution of 1910 transformed a semi-feudal
economy into one of rapid economic growth, following distribution
of land to peasants, and the spread of education. (Nationalization
of oil and the railroads came later, in the 1930s: an international
crisis over the expropriation of foreign property was narrowly
avoided.) Since 1940 there has been a boom reminiscent of the
great expansion in the United States in the nineteenth century.
This expansion in the economy from 1940 is partly explained by
the close co-operation between the United States and Mexico with
heavy U.S. investment, the annual migration of Mexican agricultural workers to the States, and the exchange of students and tech-
nicians; in addition Mexico is very dependent upon the U.S.
tourist trade to stabilize its economy.

Urban centres of modern commerce and secondary industry
with relatively large wage-earning populations have developed as a
direct result of the rapid expansion of cash-crop production in
Africa; the outstanding feature of the increased product is, however, that it has mainly been used to purchase imports — also a
notable feature of the Japanese economy in early stages of
development.

There may still be some who believe that Communist revolution
can solve the problem of agricultural development.

We take first the experience of Soviet Russia.

Taking (except for 1913) averages of three years at a time to
smooth out weather anomalies, we see that the first effect of the
1917 revolution was a drastic reduction in food supplies per head.
Accentuated by drought, this led to a disastrous famine in a number of regions in 1921, which induced Lenin to restore freedom of
production and property ownership to the farmers, subject to
their selling a specified part of their output to the Government at
proclaimed prices. This led to a rapid restoration of agricultural
productivity, though even in the best period supplies per head of

TABLE XIX. AGRICULTURAL PRODUCTION IN SOVIET RUSSIA

	1913	1921–3	1926–8	1932–4	1937–9	1951–3	1957–9	1960–2	1963–5	1966–8
Agricultural production	147·2	111·3	150·5	127·2	163·9	194·0	247·5	265·4	281·4	342·0
Population (millions)	139·3	132·0	148·7	158·8	168·1	191·0	207·0	217·8	227·7	235·5
Production per head, tons of wheat equivalent/year	1·06	0·84	1·01	0·80	0·97	1·02	1·19	1·22	1·23	1·45

Production measured net of seed and feeding stuffs and including fibres. In millions of tons of wheat equivalent (world price weights of 1934–8). To 1957 from Colin Clark, *The Real Product of Soviet Russia*, U.S. Senate Committee on the Judiciary, 1961; subsequently from United States Dept. of Agriculture (also calculated net of seed and feeding stuffs) linked on 1953–5 (see U.S. Dept. of Agriculture, ERS Foreign 115, 151, 259).

population were less than they had been in 1913. In 1929 Stalin reversed course and decreed the collectivization of all farming, which led to another great decline in output and a disastrous famine in the Ukraine and the north Caucasus in 1933. Recovery was slow, and it was not until the late 1950s, after Krushchev had relaxed the rigour of Stalin's agricultural policy, that even the consumption standards of 1913 could be recovered. To see any increase in food supplies as a result of Communism, the Russian people had to wait nearly half a century — and meanwhile there had been steady increases in nearly all other countries.

The experience of Communist China has been even more discouraging.

	Food production millions of tons wheat equivalent				Population millions	Production per head kg./year wheat equivalent
	China Quarterly	U.S. Consulate Hongkong	Dawson	Larsen		
1929–37	248				564	440
1952–4	243				562	432
1955–8	259		259	259	596	434
1957	257	257	255	260	601	428
1958	266	270	282		611	435–61
1959		234	235		616	380
1960		222	220		615	359
1961		232	234		615	378
1962		247	248⎫	256	619	400
1963		249	255⎭		622	400–10
1964		254	269	253	629	400–27
1965		250	272	253	636	392–426
1966				253	643	

Production net of seeds and feeding stuffs from *China Quarterly*, Jan.–Mar. 1965, p. 152. Relative prices taken as U.S. *retail* prices of 1950. Other recent data are estimates based on grain and potato production only, linked to the *China Quarterly*, series on 1955–8 or 1957. For the two former series, see U.S. Joint Economic Committee, *An Economic Profile of Mainland China*, 1967; for Larsen's estimate, see International Federation of Agricultural Producers *News*, Sept. 1966. Population from Colin Clark, *Population Growth and Land Use*, 1967, p. 58, and *Population*, Nov. 1966.

In view of the complete cessation of publication of statistics from China since 1959, estimates made by outside experts have had to be used. We do have, however, one interesting confirmation from Chou En-lai himself. While travelling in Africa in 1964, he admitted[1] that 1963 grain and potato production was below 190 million tons (1957 having been 185 million tons).

The supply of food in China in the 1930s was above the sub-

[1] Interview with Edgar Snow at Conakry, 23 Jan. 1964, quoted in *Population*, May–June 1965, pp. 508–10.

sistence level, though not by a wide margin. Buck's studies show that, in the absence of a satisfactory system of transport and commerce, wide differences between villages prevailed, some having abundant food and others being below subsistence level during the year of investigation.

After the revolution, in the 1950s, and while collectivization was still tentative, agricultural production per head recovered to a level a little below that of the pre-revolutionary period, as it did in Russia. But after 1958, 'The Year of the Great Leap Forward', when farms were organized into 'communes', production fell disastrously, and about 1960-1 there was widespread famine.

It appears that there has been an actual loss of cultivated land.[1] During the 1950s, damaged irrigation works were restored and cultivated land rose from 108 million ha. in 1949 to 112 million in 1957. By 1963, because of grandiose but impracticable irrigation projects and mismanagement leading to soil salination, the cultivated area was down to 106·7 million ha.

The population estimates, which are the best which can be made, are considerably lower than those generally quoted. If in fact population is higher, then food supply per head must be even worse than is shown by the table.

It must also be noted that the table ends in 1966, the year in which the Red Guards and the Cultural Revolution appeared, which must have caused considerable further damage to production and transport.

[1] Joint Economic Committee, *An Economic Profile of Mainland China*, 1967, p. 82.

CHAPTER VI

Labour Productivity and Requirements

From these figures of national agricultural product, necessarily limited to countries for which reasonably good national statistics are available, we now turn to information on productivity based on general local observation, or studies of individual farms, or groups of farms. To have such information in the form merely of round-figure general averages is a useful start: but it is much more interesting if we are able to compare farms at different levels of labour input/ha., so that we can estimate the marginal productivity of labour, or of land. These procedures have not yet been carried out satisfactorily in any great number of cases by agricultural economists even in the advanced countries, and we must be content with rough and ready measurements. Nevertheless, they are of great interest and importance. Finally, we can test our results by applying the basic economic theorem, that the wage paid to hired agricultural labourers should be approximately equal to the marginal product of labour.

There has been a widespread belief that the poor countries have a large 'surplus' of agricultural population, with low or zero marginal productivity, which could therefore be transferred to industrial work, to their country's great advantage. But any such plans come up against the fact that the requirements for labour are far from being evenly distributed throughout the year. Periods of idleness, sometimes prolonged, in countries with a long dry or cold season, are followed by periods of intense activity, when every hand is needed, including children, and any labour withdrawn from agriculture at this season has serious consequences for output.

In no country has this question been more disastrously misunderstood — or the consequences more grave — than in China.

The distribution of work throughout the year of Chinese farms was carefully investigated by Buck who showed that the average amount of time lost was only 15 per cent (1·8 months); and that this was practically confined to the winter months. Even at the time of Buck's enquiry, 65 per cent of the villages reported some labour shortage at harvest time. Only 19 per cent of the villages reported that they never experienced labour shortage. It may seem paradoxical to talk about a labour shortage in China. But set out to cultivate a country of that size almost entirely with hand-tools, and you will soon find that you need 600 million population.

But Mao had other sources of information. 'Under present conditions of production', he wrote in his book, *Socialist Upsurge*, 'there would be a one-third manpower surplus in rural areas.' And, having written it, he probably believed it. Possibly he was basing his judgement on India, where only two-thirds of the available labour is occupied. But in comparison with China, this might be called 'technical unemployment'; India is more 'technically advanced' than China, using ox ploughs which require less labour.

Never has a mistake in information on agricultural economics had more serious consequences. It was the belief in the existence of this 'one-third surplus' of labour among the rural population which led to the massive diversion of rural labour to all sorts of other projects during the 'Great Leap Forward' which began in 1958, many of them quite futile, such as the rural blast furnaces which had to have most of their materials carried by hand, and ended up by yielding an unusable product. It was this artificially created labour shortage which has been primarily responsible for the food shortages of subsequent years, not floods and droughts.

It is not that Mao did not have warning. Ma Yin-chu, President of the University of Peking, one of the few independent thinkers in China (he believes that population growth should be restricted) pointed out[1] that there were critical labour shortages at a vital period of the year described by the Chinese proverb 'in the morning yellow, in the evening green' (when peasants are harvesting the first rice crop, but having to transplant the seedlings for the second rice crop in the cool of the evening of the same day). Even in 1956, the government had ordered excessive planting in Chekiang Province beyond the capacity of the labour available, with the result that transplantation of the second crop was not performed over a wide area, and over a larger area was left very late, with consequent very low crop yields.

For China, Ma Yin-chu advocated the use of machinery —

[1] *New Construction*, Peking, November 1959 (Chinese text). We are indebted to Dr. K. R. Walker, School of Oriental Studies, University of London, for these quotations.

'The future key to rich increases in rural production', he wrote, 'is in mechanical assistance during the excessively busy period.' He may have been right, if the demand for labour in China is really very sharply peaked: though the matter requires very careful examination, in view of the capital cost involved.

The most extreme seasonal inequalities in the demand for labour arise in the agriculture of monsoonal countries, where work has to be concentrated in a short wet season. (Countries with very cold winters have a less extreme seasonality of demand for labour.) It is true that the better distributed the rainfall, the better distributed also the demand for labour; but even where rainfall is uniform, there are still peak demands. In some parts of India, where the rainy season is very short, this peaks the demand for labour in a most alarming manner. Instead of being in embarrassing surplus, labour suddenly becomes the critically scarce factor of production. If any able-bodied man or woman is incapacitated by illness (e.g. the malaria which is prevalent in many of these countries) during this period, the loss of production may be very serious.

TABLE XX. UTILIZATION OF LABOUR IN AGRICULTURE AS PERCENTAGE OF AVAILABLE LABOUR SUPPLY

| | | India | | Ghana[d] | Iraq[e] | |
| | | Madhya[b] | Maha- | Cocoa | Middle | Best area |
Month	China[a]	Pradesh	rashtra[c]	farming	Tigris	(Diyala)
January	47	29	65	57	22	24
February	78	29	62	18	23	27
March	94	41	66	30	23	26
April	97	41	32	28	35	39
May	98	52	34	30	70	92
June	96	33	42	30	72	94
July	94	127	55	47	56	76
August	96	127	60	57	60	76
September	97	93	47	75	52	43
October	92	96	52	100	53	45
November	82	82	100	90	54	52
December	57	82	94	65	25	35

Note: Figures in excess of 100 indicate temporary agricultural work done by non-agricultural workers of the village.

[a] Calculated from Buck, Land Utilization in China, Vol. III, Statistics.
[b] Shiwalkar, Indian Journal of Agricultural Economics, March 1954 (refers to periods beginning about the middle of the months specified).
[c] Institute of Agriculture, Anand. Bulletin No. 4, March 1958.
[d] Beckett, London School of Economics Monograph on Social Anthropology, No. 10.
[e] Hunting Technical Services. Final Report to the Government of Iraq, Diyala and Middle Tigris Project.

TABLE XXI. EGYPT (NUMBER OF DAYS OF WORK
REQUIRED FOR PLANT PRODUCTION PER PERSON IN
PERMANENT LABOUR FORCE)

Month	Men		Women & Children		Men and Women & Children	
	1955	1960	1955	1960	1955	1960
January	6	7	2	3	5	5
February	14	16	2	3	9	11
March	7	8	6	7	7	8
April	18	20	8	8	14	15
May	27	28	9	10	19	21
June	21	23	32	36	26	29
July	12	13	22	26	16	18
August	10	11	25	30	16	19
September	17	19	31	37	23	26
October	17	19	16	18	17	20
November	9	9	6	6	7	8
December	9	10	2	3	7	7
Total	168	184	161	187	166	185
Average	14·0	15·3	13·4	15·6	13·8	15·4

It is only recently that scientific tests have indicated how serious can be the effects of even slight delays in planting, in climates where the wet season is so short. Akehurst and Sreedharan[1] have shown that a month's delay in planting maize in Tanzania may cause only a 15 per cent loss, but in other years may cause 50–80 per cent loss. A number of experiments on cotton throughout Africa[2] show an average loss of 8 per cent for each week's delay. With the best will in the world, farmers cannot keep absolutely precise schedules. 'If farmers carried out every operation at the time indicated by agricultural officers to be necessary for optimum yields, they would in effect have to cope with a number of insurmountable peaks of labour demand.'[3]

Experience in some European countries such as Italy and Greece shows that the cultivation of fruit and the keeping of livestock spread the demand for labour better over the year. These countries too, however, have a problem of labour shortage at the peak period. Precise details of monthly or weekly labour requirements through-

[1] *East African Agricultural and Forestry Journal*, Jan. 1965.
[2] Dept. of Technical Co-operation, Miscellaneous Report No. 2, 1962.
[3] Judith Heyer, quoted in de Wilde, *Agricultural Development in Tropical Africa*, Vol. II, pp. 101–2.

CHART III

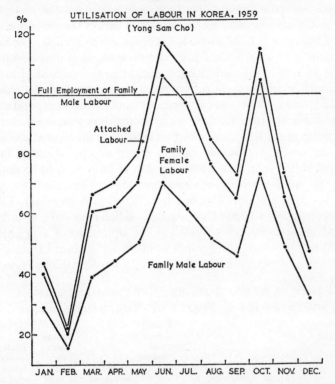

UTILISATION OF LABOUR IN KOREA, 1959
(Yong Sam Cho)

Full Employment of Family Male Labour

Attached Labour

Family Female Labour

Family Male Labour

out the year have been estimated nationally for Egypt[1] (Table XXI), and are also available for a sample area in Korea[2] (Chart III). It will be seen that Egypt has two peaks of really acute labour shortage at the time of rice planting and cotton harvesting. A similar situation is apparent in Korea, where the principal crop is rice.

Labour shortages are frequently alleviated by hiring from surrounding areas. But this is only a temporary remedy. Even if the men like it, industrial employers in the long run are going to prefer a regular labour force, which will be much more efficient. Before long it will be urgently necessary to smooth out these peaks of labour demands, and the problem may have to be faced in countries which have not the capital or the knowledge to intensify in the way that the countries of Southern Europe have done, by growing fruit, keeping livestock, etc.

[1] Mona El Tomy and Bent Hansen, *Seasonal Employment Profile in Egyptian Agriculture*, Institute of National Planning, Memo. No. 501, 1964, p. 12.
[2] Yong Sam Cho, *Disguised Unemployment in Under-developed Areas.*

A particularly thorough study was made by Kitsopanides[1] in the Florina district of Greek Macedonia, a mountainous district right on the Albanian border, where we would expect the problems of underemployment to be worse than for Greece as a whole. For the first time, it appears, he has measured the amount of time devoted by the women to domestic labour, indicating the amount of time left available for farm work. Of the available time of the able-bodied women, 38 per cent is occupied in domestic work, and the remainder is available for farm work. In the busy summer months the women are able to defer a certain amount of the domestic work until the winter. Greek law requires children to be educated, but law and custom permit a certain amount of farm work to be done by the children (estimated at 16 hours in May, 18 hours in June, 36 hours in July, 50 hours in August, 22 hours in September). The average farm is 5 ha., and has 1·84 able-bodied men and 2·05 able-bodied women (the latter treated as the equivalent of 1·54 able-bodied men). Sundays and public holidays are excluded from the calculations of available labour supply. In a mountainous region,

TABLE XXII.   LABOUR REQUIREMENTS IN A
MOUNTAINOUS DISTRICT OF NORTHERN GREECE

Month	Available labour[a]	Domestic labour	Family labour on farm[b]	Family labour not required on farm or in home	of which employed elsewhere	Unoccupied family labour as % of available	Non-family labour hired on farms
			Hours/man equivalent[c]/month				
January	216	70	35	111	21	42	—
February	221	64	54	103	26	35	—
March	250	67	78	105	27	31	5
April	275	73	90	112	25	32	6
May	320	63	132	125	21	33	18
June	341	56	193	92	19	21	26
July	347	51	246	50	15	10	25
August	382	55	240	57	15	12	20
September	319	59	168	92	18	23	11
October	275	66	113	96	30	24	10
November	250	68	49	113	39	37	1
December	216	73	38	105	29	35	—
	3380	716	1438	1226	295	28	124

[a] Sundays and public holidays are excluded from the calculations of available labour supply.
[b] Child labour included in the high figures for the summer months: maximum assumed for the man himself, 300 hours/month.
[c] Women treated as 0·75 man-units.

[1] G. Kitsopanides, privately communicated.

Labour Input man hours/hectare/year

	Africa—general	Came-roun	East Africa	Gambia	Ghana	Haute Volta	Nigeria	Uganda	Guate-mala
Rice, rough				1534k		760			
Maize	900				650	416	305		565
Millet	500c			544		390		820	
Sorghum		700	455	166		390			
Sweet potato	1160					585			
Cassava	1870					260	355		
Yams	2330		1030		1665	591	1085		
Groundnuts in shell	1515	730	1160	650		520			
Sesame						390			
Beans		515							
Voandrou						390			
Cowpea							240		
Guinea Corn							770	1160	
Bananas									
Vegetables		830			10500	715	450		
Cotton unginned	1095								
Cocoa									
Tobacco						780			

Product kg. wheat equivalent/man hour

	Wheat Equivalent	Africa—general	Came-roun	East Africa	Gambia	Ghana	Haute Volta	Indo-nesia	Malawi	Nigeria	Uganda	Guate-mala
Rice, rough	0·80				0·51f		0·67	1·20	0·43h			3·64i
Maize	0·75	1·49			0·68		1·15		0·87	1·22		
Millet	0·68	1·30			0·32		0·61		0·29g		0·34	
Sorghum	0·60		0·87	1·56	0·64	0·82	0·69					
Sweet potato	0·30	1·58					1·34					
Cassava	0·23	1·75	1·56				1·98		3·30h	0·97		
Yams	0·23a	0·97		0·75		1·36	0·46		2·28			
Groundnuts in shell	1·10	1·35	0·86	0·84	0·91		0·94		0·85h			
Sesame	1·77						0·68					
Beans	1·12b								0·35			
Voandrou	1·12b		0·89				0·86					
Cowpea	1·12b								0·54			
Guinea Corn	1·12b								0·19			
Bananas	0·32							2·05j				
Vegetables	0·65		2·94				0·93					
Cotton unginned	2·94	1·24				2·51e	0·82		0·26			
Cocoa	4·50								1·42			
Tobacco	8·00						2·56					

a Assumed on cassava. b Assumed on pulses. c Eleusine. d Resembles groundnut. e Return for work on bearing bushes 50 per cent higher, but considerable work has to be done on non-bearing bushes. f Return only 0·14 on upland rice. g Eleusine. Return only 0·08 in a hill village. h Lakeside village. Return from groundnut only 0·36 in foothill village. i High yield from rotating cultivation. j Inferior bananas suitable only for beer-making, about half the output by weight, reckoned at half the value of good bananas. k This exceptionally high figure may be explained by the unusually heavy soil, cultivated entirely by hand, and long distances walked between compound and plots.

Sources: Africa — general Higgs, Kerkham and Raeburn, Report of a Survey of Problems in the Mechanization of Native Agriculture, Colonial Office, 1950.

Cameroun Guillard, Golonpoui.
East Africa Fuggles Couchman, East African Journal of Agriculture, March 1939.
Gambia Haswell, Economics of Agriculture in a Savannah Village, Colonial Office, 1953.
Ghana Beckett, Akosoaso, London School of Economics Monograph on Social Anthropology No. 10, and Gold Coast Department of Agriculture Year Book, 1930.
Haute Volta Gérardin, Le Développement de la Haute Volta, Institut de Science Économique Appliqué, Supplement 142, 1963.
Indonesia Terra, Netherlands Journal of Agricultural Science, August 1959.
Malawi Platt, Nutrition Survey 1938 (Colonial Office Library). All expressed in terms of man-hours of labour of a fully able-bodied man.
Nigeria Upton & Petu, Journal of Tropical Agriculture, July 1966.
Uganda Pudsey, private communication.
Guatemala Sol Tax, Penny Capitalism.

TABLE XXIV. GENERAL ESTIMATES OF AFRICAN PRODUCTIVITIES

| | General Estimate for all Africa[1] | | | | Malawi 1938[2] | | | Ghana[3] | | | |
| | | | | | Kg. wheat equivalent/man-hour[b] | | | | | | |
	Labour input[a] man-hours /ha.	Crop kg. /ha.	Kg. wheat equivalent /ha.	/man. hour	Hill village	Foothill village	Lake village	Labour input[a] man-hours /ha.	Crop kg. /ha.	Kg. wheat equivalent /ha.	/man. hour
Maize	900	1790	1340	1·49	1·19	0·86		650	712	533	0·81
Eleusine millet	500	953	650	1·30	0·08	0·28					
Cotton (unginned)	1095	462	1358	1·24		0·26					
Groundnut (shelled)	1515	1116	2040	1·35			0·94				
Cassava	1870	14280	3285	1·75			3·39				
Sweet potato	1160	6080	1824	1·58							
Yams	2320	9790						1665	9850	4660[c]	2·96
Beans						0·41					
Rice (rough)		795	646			0·45					
Tobacco (dry leaf)		392	3135								

[a] Assuming 6½ hours/day.
[b] Expressing women, children, infirm men, etc., as 'first-class men' equivalent.
[c] Converted on local prices for maize and yams, which are more favourable to yams than is indicated by their relative nutritive value.

[1] J. W. Y. Higgs, R. K. Kerkham, and J. R. Raeburn, *Report of a Survey of Problems in the Mechanization of Native Agriculture in Tropical African Colonies*, Colonial Office, 1950.
[2] B. S. Platt, *Nutrition Survey*, Colonial Office library, mimeographed.
[3] *Gold Coast Department of Agriculture Yearbook*, 1930, p. 226.

with considerable snowfall, only 5 hours/day of work is considered possible in the winter months; but this is offset by expecting 12 hours/day in the summer. Even so, underemployment in the winter is marked.

Farm family members, it will be seen, do a certain amount of work away from their own farms; while at the same time a certain amount of hired labour is engaged in the busy season, much of it coming across the mountains from Yugoslavia.

Bearing in mind the all-important question of seasonality of demand for labour, we now examine available information about the productivity of labour in subsistence agriculture, where possible distinguishing marginal from average product.[1] We have some general estimates of African productivities.

For East Africa we are fortunate in having a pioneer study of the 1930s.[2] At a time when 1s. would buy 15 kg. of maize (a quite exceptionally low price — high transport costs kept East African maize prices well below world price, which itself was then very low) the *gross* returns, expressed in kg. maize equivalent/hour, ranged from 2·0 for groundnuts (in the year in question, which was very dry, the return was half this, but 2 is regarded as normal), to 2·1 for cassava, and 2·6 for sorghum or cotton. There are several factors explaining this much higher level of productivity, as compared with West Africa; the soil is rich, whereas West African soils are deficient in phosphorus; the climate is more favourable, with a shorter dry season. On the other hand, Couchman was examining the records of farmers who still worked with hand hoes. Male and female labour was used in approximately equal quantities, and he computed his averages without distinguishing between them.

In a thorough survey in a village in Gambia, to which a whole year was devoted, one of the authors obtained results much below Raeburn's figures shown in Table XXIV (both climate and soils in Gambia, however, are less favourable than in many regions of Africa).[3]

Relative prices in the local markets appear to have been similar to the FAO relative weights, except that rice was priced locally extremely high relative to the other crops. Regarding the marked

---

[1] An explanation of the mathematical function used is given in Chapter X.
[2] Fuggles Couchman, *East African Journal of Agriculture*, March 1939; and Clayton, *Journal of Agricultural Economics*, May 1961.
[3] M. R. Haswell, *Economics of Agriculture in a Savannah Village*, Colonial Research Studies No. 8, 1953.

TABLE XXV.   GAMBIA: AVERAGE RETURNS TO LABOUR
IN KG. PER MAN-HOUR

	Actual Returns	Wheat equivalents (FAO weights)
Late millet	·47	·32
Early millet	·48	·33
Sorghum	1·06	·64
Digitaria exilis	·99	·67
Maize	·91	·68
Rough rice: swamp[a]	·64	·51
upland[b]	·17	·14
Groundnuts (unshelled)	·84	·91

[a] flood irrigated.   [b] entirely rainfed.

CHART IV

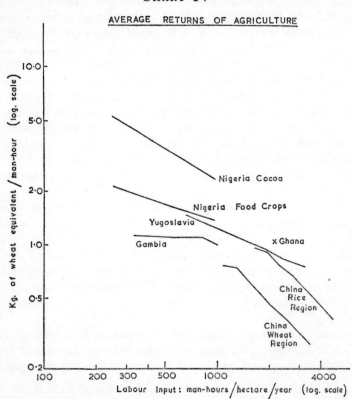

difference shown in returns per hour in Gambia, favoured soils for
growing groundnuts are rather scarce, and farmers are reluctant to

extend their groundnut plots to the less well-drained soils to which these give way. Maize can only be grown on very limited areas of land near the houses where domestic animals roam and manure is available. Digitaria and, to a less extent, sorghum are unpalatable, and limited amounts are grown each year as famine reserves. The comparatively high return from swamp rice has indeed led to a great expansion of its production in the ten years since the first survey; though this extension has only been made possible by the building of causeways into the swamp. The growing of the unremunerative upland rice continues, the work being done entirely by the women, who appear to calculate the return to their labour less nicely than the men.

We may now examine those data giving comparisons between farms with varying inputs, from which we can estimate marginal productivities of labour and of land.

CHART V

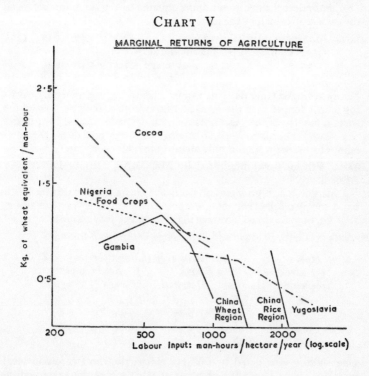

Notes and Sources to the diagrams, average returns of agriculture and marginal returns of agriculture:

CHINA: Buck, *Land Utilization in China*, Statistical Supplement, pp. 298, 302.

Wheat Region		Rice Region	
Crop ha./man equivalent	Tons grain equivalent/man equivalent	Crop ha./man equivalent	Tons grain equivalent/man equivalent
0·70	0·68	0·51	0·94
1·00	0·96	0·72	1·33
1·26	1·18	0·88	1·65
1·54	1·44	1·05	1·87
1·98	1·86	1·27	2·26
2·33	1·93	1·55	2·43

(For conversion to man-hours, assumed 2500 worked per year)

GAMBIA: Haswell, *Economics of Agriculture in a Savannah Village*, Colonial Office Research Study no. 8, 1953, p. 56, and Haswell: *The changing pattern of economic activity in a Gambia Village*, Department of Technical Co-operation Overseas Research Publication No. 2, 1963.

1 kg. undecorticated groundnuts equated to 1·3 kg. grain: refers to the cash crop grown by the men.

Data: Man-hours per ha. per year	322	570	817	1065
Grain equivalent per man-hour, kg.:				
Average	1·13	1·10	1·10	0·98
Marginal	0·88	1·18	0·88	0·30

Hours averaged 6 per day (the women cultivating rice generally working a little longer than the men) and farm work is only performed for some 9 months of the year, because nothing useful can be done in the dry season February–April. Allowing for some rest days, the total labour input per worker is only about 1350 hours per year.

GHANA: Privately communicated by Mr. Torto, Deputy Director of Agriculture.

Itinerant maize growers on worn-out cocoa lands cultivate (with hand tools) 0·8 ha. per man, cropping two times a year, obtaining 1820 kg. of maize in all. Average man-hours per year assumed 1750.

NIGERIA: Galletti, Baldwin and Dina, *Nigerian Cocoa Farmers*, p. 337.

Hours per acre per year	Returns in shillings per hour			
	Cocoa Farms		Food Crops	
	Average	Marginal	Average	Marginal
100	3·16	1·30	1·28	0·80
200	2·11	0·87	1·02	0·67
300	1·66	0·60	0·89	0·60
400	1·38	0·50	0·81	0·55

One shilling is equated to 1·68 kg. maize, the most common local grain (p. 419). The price of cocoa at the time of the investigation (1951–2) was, per unit of weight, 5·3 times the price of maize. Equations were established (pp. 314, 328) showing:

Yield in lb. cocoa $= 53 \cdot 54$ Acreage$^{\cdot 675}$ Man-hours$^{\cdot 325}$

Food crop yield/acre, shillings, before debiting seed =
$$5 \cdot 78 \text{ (man-hours/acre)}^{0 \cdot 67}$$

Food crop yield/acre, shillings, after debiting seed =
$$2 \cdot 68 \text{ (man-hours/acre)}^{0 \cdot 76}$$

Food crop yield/acre, thousand calories, before debiting seed =
$$(7238 \text{ man-hours/acre})^{0 \cdot 5}$$

The relative prices of the different crops do *not* vary according to their calorie content: cassava, per thousand calories, is the least liked, lowest priced and lowest protein crop. Comparing one equation with the other, the money value per thousand calories is found to *rise* (i.e. a tendency to grow a greater proportion of high protein and more palatable products) as labour input per unit rises. Wages averaged 7d. (cocoa farms $7 \cdot 4$, food crops $6 \cdot 6$) per hour, i.e. $0 \cdot 98$ kg. of maize or $2 \cdot 94$ tons per man-year. This is about the marginal product of both cocoa and food crops at a density of 10 labour units per sq. km.

	All work	Farm work
Average hours of work per year: males	1309	1112
females	1552	164

YUGOSLAVIA: Paper by Bicanic at International Association for Income and Wealth Conference, De Pietersberg, 1957.

	Under 2	2–3	3–5	5–8	Over 8
			Size of holdings in ha.		
Average size, ha.	$1 \cdot 4$	$2 \cdot 5$	$4 \cdot 0$	$6 \cdot 5$	$11 \cdot 7$
Labour force[a]	$2 \cdot 68$	$3 \cdot 02$	$3 \cdot 40$	$3 \cdot 53$	$3 \cdot 87$
Do. excluding non-farm labour[b]	$2 \cdot 34$	$2 \cdot 74$	$3 \cdot 17$	$3 \cdot 31$	$3 \cdot 71$
Labour units per sq. km.	167	110	79	51	32
Average product per man-year tons grain equivalent[c]	$1 \cdot 49$	$1 \cdot 75$	$2 \cdot 06$	$2 \cdot 44$	$2 \cdot 97$
Marginal per man-year tons grain equivalent[c]		$1 \cdot 0$	$0 \cdot 94$	$1 \cdot 41$	$1 \cdot 56$

[a] Computed from total number of persons on holding assuming, per 100 total population, 40 male labour units + 24 female, equivalent to 57 male labour units in all.

[b] Non-farm labour deduced from non-farm earnings, assuming that the average non-farm rate of pay was 200,000 dinars per man-year.

[c] Net farm income before tax converted on 32,000 dinars = 1 ton wheat.

Assumed number of man-hours per year, 2,000.

Charts IV and V measure not only the average product but also the marginal, that is to say, the additional grain equivalent obtained when an additional man-hour of labour is applied to the same land. For Gambia these show a nearly horizontal relationship (marginal product about the same as average product) up to a labour input of some 700 man-hours per ha. — after which the marginal product falls rapidly. The author's experience in the village showed that cultivators did in fact stop putting any further labour into cultivation at about this point. The Gambian male cultivator may not be able to read or write, but he knows the difference between marginal and average product, which is more than can be said for some highly educated accountants. In any

CHART VI

MARGINAL RETURNS IN INDIA
(C. P. Shastri)

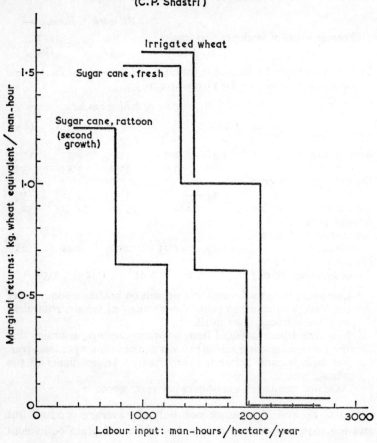

case, since available lands were not scarce, we should, on the whole, expect marginal product to be similar to average.

Of quite a different order of magnitude are the results obtained by rice growers in Wellesley Province of Malaysia, a highly productive area.[1] The average net return (after paying for fertilizer, etc.) of a rice grower is as high as 2·55 kg. paddy/man-hour worked. Wage workers receive the equivalent of 1·2–1·5 kg./man-hour of paddy, higher in the harvest season.

Luning[2] considered that in Northern Nigeria (principal crop groundnuts) marginal returns to labour became zero at an input

CHART VII

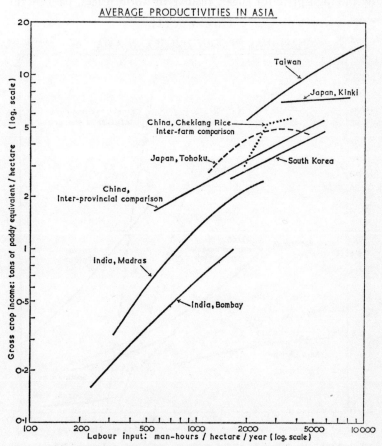

AVERAGE PRODUCTIVITIES IN ASIA

[1] Purcal, Ph.D. thesis, Australian National University.
[2] Luning, *Netherlands Journal of Agricultural Science*, Nov. 1964.

of about 1000 man-hours/hectare/year, an input of 400 being normal.

For India, a pioneering study comparing yields on farms with different levels of labour input was made near Agra by Shastri[1] in 1956. The average product of wheat on irrigated land is a little over 1 kg./man-hour. Rather surprisingly, at the lowest levels of labour input (below 1500 man-hours/ha./year) marginal product is higher than average, i.e. the labour input has been inadequate. Marginal product however falls rapidly nearly to zero with higher labour inputs. Marginal product of sugar cane, measured at world prices, also falls off similarly — though this effect has been masked by the high price for sugar, relative to world prices, paid by the

CHART VIII

MARGINAL PRODUCTIVITIES IN ASIA

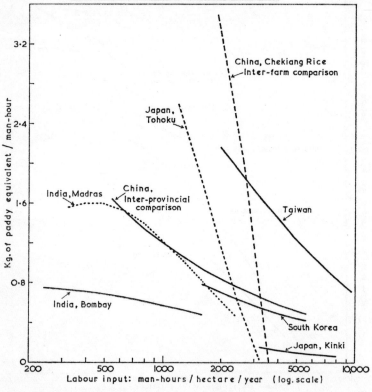

[1] C. P. Shastri, *Indian Journal of Agricultural Economics*, January–March 1958. Sugar cane assumed 11 per cent sugar content which is converted to wheat equivalent on FAO factor of 1·03 kg. sugar = 1 kg. wheat.

Indian government (which has led now to India's producing more sugar than she can consume).

Many data for Asia were assembled by Ishikawa.[1] As in the previous diagram, the Chinese data from an inter-farm comparison in one province appeared to fall to zero, though at a higher level of labour input than there shown. But conclusions drawn from a Chinese inter-provincial comparison, and also from South Korea, show marginal product remaining positive. Most striking are the results from Taiwan, where average product (due largely to double cropping) is so high, but which also shows a substantial positive marginal product at a labour input as high as 10,000 man-hours/ha./year.

TABLE XXVI. MARGINAL PRODUCTIVITIES IN RHODESIA

| | Tribal Tenure Area (Chiweshe) | | | Freehold Area (Darwin) | | |
	Maize	Ground-nuts	Millet	Maize	Ground-nuts	Millet
Returns measured in kg. crop/physical unit input:						
Land (hectare)	254	62	112	1800	581	580
Weeding labour (hour)	0·41	0·26	0·38	0·95	0·33	1·42
Farmyard manure (ton)	108			48		
Returns measured per unit of money input:						
Fixed capital (net)[a]	0	0·116	0·033	0·132	0	0·083
Chemical fertilizers	1·69			2·94		
Average price[b] of crops £/ton	10·5	42·5	33·6	10·5	42·5	33·6

[a] Net fixed capital (after depreciation) estimated at three-quarters of gross. Measured as annual returns (i.e. from 0 to 13 per cent).
[b] Millet is the grain most traded locally, and its price should be used for converting results into grain equivalents, for comparison with other African results. On the F.A.O. system of weights millet stands at 0·68, groundnuts unshelled at 1·10 and maize at 0·75 (wheat = 1). Groundnuts sell at a relatively low price in terms of millet, and maize at an exceptionally low price, because they have to meet transport costs for sale in distant markets — maize for export to Europe. Maize, commanding these low prices, is seen to be grown only on land giving a high marginal return.

In Jamaica, where a great diversity of crops are grown, Edwards[2] found a fairly uniform distribution of demand for labour throughout the seasons of the year. He gives records for farms with labour input ranging from a little over 500 to over 4500 man-

[1] *Economic Development in Asian Perspective.*
[2] D. Edwards, *An Economic Study of Small Farming in Jamaica*, 1961.

hours/ha./year. At inputs over 2500 man-hours/ha./year, both marginal and average product appear to stabilize at about $\frac{1}{2}$ kg./ man-hour wheat equivalent. Average returns, however, might be four or five times as large as this on the less labour-intensive farms. In Jamaica there is extensive cultivation of banana, which requires considerable attention throughout the year.

An original study by Massell and Johnson[1] has thrown a great deal more light on marginal productivities in Rhodesia, distinguishing a traditional tribal farming area from a modern farming area in which comparatively large holdings are occupied by more skilled African farmers.

Massell and Johnson make the interesting point that, at any rate under hand labour conditions, the amount of labour devoted to planting and harvesting is fairly closely determined by the area planted and by the weight of the harvest respectively. The most flexible element in the labour input is the time devoted to weeding. Marginal returns are here seen to be low, though higher in the Darwin area.

CHART IX.

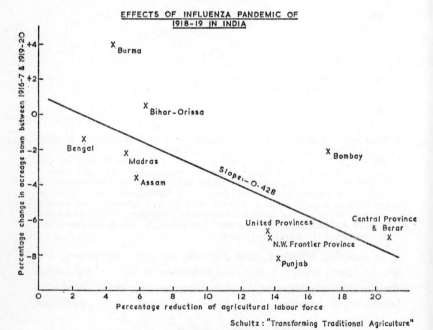

EFFECTS OF INFLUENZA PANDEMIC OF 1918-19 IN INDIA

Schultz: "Transforming Traditional Agriculture"

[1] *Economics of Smallholder Farming in Rhodesia.*

It is clear that there is no general rule about the ratio of marginal product to average product. There are cases where marginal product is almost as high as average, and there are cases where it is zero. But the opinion has been expressed by several workers that, under subsistence agriculture conditions, the general order of magnitude of this ratio may be 0·4. This theory received striking confirmation from a recent study by Schultz.[1] The world-wide influenza pandemic of 1918 happened to be particularly virulent in India, was very varied in its incidence between provinces, and, for some unknown reason, selectively attacked able-bodied men. This unhappy conjuncture of circumstances, however, provided a unique opportunity of testing this theorem, by removing various proportions of labour from the different provinces, all other things remaining equal.

A slope of approximately 0·4 is observed. (Chart IX).

From the information assembled we now have some knowledge, though much less than we would wish, on the falling off of the marginal returns to further labour inputs on a given area. In some cases the curve of marginal return plunges downwards steeply, and we can estimate fairly precisely the maximum feasible labour input per hectare for a given crop.

We seek to proceed from this to answer the more general question, namely how much land does a given agricultural population need or, conversely, on a given area of land, at what level of population density can we say that the land is overpopulated in an agricultural sense?

This question, apparently simple, raises a number of difficult subordinate questions. We have seen in Chapters II and III how the land required to feed one person may be as high as 10 sq. km. for a primitive people living entirely by hunting and fishing; may fall to 10 ha. (100 ha. = 1 sq. km.) for the simplest neolithic-type cultivators and herdsmen; for shifting cultivators, including the land waiting and regrowing trees for a 12–20-year period, still only 5 ha. for each person may be required, or even less in some fertile areas. The actual amount of land cultivated in any one year, if we take the Iban as an example, may be only about one-third ha./year. When pressure of population finally forces the shifting cultivator to become a sedentary cultivator, fallow land will disappear, or will be greatly reduced, but the per person requirements of land actually cultivated will be increased. The sedentary cultiva-

[1] *Transforming Traditional Agriculture.*

tor in India, for example, has to do without those reserves of fertility in the soil which most African cultivators are still able to replenish through their shifting cultivation; the Indian in consequence gets considerably lower yields per ha. for most of the important crops.

So far however we have been considering communities whose aim was to produce their subsistence, with a small margin to spare, perhaps desiring to exchange to a very limited extent — the Hanunóo, for example, trading 10–15 per cent of their product. Once we introduce the consideration that a community can produce cash crops, and can sell them, the amount of the land which they require, and the amount of labour which they devote to agriculture, may be expected to be greatly increased.

We may, however, make the assumption, mistakenly, that once a community has discovered the opportunity of earning and spending cash, it will promptly seek to work all the hours that are physically possible, in order to earn more. In fact, as we shall see below, such communities have very definite ideas about the amount of leisure which they consider desirable or, to speak more precisely, the proportion of their time which they wish to devote to non-agricultural pursuits. We must remember that out of their total of non-agricultural hours they have to find time to make their clothes, build and repair their houses, perform numerous religious and civic duties, and many other tasks which we have performed for us, before they have time for what we would regard as leisure and rest.

It is, on the other hand, true that the nearer and more insistent the opportunities are for earning and spending cash, the more the cultivator is likely to revise his ideas about leisure, or the relative numbers of hours to be devoted to agricultural and non-agricultural pursuits. He may not only take less leisure, but also pay someone to build his house, and perform similar tasks, if industrial goods are readily available for sale at low prices, as in Japan, for example. Conversely, in the remoter parts of Africa where few industrial goods are available, and those that are at a high price after all the expenses of transport and distribution have been met, the cultivator still builds his own house, etc., and also appears to take abundant leisure.

After cash cropping has begun, and after we have taken account of varying leisure preferences, we must still take account of changing methods of agriculture. When the cultivator has some margin to spare over his most immediate requirements for food, and for other goods for which he exchanges part of his crop, he also finds (as we saw in Chapter IV) that he has enough cereals to provide part of the ration for draught animals. Use of draught animals increases the area which one man can cultivate in a given time. In certain monsoonal climates, where the period in which cultivation is possible is very short, as in northern (but not southern) India, the use of draught animals may indeed be a necessary condition without which agriculture would not be possible at all. The employment of draught animals further increases the required acreage, because part of their food has to come from fodder crops or grass, in addition to cereals.

So far we have assumed that the draught animals pull only a simply designed plough and harrow. Later, as in America and Europe up to the 1920s, while animals still provided the power, nevertheless a great variety of improved implements were designed for them to draw, greatly increasing the area which one man could economically handle. The whole process culminated in the introduction of the tractor.

So, after the introduction of cash cropping, land requirements per man increase for two separate reasons; firstly, the increasing proportion of the working year which each man is willing to devote to agriculture, and secondly the technical improvements, which increase the area which he can handle in a given time.

We must of course carefully distinguish this definition of the area 'required' by each man, as between the amount of land which he would like to have in order to earn an economic living, and the area 'required' to produce his subsistence.

With such figures in our mind, not constant, but changing slowly with decreasing leisure preference, and changing sometimes rapidly with technical improvements, we may then examine the amount of land actually available, and if it falls short of 'requirements' we may complain (legitimately, so long as the definition of the words is carefully borne in mind) of 'underemployment', or of 'rural overpopulation' — the two phrases are reciprocal ways of describing the same thing.

The amount of labour which can be economically expended on a given area of land varies greatly both with the crops cultivated and the agricultural methods available. We have considered predominantly so far the marginal returns, and the economic limits to labour expended on cereal cultivation, for the reason that this must be the primary concern of subsistence cultivators. A good deal more labour can be economically expended on a given area when growing cassava and other root crops. But we should not take this too much into account; if people depend upon these crops for more than a certain proportion of their diet, they will suffer from protein shortage. Some of the cash crops, such as cotton, and above all tobacco, can have very large amounts of labour expended upon them. But the production of these crops depends upon adequate access to markets, requires considerable skill, and in any case the farm communities which we are considering will still have to devote the main part of their energies to producing their subsistence requirements, and only a fraction of their land can be under commercial crops.

De Vries thought that the introduction of draught animals was not economically feasible until production had reached 500 kg. grain equivalent/person/year. (He did not consider the exception discussed above, namely monsoonal climates with a very short rainy season, where the use of draught animals may be unavoidable, however poor the cultivator may be.) One of the facts which emerges is that the draught animals are as likely to suffer underemployment as the men. In the East Bengal Province of Pakistan, admittedly a very densely populated area, provincial agricultural officials[1] have estimated that draught oxen are capable of working 1200 hours/year, that there were about three times as many oxen in the Province as were actually required to do the work, and that much of the cultivation was done at a pace far slower than that of which the oxen were capable. Shastri[2] has estimated that the percentage of the capacity of the draught oxen utilized in India varies from 24 per cent on the smallest farms to 40 per cent on the largest. In the Punjab on the other hand, an area of comparatively large farms, the oxen are estimated to be employed for a full working year of 161 days (the animals working fewer hours each day than the man, as has always been the case).

A valuable pioneer study of underemployment in India was made by Tarlok Singh.[3] He devised an ingenious method of estimating the labour input required for a given amount of land in various areas, based on the numbers of ploughs and plough teams. We have seen above that nearly all the draught oxen in India work well below their theoretical capacity (although at the same time

[1] Private communication.
[2] *Economic Weekly*, 29 October 1960.
[3] *Poverty and Social Change*, 1945.

most of them are fed at a rate far below that required for doing a full year's work). Tarlok Singh, in effect, based his calculations on the assumption that the degree of underemployment of draught

TABLE XXVII. UNDEREMPLOYMENT IN INDIA

	Estimated Ha./Man required for Full Employment	Actual as Percentage of Full Employment	
	Tarlok Singh	Tarlok Singh	Congress Agrarian Reforms Sub-Committee
Bengal	2·8	58	60
United Provinces	3·2	59	59
Bihar	3·2	61⎱	not over 67
Orissa	3·2	79⎰	
Assam	3·2	76	
Madras	4·0	77	
Punjab	4·9	92	50
Central Provinces and Berar	4·9	100	
North-west Frontier Province	4·9	68	
Delhi	4·9	67	
Ajmer-Merwara	6·1	70	
Bombay	7·5	86	83
Sind	8·0	112	

oxen would be fairly uniform. At any rate, his results for Bengal came out very close to those which Ghosh and Das calculated by quite a different method.

Tarlok Singh's estimates of actual as a percentage of full employment are compared with those published by the Agrarian Affairs Sub-Committee of the Congress Party in 1949 (treating 300 days as a full year's work). The data were computed from the 1941 Census, with the names of the Provinces as they were then, including a good deal of what is now Pakistan territory. The territories of what were then 'Indian States' have been omitted.

The two methods agree quite well for the most densely populated area, Bengal. (The Agrarian Reform Sub-Committee figure is on the assumption that both jute and rice are grown; if jute only is grown, the figure should be halved.) Agreement is also good for Bombay Province (now Maharashtra and Gujarat States), the

E

most industrialized part of India, where we would expect that some of the rural underemployed would be drawn into industrial work. For Sind (now part of Pakistan) Tarlok Singh estimated that the labour supply was actually inadequate, and barely adequate for Punjab (for which region the Agrarian Reforms Sub-Committee however got a very different result). Sind is entirely, Punjab almost entirely, dependent upon irrigation water, which is chronically scarce. This situation may have affected Tarlok Singh's method of calculation. Provincial officials in Punjab have stated that where sufficient water is available to grow two crops a year, one man is fully occupied on $2\frac{1}{2}$ ha. (the same has been stated by provincial officials in the North-west Frontier Province of Pakistan). The International Labour Office Advisory Committee for Asia made their estimate higher, but still at only $3\frac{1}{2}$ ha., for the land required to keep a man fully occupied in the double-cropped areas of Pakistan. (In this latter case they specified that two pairs of bullocks would be needed to every three men.)

These Indian figures show how variable is the amount of land required to keep a man occupied. While the rainfall is high (as in Bengal), or on irrigated land where ample supplies of water are available, the figure may be only $2\frac{1}{2}$ ha. On these lands a high proportion of the most labour-demanding crops may be grown. On the lower rainfall lands a higher proportion of the simple cereal crops may be grown, if only for needs of subsistence. Also, as agricultural knowledge advances, labour-saving methods may be introduced, whereby one man can handle a larger area.

The most convenient unit of measurement, where possible, is the number of ha. of cultivated land/adult male engaged in agriculture.[1] Undoubtedly a good deal of agricultural work is done by women, and some by children, particularly in Africa. In some modern countries, including Japan, Germany and France, every farmer's wife is recorded by the Census as a full-time agricultural worker. This appears to be largely for political reasons, to enhance the supposed importance of agriculture in the national economy. As the method of recording female labour varies so greatly between countries, the only statistically safe procedure is to work on male

[1] Cultivated land as defined by FAO, including fallows and orchards. In countries where land is very scarce, it is a reasonable assumption that all land capable of cultivation is being cultivated, and that grazing is confined to mountains, swamps, heathland, etc. But in less crowded countries we must bear in mind that a great deal of land is grazed which would be capable, physically, of arable farming.

labour only. In Yugoslavia it was estimated (Chapter VI) that for each 100 of farm population we should expect 57 man-years of total labour input, if we convert women's and children's labour to adult male equivalents, or 40 units of adult male labour. For most subsistence economies, however, with a higher proportion of children, the number of males engaged in agricultural work may be taken at one-third of total agricultural population. Sometimes we only have figures of total population of a rural area, which include presumably a certain number of village craftsmen and traders. In this case, the number of males engaged in agricultural work may be taken as one-quarter of the whole.

We will also assemble a number of estimates on the extent of underemployment. Relating these to the figures of the amount of land cultivated/man, we can deduce in effect the amount of land required to keep a man fully occupied, in the opinion of the constructors of these estimates.

We need not take into account here regions where the supply of land is clearly abundant. Thus in Mexico[1] agricultural population has been growing at the rate of 25 per cent per decade, but the amount of agricultural land has been expanding at about the same rate, and available land is nearly 10 ha./man.

About the same average prevails for Brazil.[2] The national average in 1940 was about 9 ha., falling to $4\frac{1}{2}$ in São Paulo, the most developed and the most populated province, and rising to over 30 in Maranhão.

Some of the most intensively cultivated land in the world is in Egypt, where on the average 1·4 crops/year are taken from each unit of land. Large quantities of fertilizer are used; and, contrary to expectations, it is still proving practicable to carry double cropping further than this. Issawi[3] has estimated that the true labour requirements per ha. are 155 man-days (of 10 hours) + 60 women- and child-days. If we take 300 days as the full normal working year, and assume that the ordinary amount of women and child labour is also available, then land requirements for a man are 1·9 ha. A figure of 2 ha. was also estimated by Bonné.[4]

The present Egyptian figure of only a little over 0·6 ha./man is clearly too low to provide full employment, though not to the extent indicated by the above figures. On a recent official survey of

[1] *Commercio Exterior*, September 1957.
[2] Lopes, *International Labour Review*, November 1941.
[3] C. Issawi, *Egypt at Mid-Century, an Economic Survey*, O.U.P., 1954.
[4] *Economic Development of the Middle East*, 1943.

hours worked,[1] if we take a 60-hour week as normal (less public holidays, which had been excluded from the survey), it appears that 42 per cent of the agricultural population were fully occupied at the time of the survey. The average week worked by the whole agricultural population was 79 per cent of the assumed full working week, indicating that, at the present rate of double cropping, 0·8 ha./man would provide full employment. This order of magnitude is indeed confirmed by another statement by Issawi himself. The present state of underemployment, he says, only became apparent during the present century. In the nineteenth century the general complaint in Egypt was of shortage of labour. At that time there was not much double cropping. The figures of ha. of cultivated land/man stood at 1·2 in 1886 and just about 1 at the end of the century. It was only after that date that double cropping became important.

The amount of cultivated land in Egypt[2] rose from 0·6 million hectares in the eighth century A.D. to 2·1 million at the end of the nineteenth century. Owen thinks that these acreages were approximately proportioned to the population at these two dates. He states that double cropping began about 1870. By 1897 the ratio of cropped to cultivated area was 1·33, and by 1960 (on a total cultivated area which had risen to 2·35 million hectares) the ratio of cropped to cultivated area had risen to 1·77, water being used to an average depth of 1·84 metres.

	Japanese Average		Farms below 0·5 ha. (sample)	
	Male	Female	Male	Female
Number of persons/farm engaged in farm work	1·41	1·45	0·63	0·98
Hours worked/person/year	2306	1770	2810	1377
Of which non-farm work	474	148	1320	238
(average working day about 9 hours)				

Buck[3] ranged the farms in China by size groups. The smallest had about ½ ha./man, the largest 2. The number of idle months/man-year stood at 1·7 or 1·8 (in mid-winter), almost irrespective of size of farm. It is true, as we have seen, that the occupiers of the smallest farms were driven by poverty to extend their labour to a point

---

[1] *International Labour Review*, November 1960.
[2] Owen, *Land Economics*, August 1964.
[3] J. L. Buck, *Land Utilization in China*, 1937.

where it was bringing in almost zero marginal return; nevertheless these results show that a farm population using only hand tools can be fully occupied even on these very small areas.

In Japan also, with an average of only 0·7 ha. cultivated land/man, all the signs indicate very full occupation of men, women, children and old people, although here again labour input has been carried to a point of almost zero marginal return. Much of the 'surplus labour' from small farms finds non-farm employment.[1]

A very strong indication that these low land/man ratios are regarded as normal in many parts is shown by the following extraordinary figures from Indonesia.[2]

TABLE XXVIII.   INDONESIA — LAND/MAN RATIOS

HA./MAN ENGAGED IN AGRICULTURE (ASSUMED ¼ OF TOTAL POPULATION)

	Total area	Area of arable land (including estates)	Area harvested (double-crop land counted twice) of food crops plus planted area of commercial crops and estates
West Java	1·07	0·63	0·63
Central Java	0·79	0·59	0·61
East Java	0·97	0·63	0·74
Java and Madura: Total	0·94	0·63	0·65
Outer Islands	18·2	1·3	0·69

In Central Java, where population is very dense, the total land area is only 0·79 ha./man engaged in agriculture, of which 0·59 is cultivated, with a little double cropping. Double cropping appears to be more common in Eastern Java where population density is less. But in the Outer Islands of Indonesia, where the amount of land available per person is twenty times what it is in Java, the amount actually harvested per person is hardly any higher. (In the Outer Islands, the figure for arable land is approximately double the figure for harvested land because there is no double cropping, and the cultivators can afford to fallow half their land each year.) Wertheim[3] considers (on Indonesian experience) that the amount of irrigated land required is somewhere between 0·5 and 1 ha./

[1] Tobata, *Japanese Agriculture*, 1952.
[2] Dr. Hilde Wander, quoting Bino Pusat Statistik, *Penduduk Indonesia*, 1959, and *Statistical Pocketbook of Indonesia*, 1950.
[3] Privately communicated.

person to provide economic equilibrium, without either unemployment or labour shortage. For dry land he puts the figure at 5 ha. — presumably allowing for extensive fallowing. Koentjaramingrat[1] estimates requirements in the village of Bontoramba (Celebes) per person at 0·09 ha. rice land plus 0·11 ha. dry land (6·1 persons per family).

It has been estimated[2] that lands with similar labour inputs per hectare yielded (at prices of the 1930s) 100 guilders/hectare under subsistence agriculture, 500 under rubber, tea or cocoa, and 1000 under sugar or quinine. Nevertheless the Javanese seem to have been reluctant to grow them.

These customs appear to be of very ancient standing. Some eight centuries ago, before the Moslem invasion, when Java was a Hindu country, and when population pressure was very much less, the customary family holding of irrigated land was still only 0·7 hectares.[3] De Vries goes on to make the interesting observations that the irrigated land was taxed, at a rate not exceeding 20 per cent, which represented the difference between what the cultivator could expect to get from a given amount of labour expended on irrigated rice, and on upland rice. If the tax authority attempted to collect any more, people would take to the jungle. This however was on very fertile Javanese soil on which (according to Van Beukering's estimate) a square kilometre could support 40 persons by subsistence agriculture, as against Allan's estimate (previously quoted) of only eight in Africa.

Terra also estimated[4] that, in the case of a cultivating family without draught animals, the difficulty of weeding in a tropical climate imposed a maximum holding of 2–3 hectares for dry crops, but of 5 for rice (the inundation necessary for the growth of the rice also checks weeds). This is a little larger than the 0·87 hectares/ person which Grove considered the maximum in Africa (previously quoted).

Similar densities are sometimes found in the high rainfall districts in Africa. In Ruanda-Urundi[5] population density rises to 550 persons/sq. km. in some areas. Taking a quarter of the total population as men engaged in agriculture, this gives them approximately $\frac{3}{4}$ ha. each on high rainfall land growing continuous banana crops.

[1] *Villages in Indonesia*, p. 205.
[2] Terra, *Netherlands Journal of Agricultural Science*, May 1961.
[3] De Vries, World Population Conference, 1965.
[4] *Netherlands Journal of Agricultural Science*, August 1959.
[5] P. Gourou, *Mémoire de l'Institut Royale Coloniale Belgique*, No. 6, 1953.

Gourou[1] quotes other densely populated areas. The highest densities in Europe are 0·9 ha./man engaged in the Valencia district in Spain, and 0·6 in some parts of southern Italy. The world record appears to be shared by the Adiwerno district in Java, totalling 93 sq. km. in area, engaged in growing sugar cane as well as rice, where the figure falls to 0·24, and by certain areas in Viet Nam.

But Gourou has also pointed out[2] that the high or low density at which land of a given climate is occupied is very much the matter of historical chance. The Sikiang Delta in China, which has a population density of 700 persons/sq. km., is homoclimatic with the Paraná Delta in South America, with a density of 10. The Red River Delta in Vietnam has 500, and its homoclimes the Zambesi and Niger Deltas have 20 and 12 respectively. Java may be exceptional because of its volcanic soil; but the adjacent island of Madura, with poor soil, has a density of 300, compared with its homoclime the Marajo Islands in the Amazon Delta, with a density of 5. To turn to cooler climates, the Landes in France have a density of 15, but Gândara in Portugal, with similar poor soil and dry climate, has 120. Iowa with its density of 10 is homoclimatic with the Hopei plains in China, with a density of 300.

The highly productive soil area of the delta of the Tonkin in Vietnam, an area of 15,000 sq. km., is one of the most densely populated agricultural areas in the world. Gourou, who made a study[3] of the human geography of the Delta, recorded an average rural population density (again taking men engaged in agriculture at one-quarter of the whole population) of 0·88 ha./man falling to 0·5 over one-seventh of the area and to 0·24 in a few districts, just matching the figures for the most heavily populated district in Java. The lands of the Tonkinese Delta are exploited with the utmost intensity. Certain techniques practised on these fertile soils consume exceptional quantities of manual labour for the production, wherever possible, of two crops of rice, or one of rice and one of a dry land crop, per year; the help contributed by draught animals is negligible, equipment is neither important nor costly, consisting only of a few tools of wood or bamboo, and land is minutely divided. The poor Tonkinese peasants who inhabit the region work hard for an average of 230 kg. rough rice/person/year

[1] P. Gourou, *The Tropical World*, 1961.
[2] *Impact*, 1964, No. 1.
[3] P. Gourou, *The Standard of Living in the Delta of the Tonkin*. Institute of Pacific Relations, 9th Conference, French Paper No. 4.

supplemented, probably inadequately, by small fish caught in ditches, edible herbs collected off the marshes, fruits, and numerous insects. At this level of food consumption, with a yield of 4 tons rough rice/ha./year, and with 20 per cent of the soil not in rice fields, the land should be capable of feeding a total population of 14 persons/ha. (0·285 ha./man engaged). Where density surpasses this figure, some resources from outside the locality become essential. In these circumstances, income is supplemented by earnings from seasonal migrations to other areas at the time of harvest, or by migrations over a more prolonged period into coal mines on the borders of the Delta, or from peddling.

Other Asian countries with low figures of ha./man engaged in agriculture are Korea and Ceylon with 0·9. Ceylon however still has a large proportion of its total area uninhabited — it is true that this has lower rainfall than the inhabited area, but areas in India and other countries with similar rainfall are capable of supporting large populations. Thailand, Burma, Philippines and Malaya have considerably larger areas of cultivated land for each man in work, and also large areas of potential cultivable land not yet developed at all.

For India, Qayum[1] estimated that the amount of agricultural work actually done in 1950–51 was 18·3 billion man-days. He assumed that each man in the rural population could be available for 300 days a year, each woman for 120, each adolescent for 150. He then, however, knocked off a round figure of one-third for time required for subsidiary occupations, and concluded that the amount of labour available for agriculture was 26·5 billion man-days. The work actually done was thus almost exactly two-thirds of the available labour. Sen[2] estimated that 'even on the basis of existing antiquated techniques', surplus labour was equivalent to 15 to 20 million workers, or 4½ to 6 billion man-days. If we accept Qayum's figure of the amount of work actually done, Sen's result indicated that this was 78 per cent of the amount of labour available. Underemployment is generally considered to be at its worst in southern India. Srinivasan,[3] surveying seven villages near Coimbatore, assumed 260 days as a normal year. He found that labour utilization as a percentage of actual varied from 53 per cent to 81 per cent, with a median of 65 per cent.

---

[1] Conference on Research in National Income, Delhi, January 1957.
[2] World Population Conference, 1954.
[3] *Indian Journal of Agricultural Economics*, April–June 1957.

These figures for India however will be considerably modified when we consider below the extreme seasonality of demand of labour in India.

We may now consider land requirements in some of the more densely populated eastern European and Mediterranean climates.

TABLE XXIX. LAND REQUIREMENTS IN SOME OF THE MORE DENSELY POPULATED EASTERN EUROPEAN AND MEDITERRANEAN CLIMATES

	Ha. agricultural land/male actively engaged in agriculture[a]	
	1900	1950
Poland	5·9	6·0
Czechoslovakia	4·5	6·9
Hungary	5·4	4·6
Roumania	5·1	3·9
Bulgaria	6·9	3·4
Yugoslavia	5·1	4·5
Italy	3·5	3·6
Spain	7·0	6·2
Portugal	4·2	3·7

[a] These figures include pasture land

In these countries, agricultural populations have been declining and the amount of land per head increasing, but there have been exceptions.[1]

In Hungary, for example, cultivated land was only 3·5 ha./male engaged in agriculture in 1938. A variety of estimates have been made of the ratio of actual to potential labour, whose median seems to be about 75 per cent.[2] For Yugoslavia, Krasovec gives the following figures (Table XXX).[3]

Bicanic[4] estimated for the 1930s labour utilization at 62 per cent of available labour, for the whole country. The same author,[5] in a more detailed study in the 1950s, showed how the smaller holdings sent a larger proportion of their workers to work in the rural industries, which are now becoming distributed around Yugoslavia, as indeed they are also in Japan, and may soon be in India.

[1] F. Dovring, *Land and Labour in Europe, 1900–1950*, The Hague, 1956.
[2] Rudzinski, *Polish Economist*, July–September 1942. Also *The World To-day*, Institute of International Affairs, March 1947.
[3] Krasovec, International Conference of Agricultural Economists, 1955.
[4] Bicanic, *Geographical Review*, January–February 1944.
[5] 1957 Conference of International Association for Research in Income and Wealth; and private communications.

TABLE XXX.   YUGOSLAVIA — LAND/MAN RATIOS

	Ha./man, all agricultural land	Ha./man, cultivated land only
Serbia	3·0	2·2
Voivodina	4·5	3·9
Croatia	3·8	1·9
Slovenia	4·0	1·3
Bosnia-Herzegovina	3·7	1·8
Macedonia	4·1	1·8
Montenegro	5·0	0·6
All Yugoslavia	3·5	2·0

Size of holding, ha.	Under 2	2 to 3	3 to 5	5 to 8
Average area, ha.	1·4	2·5	4·0	6·5
Man-year equivalents (women 70% of men) available/ holding	2·68	3·02	3·40	3·53
Do. engaged in non-farm work	0·34	0·28	0·23	0·22

Bicanic estimated the average working year of those engaged in farm work still to be below 2000 hours.

Bulgaria, until recently at any rate, has been a country with comparatively little industrialization and, as population rose, the amount of the land per man declined heavily. An estimate for the 1930s[1] showed 355 million man-days of work to be done each year, which, taking 290 days/year as full employment, represented 90 per cent of the available male labour supply, or 63 per cent of male plus female. In the Stara-Zagora district the figure of cultivated land/man fell to 0·8 ha.[2]

Greece,[3] with 3·57 million ha. of farm land (including a limited amount of grassland) in 1960, was estimated to require 86·9 million 'man-productive days' in the busiest three months of the year, with only 84·7 million available, i.e. a deficiency of 2·6 per cent. The authors think that Greece passed from being a country of chronic labour surplus to one of labour deficiency in 1955. However, they define labour availability on the curious assumption, which appears amusing to dwellers in more rainy climates, that 'rainfall of at least

[1] Egoroff and Mollow, quoted Institut für Konjunkturforschung, *Weekly Bulletin*, 29 June 1939.

[2] A. Suha, *Economic Problems of Eastern Europe*. This author quotes figures of 1·7 ha./man in the Cracow district of Poland and 1·5 ha./man in a district of Slovakia.

[3] Pepelasis and Yotopoulos, *Surplus Labour in Greek Agriculture, 1953–60*, Centre of Economic Research, Athens, Research Monograph No. 2.

1 millimetre, or rainfall that accumulates less than 1 millimetre and lasts for more than three hours, usually causes the loss of a full day's work'. As we shall see below, there are large seasonal fluctuations in the demand for labour; and also the situation in some of the mountain regions is worse than the national average.

The above figure relates to the supply of man-productive days in the spring quarter of the year. For the whole year 1960 the figure was 357 million. This is calculated on the low basis of 255 days/year, omitting males below 19 and over 65, and with females weighted to convert them into adult male equivalents. The number of male man-years (without weighting ages) was 1·07 million. This implies a ratio of $3\frac{1}{2}$ ha./man (a small amount of pasture is included here). With the number of hours/year devoted to agriculture by the average Greek farmer, this provides something very close to full employment.

For Hungary we have estimates[1] of an average of 200 days actually worked per year on the basis of a 12-hour day. On a 10-hour day we may equate them to 80 per cent and 60 per cent of full employment (300 days). An alternative estimate[2] for 1930, computed on male labour only, indicated actual as 76 per cent of potential work. For 1947,[3] on male and female labour taken together, actual employment was estimated at only 53 per cent of potential labour supply. For the Hungarian type of agriculture, which includes a good deal of grazing, it appears that $7\frac{1}{2}$–10 ha./man are necessary in all. Hectares of *cultivated* land/man were 3·3 in 1930 and 2·5 in 1947.

Russia in 1913, with 4 ha. cultivated land/man, was estimated[4] to be 74 per cent occupied: again in 1928,[5] when the area had fallen to 3·6, 78 per cent occupied.

Spain in the 1930s was estimated[6] to have $7\frac{1}{2}$ per cent complete unemployment and 5 per cent partial among rural workers. At this time cultivated land/man was 5 ha. For 1903–12 an estimate[7] of actual at 83 per cent of potential employment was made.

In Italy in 1951–2[8] rural working population (of whom a few are female) included 4·93 million occupiers of land, who lost on an average 88 days/year, and 1·88 million wage workers who lost on an

[1] *International Labour Review*, Vol. 25, p. 673, and Vol. 28, p. 525.
[2] Nadujfalvy, *Revue Hongroise de Statistique*, 1947.
[3] Meszaroa, *Statisztika Szemle*, 1952.
[4] Marcus, *International Labour Review*, Vol. 53, p. 356.
[5] *International Labour Review*, Vol. 27, p. 349.
[6] De Arlandis, *Weltwirtschaftliches Archiv*, September 1936.
[7] Vandellos, *Metron*, 1925.
[8] *Banca Nazionale del Lavoro*, June 1955.

average 150 days/year, out of an assumed total of 275 potential working days. The weighted mean of days lost was therefore 94 (63 in the north, 112 in central Italy, 117 in the south and islands). A higher pre-war degree of utilization is shown[1] by Vitali and Angelini, with the average rural worker and farmer estimated to be working 2250 and 2500 hours/year respectively, as against a supposed norm of 3000.

Italy in 1950 had 3·6 ha. agricultural land/man engaged, as shown in Dovring's table, and only 2·3 ha. cultivated land. From the above estimates of underemployment we may conclude that 3·5 ha. cultivated land/man engaged and 5·5 ha. total land are necessary for full employment, with Italian-style agriculture — not quite as intensive as Greek. (It is worth recollecting that Cato in *De Re Rustica* stated that one full-time man was necessary for every 4·8 ha. of olive or 1·6 ha. of vineyard.)

There appears, however, to be some uniformity between the figures for Mediterranean countries. In the Mediterranean, cereal harvesting is generally completed by June, and is followed by a hot dry spell, in which some underoccupation is likely, though less so if there is a grape harvest to be gathered. The League of Nations Conference on European Rural Life in 1939 concluded that $5\frac{1}{2}$ ha./man engaged was inadequate in Lithuania, but that 2 ha. was not seriously inadequate in east Flanders. An adequate system of transport and communication (they might also have added an abundant supply of fertilizers) makes all the difference, in making possible more labour-intensive crops and livestock than those of less developed peasant populations.

Cases of extreme congestion or 'rural overpopulation' represent an unhappy by-road from the normal course of economic development. But the country travelling down this road may reach a point of no return. The normal and fortunate course of economic development is that, when the productivity of a country's agriculture can considerably exceed the required standards of consumption of the rural population, and when other circumstances are favourable too, urban and industrial population begins to grow. Some of the goods and services which the urban population can supply may in their turn contribute a good deal, as we shall see shortly, to the further productivity of agriculture. But if this normal urban growth is in some way checked, and rural population

---

[1] Quoted in *Foreign Agriculture*, United States Department of Agriculture, May 1945.

continues to grow so that the amount of cultivable land per man falls, marginal productivity may also fall, and then, even though standards of consumption per head may fall, the difference between production and consumption, and in consequence the ability to feed an urban population, also diminishes. Such a country may therefore become relatively more dependent upon agriculture than ever. We then see a substantial proportion of the rural population having just about enough to eat but not much of anything else, unoccupied or unemployed for many months of the year. Such a situation is of course accentuated if the climate is difficult, as in India.

This state of affairs, so regrettably common in the present-day world, was also — this is not generally recognized — the lot of rural England for a long period, probably for several centuries, in the past. In 1688 Gregory King estimated that, out of a total population of 5·5 million, 1·3 million represented 'cottagers and paupers' and their families, a seriously underoccupied rural population, receiving an average family income less than half that of a regularly employed labourer. This persistent rural unemployment in England did not disappear until the middle of the nineteenth century, and in Ireland is present to this day. It required a rapid growth of urban employment relative to population — more rapid than that of which the seventeenth and eighteenth centuries were capable — to solve this problem, even in a country so favourably situated as England.

But urbanization, or to use a more precise phrase, the development of non-agricultural employment generally, is not to be had just for the asking. We know that it requires a combination of factors, not always easily brought about, to make such development possible. We have clear evidence that England in 1688 or Germany in 1800 had an agriculture which, though very unproductive by present-day standards, nevertheless could produce a good deal more than was required for the food consumption of the rural population.

Even in the ancient world similar relationships prevailed. When population had passed a certain density, an urban civilization generally developed, producing manufactured goods which it traded in order to obtain primary products from more distant areas. A state of rural overpopulation can best be defined and considered in the light of the converse phenomenon, failure of an adequate urban population to develop. The most striking examples of this, indeed, are in countries which we know to have had a great urban development in ancient times, but which have failed in the modern world to establish even that degree of urbanization which they possessed in the remote past, e.g. Egypt, Greece, the Indus valley, the centres of the Maya, Aztec and Inca civilizations in America.

This phenomenon of rural overpopulation is in some ways analogous to the phenomenon of super-cooling or of metastable equilibrium in physics or chemistry. We seem to settle down for a considerable period in a situation considerably removed from that demanded by true economic equilibrium. We may perhaps press the analogy further to predict that, once the metastable equilibrium is disturbed, the progress towards true equilibrium will then be rapid.

It is hard to give any generalized reason as to why this state of affairs should come about. On the whole we must seek for political and historical rather than for narrowly economic reasons. Historically, some deficiency in the political order often prevented or impeded the development of towns and of commercial activities. In many cases this can be attributed to the despotic rule of absolute monarchies, particularly where arbitrary and oppressive taxation is imposed, as was particularly the case in all territories formerly part of the Turkish Empire. To take another example, in the eleventh century south Italy and Sicily supported a great many more people per unit area than Belgium, and apparently at a considerably higher standard of living. Their subsequent lapse into a state of under-employment, from which they have not recovered to this day, must probably be blamed upon political factors.

Enough information is now available to make some review of the economics of ox-ploughing, either with own team and equipment or by contract, on subsistence farms — bearing in mind de Vries's rule that in general this only becomes possible when production exceeds 500 kg./person/year grain equivalent. In a few cases contract cultivation by tractor can also be considered.

The first question is on the number of cultivations required, on which there is considerable difference of opinion. Cotton in Pakistan[1] requires three ploughings, sowing, and inter-cultivation. Rice in Vietnam[2] requires ploughing, harrowing and rolling (once planted, the water suppresses the weeds). Estimates for tractor

---

[1] Rafiq and others, *Pakistan Development Review*, spring 1968.
[2] Sansom, University of Oxford thesis, 1969.

cultivation in Pakistan[1] imply, however, an average of six or more operations, as has been claimed for Ceylon,[2] in an article written specifically to make a case for tractors on small farms.

The number of days/ha. required per operation has been estimated as low as 1 for inter-cultivation by a pair of buffaloes[3] (all estimates and costs below refer to pairs of animals, except for inter-cultivation by one donkey at 2 days/ha.).[4] One estimate for Vietnam[5] puts ploughing time at 5–6 days/ha., and harrowing at 1–3, but Sansom[6] considers that the three operations of ploughing, harrowing and rolling one hectare can be performed in 5 days by a buffalo team or in 8 days by an ox team.

The estimate for Ceylon,[2] which may be special pleading, estimates as much as 8 days for ploughing one hectare.

Animals tire before men. Average hours/day for an ox team have been estimated at 4[2], 5[5], 6[6], 5 with 7 for short peak periods.[1] The differences of these estimates give a partial explanation of the number of days required to cultivate one hectare.

Contractors' charges for ploughing a hectare vary to an incredible degree. In present-day Vietnam,[6] the war has led to a great loss of buffaloes — a pair of oxen will cost 4250 kg. rough rice, as against 1125 kg. in Madagascar and 700 kg. in Cameroun. There is also a labour shortage in Vietnam and the cultivation charge in terms of rough rice is now 300–400 kg./ha. — but some years earlier it was only 30.[5] The figure stands[3] at 170 in the Philippines and 150 in Madagascar[7] — both comparatively high-wage countries (although in the Philippines it appears that 6–8 men accompany the buffalo team). On the other hand five operations in West Pakistan only cost[8] 140 kg./ha. wheat. The charge[9] in Cameroun was only 25 kg./day of sorghum. In Bengal, where 'oxen work at a third of their proper pace (there are three times too many)',[10] an ox and plough can be hired[11] for only 3 kg./day rough rice.

[1] Finney, Lahore Symposium on Water Resource Development, 1969.
[2] Wijewardene, World Crops, Nov. 1961.
[3] Bureau of Plant Industry, quoted in Manila Saturday Chronicle, 25 Nov. 1967.
[4] De Wilde, Agricultural Development in Tropical Africa, pp. 107, 381.
[5] Hickey, Village in Vietnam, pp. 137–8.
[6] Sansom, University of Oxford thesis, 1969.
[7] Ottino, Cahiers del'ISEA, Jan. 1964.
[8] Rafiq and others, Pakistan Development Review, spring 1968.
[9] Guillard, Golonpoui, pp. 219–23.
[10] East Bengal Dept. of Agriculture (privately communicated).
[11] Fukutake, The Social and Economic Structure of the Indian Village.

The rate at which tractors can work, in ha./day, has been estimated[1] as high as 4, though 2 appears more plausible.[2] In Madagascar[3] their pace is estimated at six times that of the ox-plough. A careful estimate[4] for the Mwea Irrigation Area in Kenya indicates 1·8 ha. cultivated in the average day of 7·5 hours. However, the better timing of operations made possible by the introduction of tractors raises maize yields from 4·3 to 5·9 tons/ha.

Using the above figure where necessary of 4·15 hours/ha. for the average pace of tractors, the contract charge[5] for cultivating one hectare in West Pakistan was only 75 kg. of wheat (50 per cent higher if we reckon imports at their 'shadow prices'), 85 kg. rough rice in Madagascar,[3] 100 kg. rough rice in the Philippines,[2] 180 kg. maize in Kenya,[4] and 200 kg. rough rice in Vietnam.[1] Contract ploughing in Libya[6] was available at 165 kg./ha. wheat. In Thailand,[7] on the other hand, where the price of rice is kept artificially low in relation to import prices, the charges for tractor cultivation are in the 450–1200 kg. range.

In Uganda,[8] including all operations, hand cultivation is estimated to require 25 man-days/ha. of able-bodied labour; with the ploughing and harrowing done by oxen, 16 man-days (including some boy labour). Ploughing has not given the results hoped for in increasing acreage cultivated, or yields per acre.

[1] Sansom, University of Oxford thesis, 1969.
[2] Bureau of Plant Industry, quoted in Manila *Saturday Chronicle*, 25 Nov. 1967.
[3] Ottino, *Cahiers del'ISEA*, Jan. 1964.
[4] Giglioli, *East African Agriculture and Forestry Journal*, Jan. 1965.
[5] Rafiq and others, *Pakistan Development Review*, spring 1968.
[6] Meliczek, *Socio-Economic Conditions of a Libyan Village*, Technical University of Berlin, 1964.
[7] Janlekha, *Saraphi; A Survey of Socio-Economic Conditions in a Rural Community in North East Thailand*.
[8] Tothill, *Agriculture in Uganda*, O.U.P., 1940.

CHAPTER VII

Programming for Full Employment

The state of affairs in which long periods of idleness alternate with periods in which urgent labour demands cannot be met should naturally lead to attempts, scientific or rule of thumb as the case may be, to programme agricultural output in such a way as to make the demand for labour more uniform. This matter already arises with particular urgency in Japan, where nearly all farming districts are now rapidly losing the reserve of low-paid labour on which they used to count, and even the farmers and their families are being offered better-paid alternative employment in their own districts. Under these circumstances a farm has to re-programme output to provide for more regular employment if it is to survive at all.

An interesting and simple example quoted by Isobe[1] compares a farm of 1·9 ha., with 2·8 man equivalent labour units, growing single-cropped rice, vetch and mulberry, with a slightly smaller farm of 1·5 ha., and 2·4 labour units, growing double-cropped rice, wheat, barley, vetch, fruit and vegetables, and keeping poultry. Both require a certain amount of animal draught power, between April and June, though the second is better spread, not exceeding 20 hours per week, while the former may require nearly 40. The second farm is able to spread its labour requirements far better; they fall below 100 man-hours/week only for 5 weeks a year, and have temporary maxima just under 150 in June and September. The former farm on the other hand has a violent labour peak of over 300 hours required in the first week in June, and another peak in October, while for much of the winter less than ten hours a week are required.

The unevenness of labour demand throughout the year was one of the subjects of Fuggles Couchman's pioneer study.[2] On his recommended holding of 3¼ ha. (8 acres) the number of man-days/month required was as follows: November, 24; December,

---

[1] *Farm Planning with special reference to the management and improving of small-scale family farming*, Japanese Ministry of Agriculture, October 1956.
[2] Fuggles Couchman, *East African Journal of Agriculture*, March 1939.

CHART X

LABOUR DISTRIBUTION OF TWO FARMS
IN TOYAMA PREFECTURE, JAPAN

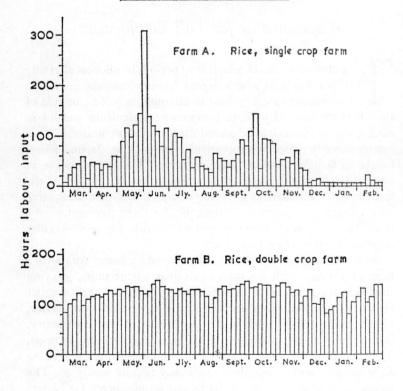

	Farm A	Farm B
Available labour on farm (man equivalents)	2·8	2·4
Size of farm (hectares)	1·9	1·5

15; January, 30½; February, 39½; March, 33½; April, 18½; May, 14½; June, 15½. It appears that the harvest was gathered from July onwards, but that this work could be spread. The February peak should be within the capacity of a man and wife both working on the holding; but, the author added (using the sort of language which would not now be regarded as permissible), 'natives do not usually work a full eight-hour day . . . a second wife and children would enable the work to be kept well in hand.'

Collinson[1] prepared a series of plans for a family with three man-equivalents labour supply, at present occupying 3 ha., but able to obtain more land if they wish, growing maize and cassava for consumption, and cotton for sale, with some livestock. At present the labour is fully occupied only during the short wet season of 3–4 months. Collinson's plans take it progressively up to full employment throughout the year. Gross and net products are expressed in maize equivalents (the local farm price is 0·22 shillings/kg. — much below world price, because of high transport costs — though the retail price is said to be two and a half times as high). The price received for cotton (unginned) is five times that for maize; in the scale of weights adopted for this book the ratio is 4. Collinson carefully debits all cash expenses, including depreciation of equipment.

TABLE XXXI

COLLINSON'S PROGRAMME FOR TANZANIAN FARMING
(3 man-equivalents per farm)

	Hectares cultivated		Proportion of year for which labour occupied	Returns tons maize equivalent/man-year	
	Total	of which cotton		Gross	Net after cash expenses
Stage I At present	3	1·2	33	3·30	3·02
Stage II Continued use of hand tools but improved methods	3	1·2	38	4·64	4·15
Stage III Introduction of fertilizers and insecticides	3	1·6	50	7·00	6·05
Stage IV Introduction of ox-ploughing	4·2	2·8	72	10·40	8·80
Stage V Alteration of methods to allow ox-drawn ridger for cotton	6·6	5·2	100	17·2	14·82

It must be added that the starting point of this programme is a farm which is already far above the African average in productivity.

[1] *Development Programme for a Rural District* (Geita), Tanzanian Ministry of Economic Affairs, 1966.

Clayton[1] used refined mathematical programming techniques for a Kenyan farm of 4·3 ha., with a farm family containing three adults, all deemed to be capable of working an 8-hour day for 300 days a year, or a potential labour input of 7200 man-hours/year. The government programme for such a farm yielded an annual income of £301, equivalent to 3 kg. maize/man-hour available (more per man-hour actually worked), i.e. at a level even higher than Collinson's. Clayton prepared a linear programme which raised the net revenue to £334, leaving (after providing 500 hours for necessary maintenance) 1388 hours still unused, mostly in the May-September period. This now represents a return of 4·1 kg. of maize equivalent/hour actually worked (compare returns of 2·0 to 2·6 kg. maize equivalent/man-hour found by Couchman in the 1930s). An improved linear programme raises the net income to £388. These programmes are based on the hiring of draught oxen; a proposal to use a hired tractor in preparing the seed bed ended up with a slight debit balance. A final programme employed all the labour available, except for the 500 hours maintenance, to be done in the off season. However, the average return per man-hour of labour actually worked was reduced to 3·85 kg. of maize. The marginal return for the 1388 man-hours saved by more refined programming thus works out at only 2·75 kg. maize/hour. The African may prefer to work these additional hours for a marginal return lower than his average; or he may prefer more leisure. But at any rate he should be grateful for the information in helping him to decide.

Kitsopanides, whose work on seasonality of employment in northern Greece was quoted in the previous chapter, also embarked on linear programming, and made a number of recommendations about changing the cropping pattern. He set himself the interesting exercise of asking whether winter unemployment (this is a cold mountain region) could be eliminated, on the interesting theoretical assumption that capital was available in unlimited quantities. Even with this assumption, it could not be done.

From his programme he was able to make precise estimates, for the different types of farm, of the marginal productivities of land, labour and short-term capital investment.

On the average farm, with a labour input already as high as 1334 man-hours/ha./year, the marginal return to labour is less than half

[1] E. S. Clayton, 'Economic and Technical Optima in Peasant Agriculture,' *Journal of Agricultural Economics*, May 1961.

CHART XI

GREEK MACEDONIA (Prof. Kitsopanides)

DISTRIBUTION OF LABOUR REQUIRED AS PERCENTAGE
OF LABOUR AVAILABLE.

—————— Labour Available
― ― ―   "   Required (average actual plan)
·········   "   "   (average optimum plan with exactly the same resources)
―·―·―·―   "   "   ("   "   "   " capital unlimited)

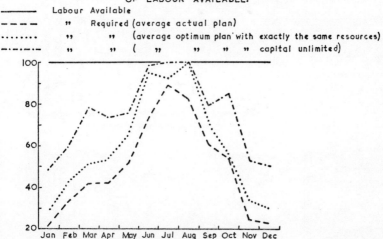

a kilogram of wheat equivalent/man-hour, a long way below the rate of wages payable for hired labour, though even at the highest labour inputs the marginal return does not fall to zero. On the larger farms, with less than 800 man-hours/ha./year labour input, it is worth while to engage labour at current wage rates.

On the smaller farms (which appear on the left of the land and capital diagrams, though they appear on the right of the labour diagram) it would be worth while paying very highly indeed both for additional land and for additional capital — if they could get them. The larger farms, it is interesting to see, are using their capital carefully, at a rate of marginal productivity which just corresponds to the expenses and interest on borrowing it. In the case of land, on the other hand, the larger farms have taken on more than they can really use, and are obtaining a marginal return lower than the rent which tenants would be willing to pay them. No doubt, however, they have family or personal reasons for holding on to additional land.

A Japanese exercise in linear programming has also been undertaken.[1] Currency has been converted to wheat equivalents on the wheat price of 45,000 yen/ton, which appears to be approximately

[1] Yajima, *World Population Conference*, 1965.

Chart XII

MARGINAL PRODUCTIVITIES IN NORTHERN GREECE

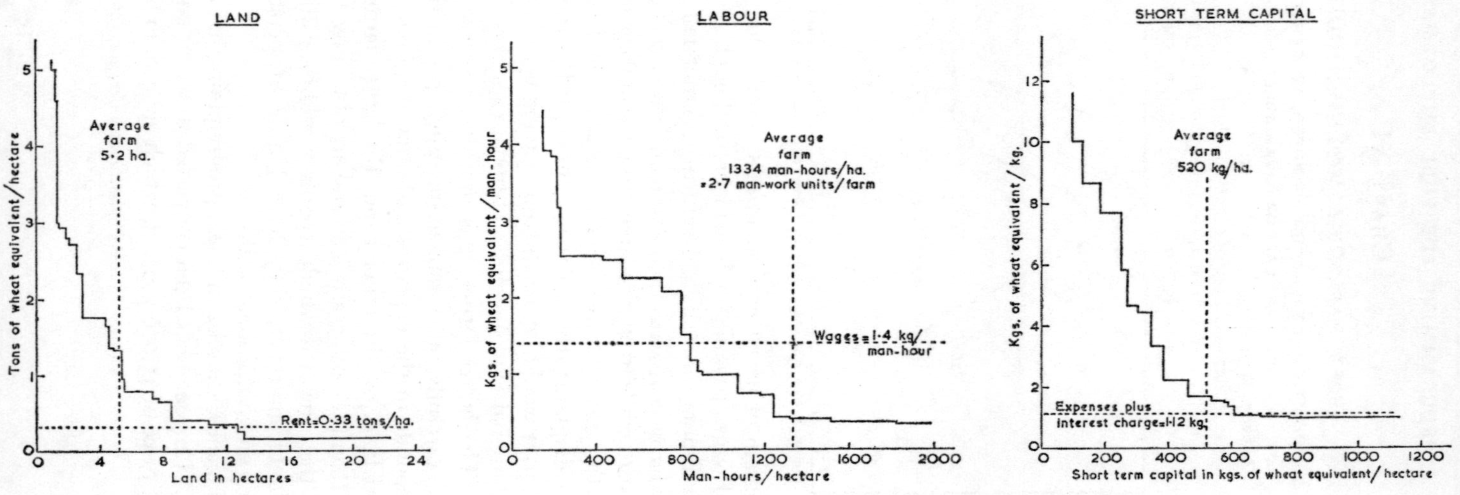

LAND
Tons of wheat equivalent/hectare
Average
farm
5·2 ha.
Rent=0·33 tons/ha.
Land in hectares
0
4
8
12
16
20
24
1
2
3
4
5
LABOUR
Kgs. of wheat equivalent/man-hour
Average
farm
1334 man-hours/ha.
=2·7 man-work units/farm
Wages=1·4 kg/
man-hour
Man-hours/hectare
0
400
800
1200
1600
2000
SHORT TERM CAPITAL
Kgs. of wheat equivalent/kg.
Average
farm
520 kg/ha.
Expenses plus
interest charge=1·12 kg.
Short term capital in kgs. of wheat equivalent/hectare
200
400
600
800
1000
1200
2
4
6
8
10
12

in line with the prices of most agricultural products. (If we converted on the price of milled rice of 95,000 yen/ton we would get much lower results. But the Government-supported price for rice in Japan appears to be out of line with that of other products.) The plan is for a family settling in Hokkaido, the cold northern Japanese island where land is fairly abundant. The family is assumed to contain 2½ labour units, each regarded as capable of working 27 days/month, 10 hours/day from May to July, 9 in September, and 8 for the rest of the year. The family is to employ draught animals, but otherwise to maintain Japanese standards of intensive cultivation. Under these circumstances, and in this climate, the programme rejected wheat, sugar beet and potatoes, and called for concentration on dairying and soya-beans.

Under these circumstances, the marginal productivity of land changes by discrete steps, indicating, for this family, an optimum holding of 12·1 hectares, yielding an income of 20·5 tons wheat equivalent. Improved yields are expected to indicate a slightly lower optimum farm of 11·5 hectares, raising the income to 26·7 tons wheat equivalent.

TABLE XXXII. MARGINAL PRODUCTIVITIES OF LAND
FOR FAMILY OF 2½ LABOUR UNITS IN HOKKAIDO

	Present methods	With expected future yield increases	
Hectares	Marginal product t/ha. wheat equiv.	Hectares	Marginal product t/ha. wheat equiv.
0– 2·5	2·55	0– 2·5	3·00
2·5– 8·2	1·60	2·5– 8·6	2·07
8·2– 8·5	1·52	8·6–11·5	2·03
8·5–10·6	1·32		
10·6–12·1	1·16		

Mathematical programmes have been prepared for a still smaller farm in Taiwan[1] with three able-bodied workers and only half a hectare of land (90 per cent irrigated). The ratio of cropped to cultivated land in Taiwan has risen, not surprisingly, from 1·16 in 1911–15 to 1·32 in 1932–5, and 1·80 in 1956–60. A shortage of feeding stuffs rules out the possibility of intensifying through keeping more livestock, beyond one pig per family, living on his ration of 400 kg./year of sweet potato, grown on 1/30th of a hectare of unirrigated land. The present family income of such a farm averages 2180 kg. milled rice (converting at 5·6 Taiwan dollars

[1] Hsieh and Lee, *World Population Conference*, 1965.

to the kg.), which is not much above subsistence level, for a family probably consisting of 6 or 7 people. Total labour input is only 224 man-days/year, of which 60 are devoted to looking after the pig and growing his fodder. Assuming an eight-hour day, this represents some 3600 man-hours/hectare/year of labour input. It means, of course, very great under-occupation of the three potential workers; in the busiest months, a total of only 28 man-days is required in February and 27 in November, while in January and June only one man-day is required in each (work on the pig being excluded throughout).

At this intensity of labour input, one would have thought that any further intensification would have yielded little or no marginal return. The authors, using a linear programming method, still accepting the constraint that no livestock must be kept except the one pig, have devised a programme which increases total labour input by 75 per cent, and more than doubles the family income, to 4630 kg. milled rice equivalent, i.e. a marginal return actually greater than the previous average return. The programme indicates two crops of rice and winter cabbage on the irrigated land, groundnut, sweet potato and cabbage on the unirrigated. The pig still receives his 60 man-days of labour annually. The other work now calls for 60 man-days in July, 59 in November and 55 in February (i.e. rather more than two men can provide); with mitigated slack periods, in which 12 man-days are demanded each in January and April, nine in September and six in October.

This remarkable study brings hope even to the most exceptionally densely populated areas — provided they have adequate water.

An original application of programming was made by Odero-Ogwel[1] in preparing a demand function for labour for the whole Nyeri District of Kenya:

Wages shilling/month	Over 75	60–75	50–60	Below 50
Labour demand (thousand)	7·8	11	13	Over 16

The present average wage is 60 shillings.

[1] University of London thesis, 1969, p. 450.

CHAPTER VIII

Wages and Leisure

The programmer who seeks to induce the subsistence cultivator to work much longer hours than he does now must
offer him a high marginal return per hour in exchange.
Does the subsistence cultivator, we are often asked, value his
leisure? Some economists have said, over-hastily, that it has no
value to them. But on examination this is seen not to be a rational
answer. If leisure really had no value, people would be willing to
work for nothing, or nearly nothing. The strange fact (disclosed
below) that, throughout all places and times for which we have
information, the rural labourer, however poor, will not do a day's
work for less than 3 kg. grain equivalent, gives us an approximate
but interesting measure of the value which the very poor put on
their leisure. And recent work, both empirical and theoretical, has
shown that as levels of real income rise, the valuation which we
put on our leisure increases; most of us require to be offered
overtime wages much higher than our average wages, to persuade
us to work any longer.

In countries where people are free, a wage or similar incentive is
necessary to attract people from agriculture to industry. The
required cash inducement is greater than one thinks. Raj[1] has
estimated that an unemployed Indian countryman will be maintained at subsistence level by his family at the cost of about
1·8 kg. grain/day. To induce him to start work, even in his own
village, he will have to be offered a wage of 3 kg. grain/day, according to region; to induce him to take work outside his own village
he will have to be offered 5 kg. grain/day or more. In Gangaikondan[2] in Madras State it was found that off-farm employment
opportunities in a cement factory 10·6 km. from the village were
attracting labour in abundance when the wage rate was 9·3 kg.
grain equivalent per day — two to three times the subsistence wage,
at which labour supply is inelastic.

The case has already been mentioned of the Land Dayak, who

[1] K. N. Raj, Director of the Agricultural Economics Research Centre, University of Delhi; private communication.
[2] M. R. Haswell, *Economics of Development in Village India*.

prefer the low-yielding upland rice in preference to the high-yielding swamp rice, because the former gives a better return per unit of labour. Gourou[1] generalized this to cover shifting cultivation throughout Africa. It was not through lack of knowledge, he contended, but a deliberate preference for leisure, which led them to use these methods rather than the more intensive methods of sedentary agriculture. His theory is demonstrated by the fact that isolated tribes can be found, hemmed into limited areas by the pressure of hostile neighbours, who have indeed practised intensive agriculture. One of the most striking was the island of Ukara in Lake Victoria, inhabited at the very high density of 4·7 persons/ha. of cultivable land. Each hectare gave a total produce of 3000–4000 kg. grain equivalent/year, including a substantial output of livestock products. Cattle were kept in sheds, yielding on an average 3 tons/year of milk, and abundant manure. The average return to labour was about 1 kg./man-hour of grain equivalent, though the marginal return was somewhat lower. The final proof of Gourou's theorem is that in recent years, when tribal tensions have diminished, much of this highly efficient cultivation on Ukara has been abandoned.

It is sometimes said that among subsistence cultivators the demand for leisure is strong (i.e. the demand for purchased commodities is weak or difficult to fulfil) so that we get the phenomenon known in economics as the 'backward-sloping supply function', whereby people actually do less work if their wages are increased. This idea has aroused a great deal of interest; but facts in support of it are few. Both theory and empirical study indicate that such a state of affairs is not likely to be found in any community with reasonable contacts with the rest of the world, where men can seek alternative employment, and where a wide range of commodities is on sale. One of the few real examples was found in pre-revolutionary Russia.[2] Here, however, we are dealing with villages physically isolated by bad communications and economically isolated by very high protected prices for manufactured goods.

However, there is some indication of these tendencies among the Dusun in Sabah.[3] Their production of irrigated rice for their own subsistence occupies some five or six months during the year. During the rest of the year they do a certain amount of

[1] P. Gourou, *Annuaire du Collège de France*, 1961, p. 248.
[2] Chayanov, *The Theory of Peasant Economy*, R. D. Irwin Inc., 1966.
[3] M. Glyn-Jones, *The Dusun of the Penampang Plains in North Borneo*, Report to the Colonial Office, unpublished.

rubber tapping for cash. Glyn-Jones pointed out that they still had, on the whole, the subsistence cultivator's outlook, because she observed that the better the land, the smaller the area the average family would cultivate. At the time when she studied them, however, they were just beginning to feel their need for more cash, or for surplus rice which could be used in exchange in much the same way as cash, in the first place to buy work animals and ploughs, and sometimes to pay additional labour for the harvest, or to rent additional land.

Economists have been grumbling about subsistence cultivators' preference for leisure, and finding it difficult to understand, ever since the days of the founder of economics, Sir William Petty (one of the authors recalls with satisfaction that he was a Fellow of Brasenose: with less satisfaction that he changed sides twice during the Civil War). Petty wrote in 1691,[1] regarding the Irish, 'What need have they to work, who can content themselves with *Potato's*, whereof the Labour of one Man can feed forty?' Petty's figure was approximately correct, and was confirmed by Arthur Young, regarding the ability of one man to produce 50 tons of potatoes per year (to feed 40 people at 8 lb./person/day); but Petty failed to observe that a substantial quantity of milk and oatmeal were also included in the Irish diet at that time.

Burgess and Musa,[2] referring to small farmers who worked on the average only about 3 hours a day, pointed out that, apart from rice production, no general effort was made to cultivate the land and it was clear that the resources for production available to smallholders were not fully utilized, largely because they did not receive a 'reasonable recompense' for the work they had done.

In Malaysia, as we have seen, ideas of what constitutes a reasonable wage stand at a much higher level than in most subsistence-agriculture countries. Wage-earners earn up to 1·5 kg./hour of paddy. Purcal[3] estimated marginal returns at about 0·8 kg./hour in fishing and horticulture, 0·4 in mat making. While this work was available, most people were unwilling to take it at these rates.

In Bengal, where the soil and rainfall are very good, some of the land is double cropped, and the labour input per ha. very high.

---

[1] Sir William Petty, *Political Arithmetick*.
[2] R. C. Burgess and Laidin Bin Alang Musa, *A Report on the State of Health, the Diet and the Economic Conditions of Groups of People in the Lower Income Levels in Malaya*, Institute for Medical Research Report No. 13, Federation of Malaya, 1950.
[3] Ph.D. thesis, Australian National University.

Nevertheless, Ghosh and Das[1] found there, from a detailed study of land registers, that families cultivated all the land which they owned (and paid rent for additional land to cultivate, in the case of the families owning least land) only up to 0·5 ha./ person. Of land owned above this limit, only about two-thirds is cultivated by the family owning it, the remainder being leased. Cultivation of 0·5 hectare in Bengal, even if we assume no double cropping, would yield about 600 kg./person/year of rough rice. It appears to be at incomes above this level that leisure preference becomes significant.

One reason why African farmers do not produce more is that while they would like to buy more industrial goods, and would be willing to produce more crops in exchange for them, they are hampered by the lack of transport, and inadequate marketing organization. This is true of crops even with high value per unit of weight such as cocoa and coffee; and there is a limit to the amount of these crops which the farmer can grow. Good roads are Africa's real priority need: without them crops have lost a large part of their value by the time they are carried to market.

Leisure preference persisted in eighteenth-century England also.[2] 'The manufacturing population do not labour above 4 days a week unless provisions happen to be very dear . . . when provisions are cheap they won't work above half the week, but sot or idle away half their time.'

While we are on the question of leisure preference, we may note that the French peasant in the eighteenth century[3] worked less than 200 days a year on his farm. He was also required, on the average, to do about 30 days a year forced labour (Corvée) on roads, etc. Cultivated and pasture land per man engaged in agriculture was about 6 ha.

Massell and Johnson[4] are also specific on the subject. 'Before the return to labour reaches zero, people refuse to work. There is ample evidence of people in the Chiweshe working short hours, even during the seasonal peaks.'

The whole issue is tersely stated in a tribal song which an administrator discovered being sung in a remote part of New Guinea, and which he translated into Australian:

---

[1] Ghosh and Das, 'Problems of Sub-Marginal Farming in West Bengal', *Indian Journal of Agricultural Economics*, Vol. V, No. 1, March 1950.
[2] Temple, Essays on *Trade and Commerce* (Quoted Cunningham).
[3] H. de Farcy, *Revue de l'Action Populaire*, April 1962.
[4] *Economics of Smallholder Farming in Rhodesia*

SONG OF THE TRIBAL ECONOMIST[1]

The primitive farmer says Cash
Is unsatisfactory trash;
  It won't keep off rain
  And it gives me a pain
If I use it to flavour my hash.

So why should I work out my guts
At the whim of these government mutts,
  My liquor comes free
  From the coconut tree
And my Mary makes cups from the nuts.

    Cash cropping is all very well
  If you've *got* to have something to sell;
    But tell me, sir, why
    If there's nothing to buy
Should I bother? You can all go to hell.

A number of comparisons have recently been made of marginal productivity of labour, and of wages paid, in India.[2] It appears that marginal products in general are substantially higher than wages paid, though less so in the Punjab than elsewhere; and that they rise on the larger farms.

TABLE XXXIII. MARGINAL PRODUCTS AND WAGES OF LABOUR IN INDIA

Rupees/day (8 hours)
(Standard errors in brackets)

		Size of farm (hectares)	Marginal Product	Wages
Punjab	Cotton	Below 6	4·1(1·0)	
		6–12	3·8(0·9)	2·56
		Over 12	7·2(2·2)	
	Wheat	6–12	5·4(1·8)	
		Over 12	8·2(2·6)	2·82
Maharashtra	Cotton	5–11	4·3(1·7)	1·37
	Sorghum	5–11	4·2(1·7)	1·40
Gujarat	All products	Below 11	4·4(2·0)	1·40

Maruta[3] made a mathematical analysis of the accounts of 30 poor farms in Kagoshima province which had, he pointed out, the highest proportion of population engaged in agriculture and the lowest per head agricultural income of all provinces in Japan, despite its favourable climate, which permits the growing of oranges and tea. Average labour input was as high as 2700 man-hours/ha./year. Maruta's equation showed that the output obtained was almost entirely explainable in terms of the inputs of

[1] Free translation of Papuan Tribal Song, Fisk, *Economic Record*, June 1964.
[2] Abraham and Bokil, *Indian Journal of Agricultural Economics*, Jan.–Mar. 1966.
[3] S. Maruta, *Memoirs of the Faculty of Agriculture*, Kagoshima University, No. 1, 1956.

land and capital. The marginal product of labour appeared to be only 50 yen/day, or 0·075 kg. wheat equivalent/man-hour (the farm price of brown, or partially milled rice, whose value on the FAO scale is precisely equivalent to that of wheat, was 67 yen/kg.). In a later study (December 1958), more refined, Maruta obtained higher figures for marginal productivity, though still very low. Distinguishing hired and family labour, he obtained marginal products of 61 and 15 yen/hour respectively. Tutiya[1] estimated marginal products at only 11 yen/hour for rice, inappreciable for wheat, barley and oranges, but at 29 for tea and 34 for sweet potato. These two latter were above the current wage level, i.e. it was worth while hiring labour to produce them.

Zero marginal output can occur in Communist agricultural economics too. A number of medium-yielding cotton farms in Uzbekistan in 1953[2] showed no change in yield as the labour input rose from 233 to 348 man-days/ha. (extremely high labour inputs in any case, even for cotton).

A most interesting new approach to the problem of marginal productivity in rice growing was Sarkar's study for Ceylon.[3] Comparing different districts in Ceylon, he obtained the equation:

Log (yield of rough rice in bushels) $=0·0802$ log (area in acres) $+0·5570$ log (labour input in man-days of 8 hours, women counting half men) $+0·2453$ log (all other costs, measured in Rs.) $-0·0141$

(1 bushel rough rice $=20·5$ kg.; wheat equivalent of rough rice $= 0·8$)

To calibrate his equation he then assumes (which does not appear to be quite the case) that the marginal product can be equated to the subsistence wage paid in the agricultural districts, which at that time was 1·9 Rs. per day (equivalent to 3·9 kg. of rough rice). Taking 268 days as a normal year, he then deduces that 28 per cent of the agricultural population is surplus. An interesting feature of this result is that the extent of surplus labour appears to be almost unrelated to the size of holding.

[1] K. Tutiya, *Quarterly Journal of Agricultural Economics*, No. 1, 1955. In Japanese.
[2] *Economic Bulletin for Europe*, November 1957, p. 00.
[3] N. K. Sarkar, 'A method of estimating surplus labour in peasant agriculture in overpopulated underdeveloped countries'. *Journal of the Royal Statistical Society*, Series A, Vol. CXX, 1957.

Taking Sarkar's equation, for a given area of land, and with miscellaneous expenditure also being given, we can rewrite it:

Log(number of labour days) = constant − log(marginal productivity of labour measured in bushels per year)/0·443

So, if we raise the number of labour days by the factor of 1/0·72 (i.e. raising it from Sarkar's computed to its actual level) the left-hand side of the equation is raised by 0·145, so marginal productivity of labour is lowered by the antilog of 0·064, i.e. 16 per cent. In this way we deduce the true marginal productivity of labour at 0·41 kg. rough rice/man-hour, as against the wage of 0·49.

The marginal productivity of land, that is to say the increase in output which can be obtained by increasing the amount of land cultivated, labour input being given, is a sort of reciprocal measure of the marginal productivity of labour. In Iraq, a comparatively advanced economy,[1] some calculations were made for a farm family of given size, if it were able to occupy holdings increasing progressively from 7·5 to 12·75 ha. Expressed in tons of wheat/ha. (the price of a ton of wheat was 20 Iraqi dinari) marginal productivity appeared to be actually increasing as the scale was ascended, beginning at 1 ton wheat equivalent/ha. and rising to 1·4.

Maruta found a marginal productivity of a hectare of land in mixed farming at about 0·6 tons of brown rice equivalent (equal to wheat equivalent); but for rice growing on irrigated land the figure was 1·2 tons for the larger farms with hired labour, and 4·1 tons (i.e., marginal productivity about equal to average) on the smaller farms without hired labour.

Bicanic's results for Yugoslavia[2] indicate a marginal return of almost exactly 1 ton of wheat/ha. for the smallest farms of 2 ha. or so, falling to 0·44 tons on the larger farms of about 8 ha. Throughout the range, it is interesting to see, the marginal return is a little less than half the average. There are some very varied results for India (Table XXXIV), some of which also indicate marginal product of labour much below that estimated by Abraham and Bokil. But we must be prepared for differences — their results related to rather large farms, and Shastri's diagram shows us how quickly marginal productivity can vary in India (as indeed elsewhere) with the amount of labour input.

[1] Government of Iraq Development Board, *Diyala and Middle Tigris Projects*, Report No. 3, 1959. Estimates by Jewett, kindly supplied by Hunting Technical Services.

[2] International Association for Income and Wealth Conference, De Pietersberg, 1957.

TABLE XXXIV. MARGINAL PRODUCTS IN INDIA

	Labour R/day	Land R/ha/yr	Equipment (marginal product expressed as multiple of input)	Fertilizer	Livestock	Bullock-pair R/day
Allahabad 1955–6	Not significant	394	1·36		0·92	
Orissa — Irrigated rice	0·5	238				
Rain-fed rice	0·6	224				
Uttar Pradesh 1963–4	1·8	175				5·3
Near Delhi 1961–2	1·27	460				5·9
Baroda 1960–1	1·44	247	1·45[a]	0·73[b]		Not significant
Ganges Valley	0·7	108				4·6

[a] Taking input (interest + depreciation) at 20 per cent of depreciated capital value.
[b] Including cattle manure purchased.

Allahabad　Wycliffe, *Indian Journal of Agricultural Economics*, Jan.–Mar. 1959. 48 farms, geometric average area 1·47 ha., employment 34 man months, equipment (including draught animals) 308 R, other livestock 377 R.

Orissa　Haswell, *Economics of Development in Village India*, pp. 71–2. Original data given in hours and converted to days by a factor of 8, and in kg. of paddy, converted by an estimated price of 0·3 Rs./kg.

Uttar Pradesh　S. P. Dhondyal, D.Sc. Thesis, University of Delhi, 200 farms.

Near Delhi　Singh & Hrabovsky, *Indian Journal of Agricultural Economics*, Oct.–Dec. 1965.

Baroda　Naik, *Indian Journal of Agricultural Economics*, July–Sept. 1965.

Ganges Valley　Hopper, *Journal of Farm Economics*, August 1965.

De Farcy,[1] reviewing a great amount of information both present-day and historical, makes the bold generalization that

[1] *Revue del'Action Populaire*, April 1962.

3 kg./day of grain represents the usual remuneration of wage labour in a subsistence economy.

A series is available for Egypt[1] for a long period.

	1914	1920–9	1933–9	1941–5	1950–1	1955–6	1959–61
Average daily wage kg. maize equivalent	3·2	4·5	3·5	3·1	5·7	3·3	4·2

Analysis shows that wages are, as theory predicts, determined by the money value of the marginal product, and that the fluctuations mostly arise in the price of cotton, not of maize. Women's wages equal men's at the seasonal peaks, but are lower in the rest of the year, when most of the work consists of tasks such as ditching.

Wages in Ethiopia[2] have been found to be 3–4 kg./day in terms of maize. In Madagascar[3] hoers receive the equivalent of 4·1 kg. *milled* rice (125 francs) plus a meal, a considerably higher amount.

Beckett's casual labourers in West Africa received the equivalent of only 3·4 kg. of maize/day in the 1930s; regular workers, including the value of their food, housing and 'customary pickings' (clandestine sale of some of the crop to itinerant buyers) earned 4½ kg. maize/day. Comparing these figures with those of farmer's average incomes, we must conclude that marginal product was high relative to average product per unit of labour. Both farmers and labourers in West Africa at that time, however, were suffering from an extremely low price of cocoa, and relatively high price of maize, far above its price in East Africa. The average wage in Tanganyika, as recorded by Couchman[4] in the 1930s was the equivalent of 6 kg./day of maize or sorghum (0·4 shillings).

The wage in this case represented only about a third of the gross product. Nigerian agricultural wages, as has been mentioned in Chapter VI, are also high, at about 1 kilogram/hour maize equivalent. More recent information indicates a wage of 6 shillings/ day (of 8 hours), representing about the same real value. In this case the wage earner appears to be paid at the rate of nearly 90 per cent of what the farmer himself can earn per man-hour.[5] The Cameroonian wage of 60 C.F.A./day on the other hand was worth only 3·25 kg/day of millet; the Tanzanian wage of 3 shillings/day was worth 10·7 kg. maize or 7·2 kg. rough rice.[6]

[1] Hansen, *Journal of Development Studies*, July 1966.
[2] Oxford University Expedition to the Gamu Highlands, Ethiopia (private communication).
[3] Ottino, *Cahiers de l'ISEA*, Jan. 1964.
[4] Fuggles Couchman, *East African Journal of Agriculture*, March 1939.
[5] Luning, *Netherlands Journal of Agricultural Science*, Nov. 1964.
[6] For sources *see* productivity comparisons in Chapter VI.

In the middle of the nineteenth century, when Ghana was almost completely a subsistence economy,[1] the average day's wage was 4–5 cowries (rare sea shells), capable of purchasing 6·3 kg. maize.

Wages in Guatemala,[2] on the other hand, averaged only 4·1 kg. maize/day, while average product was 2·9 kg./hour. The reason for this great difference is hard to see — unless some sort of serfdom prevailed. The wage labourer in Vietnam, Gourou reported, received in the 1930s 1 fr./day for a period which might vary from 120 to 200 days per year, and the equivalent of a steady 220 fr./year in kind. If we spread this latter remuneration over 200 days, his total remuneration is the equivalent of 2·4 kg./day of milled rice (equivalent to 2·85 kg. of wheat). For China, Buck quotes abundant wage data, but only in silver currency, which can be translated only into grain equivalents in an indirect manner. The day wage here however appears to average about 3½ kg. of Buck's 'grain equivalent' (which includes a considerable proportion of coarser grains).

A pioneer of village surveys of subsistence cultivators was Gilbert Slater, Professor of Economics in the University of Madras, who surveyed a number of villages in southern India in 1916. Twenty years later they were resurveyed by the University.[3]

These surveys revealed the existence, in some villages, of workers who had become, in effect, serfs. The law of British India did not recognize serfdom, nor indeed the attachment of sons for their fathers' debts, which seems to have been the way in which this quasi-serfdom arose, among poor people who were too uninformed or too frightened to seek legal redress. (Economic historians speculate that serfdom in Dark Age Europe may have originated in a similar manner.) This serfdom did, however, have the compensating advantage that the wage was paid regularly, whether work was available or not. As it came to be replaced by free contract and money payments, the workers earned money only on the days on which work was available, often as few as 100 per year in this part of India.

It appears that the situation changed little over twenty years, and

---

[1] Reindorf, *History of the Gold Coast and Asante*, 1895, quoted Anyane, *Ghana Agriculture*.
[2] Higbee, *Geographical Review*, April 1947.
[3] University of Madras Economic Series, No. 1, *Some South Indian Villages*, ed. G. Slater, 1918; No. 4, *Some South Indian Villages, A Resurvey*, ed. P. J. Thomas, 1940. 1961 data from M. R. Haswell, *Economics of Development in Village India*.

that some of the earnings were extremely low. The village of Vadamalaipuram suffers from an extremely dry climate, and there is little work outside the $2\frac{1}{2}$ months' monsoon period. Recently however a well has been installed, with an electric pump, making the growing of a variety of crops possible; and the women of the village have demanded a wage of $3\frac{1}{2}$ kg. grain/day.

The average wage in 1954 in the Madras district, as shown by the official survey, was 3·35 kg. rough rice/day for a man.

TABLE XXXV. EARNINGS OF LANDLESS LABOURERS IN SOUTHERN INDIA EXPRESSED IN KG. OF GRAIN EQUIVALENT

		Yearly wage			Daily wage		
		1916	1936	1961	1916	1936	1961
	Kg. of paddy						
Dusi	men			600[a]		2·83	3·34
	women						1·29[b]
Eruvellipet	men	412		440[c]			4
	women						2
Gangaikondan	women, peak season transplanting						3·2
	women, other hand operations						1·6
Guruvayur[d]		657	682				
Vunagatla	men	686	1144		3·0	5·2	
	women				1·5	4·2	
	boys	329			1·0	2·3	
Watakancheri	men	663	663				
	women		497				
	boys		331				
	kg. of millet						
Vadamalaipuram	men	600	454		5·4[e]		3·4
	women				2·7[f]		

[a] For 180 days' work per year.
[b] For transplanting seedlings. For harvesting, women received 2·58 kg./day paid in kind, plus a meal.
[c] For 131 days' work per year.
[d] 1925, 561 kg.; 1932, 545 kg.
[e] Work available for 54 days per year.
[f] Work available for 67 days per year.

Dharma Kumar[1] obtained figures of annual wages in grain of agricultural labour in Madras Presidency in the nineteenth century. Taking averages of the years 1873–5 (before the 1876–8 famine) and 1898–1900, she shows a striking decline in six of the seven districts, the exception being Tanjore, the granary of the south. Although agreeing that there was a famine in 1896–7, she points out that wages continued to be low in the first decade of the twentieth century.

[1] *Land and Caste in India*, Cambridge U. P., 1965.

TABLE XXXVI. WAGES IN MADRAS PRESIDENCY IN THE NINETEENTH CENTURY

	Ganjam	Vizakha-patnam	Kg. of paddy/year Bellary	Tanjore	Tirunel-veli	Salem	Coimbatore
1873–75	883	747	618	489	846	440	734
1898–1900	514	393	492	640	508	352	449

A study[1] for Kerala shows a very serious decline, which may have some bearing on the political history of the state, from 11·4 kg./day (in terms of milled rice) in 1939–40 to 4·4 in 1945–6, 3·6 in 1954–5, and 3·3 in 1960–1. (Kerala has to import rice, at high world prices.)

In the Philippines[2] the average wage of 1·63 pesos corresponds to 4·6 kg. rough rice or 7·4 kg. maize.

Thailand is known to be a country of comparatively high productivity. Wages of unskilled farm labour[3] are $7\frac{1}{2}$ kg./day of unmilled rice in the north, and $12\frac{1}{2}$ in the Central Province, and 25 in the Central Province at harvest time (the price of rice being taken at 0·8 baht/kg. on farm unmilled).

A very interesting historical series has been compiled for Vietnam, showing a rise up to the 1920s (with land development and transport improvements) followed by a decline.

	1898	1915	1923	1929	1931	1940–3	1958	1966
Average daily wage piastres	0·2	0·3	0·7	0·8	0·18	1	30	120
Kg. rough rice	10	12	20	20	13·3	16·7	12	12

Past information from Europe is also interesting in this connection. From the studies of seventeenth-century England referred to in a previous chapter, we can equate the average agricultural wage of 8 pence/day to 4·8 kg. of wheat — well above subsistence level, but only half what it had been in the fifteenth century. In 1836 Irish agricultural wages were still $8\frac{1}{2}$ pence/day, equivalent then to only 3·4 kg. wheat.

However, wages in eighteenth-century France appear to have been much lower.[4]

De Foville also quotes figures for Belgium in the neighbourhood of 3 kg./day of wheat in 1830 and 1840, and 3·7 in 1856.

[1] Pillai and Panikar, *Land Reclamation in Kerala*.
[2] Bureau of Agricultural Economics, 1962.
[3] Usher, *Economica*, Nov. 1966.
[4] Data from: de Foville, *La France économique*.

TABLE XXXVII. AGRICULTURAL WAGES IN FRANCE

Year	Man's wage Frs./day	Equivalent in kg. wheat/day
1700	0·5	2·6
1788	0·6	2·8
1813	1·05	3·5
1840	1·3	4·6
1852	1·42	6·1
1862	1·85	6·1
1872	2·0	6·5

Spanish wages appear to have been equivalent to about 11 kg./day of wheat (at farm prices) both in the 1900s and now.[1] However in one of the poorest-paid provinces, and at the worst period,[2] daily wages in Andalusia were recorded at 15 pesetas, equivalent to 3½ kg. only of wheat. In eighteenth-century Madrid[3] wages were almost exactly 3 kg./day of wheat. (The information is given for the price of bread, but the milling and baking costs would have been of a similar order of magnitude to the value of the offals, so bread and wheat prices per kg. should have been similar.) Madrid was remote from wheat-producing areas, and about one-third of the price of wheat represented transport costs.

[1] Vandellos, *Metron*, 1925, gives 2 pesetas a day for the average of 1903–12; Fr. Garavilla, Burgos (private communication) gives 47 pesetas a day for the present wage.
[2] *The Economist*, 2 June 1951.
[3] Ringrose, *Journal of Economic History*, Mar. 1968.

CHAPTER IX

Productivity of Land

W e may begin by considering some information from the ancient world. In ancient Greece, the normal wheat yield in Attica in the late fourth century B.C. was estimated[1] at 0·9 tons/ha. Michell points out that much higher yields were obtained in Egypt, Babylonia and Sicily. For ancient Egypt a figure of 2 tons/ha. has been estimated.[2]

To give the background of these figures we may note that in modern Greece in 1934–8 the figure was only 0·9 tons/ha., in India only 0·65. The Egyptian figure had fallen to 1·4 by 1830, the first year for which we have modern information, and it is only recently that it has risen again to the 2 tons/ha. of ancient times.

In mediaeval England productivity was even lower, and progress very slow:

Wheat Yields, Tons/Ha.

Year	Gross[3]	Net after seed[3]	Gross[4]
1250	—	—	0·43
1350	0·54	0·37	0·56
1450	0·57	0·40	—
1550	0·64	0·47	1·06
1650	0·74	0·57	—
1750	1·01	0·84	1·41
1850	1·8	1·6	1·8

Over a large part of the world today agricultural productivity is now the same as, or even inferior to, what it was in the leading civilized communities 2,000 years ago. This is the system of agriculture described in most interesting detail in the poetry of Hesiod and Virgil. Its basic technique was ploughing and harrowing with teams of oxen — somewhat slow and clumsy, but very much more

[1] Michell, *The Economics of Ancient Greece*.
[2] A. C. Johnson's volume on Egypt in the series, *Economic Survey of the Roman Empire*.
[3] M. K. Bennett, 'British Wheat Yield per Acre for Seven Centuries', *Economic History*, February, 1935.
[4] Richardson, *Outlook on Agriculture*, Winter 1960.

efficient than that of the bronze-age agriculture which had preceded it. Its essential implement, it need hardly be pointed out, was the iron ploughshare, a fairly recent discovery in Hesiod's time (seventh century B.C.). This was only available in communities which enjoyed not only a knowledge of iron working, but reasonably abundant supplies of this truly precious metal, and the dissemination of them to every village community. In the modern world, 1 lb. of iron exchanges against a little more than 1 lb. of wheat; in the seventh century B.C. it exchanged against some 15 lb. of wheat — but it was well worth it when the alternative was ploughing with a clumsy and short-lived wooden ploughshare.

Customary rice yields in most parts of Asia[1] over the last 50 years have been in the neighbourhood of 1 ton milled rice/ha., with a tendency on the whole to decline, as cultivation was extended into less suitable lands, without fertilizer, and with some (though probably not very serious) soil deterioration. India, Ceylon and Philippines have shown even lower yields. A figure of 0·9 tons prevailed in Japan a thousand years ago: by the sixteenth century it stood at 1·4. When the modern advance began, in the 1870s, it stood at about 1·7,[2] it now stands at 4·00 (average of last three years' yields, and assuming 72½ per cent extraction). Taking 225 kg. *milled* rice (72½ per cent extraction) as the per head subsistence requirement (including a certain amount to be exchanged for required agricultural products besides rice) for an Asian population, the area of land required to produce this amount is as follows, under varying circumstances:

India in 1930s (Cambodia or Nepal now)	0·27 ha.
India now	0·22 ha.
Japan now	0·06 ha.

The possibility is clearly open to India of supporting a much larger population on the same land, if plant breeding and fertilization can be carried as far as they have been in Japan.

Information on yields per hectare in the developing countries has become more abundant in recent years, and the FAO tables are now almost world-wide in coverage. In order to give a table of manageable size, the data for each of the continents of Asia, Africa, Central America and South America, excluding certain specified countries, have been shown as averages — their components are comparatively uniform. The countries shown have, for 1948–52,

---

[1] Wickizer and Bennett, *The Rice Economy of Monsoon Asia*, California, 1941.
[2] Wickizer and Bennett, op. cit. Also confirmed by Ike, *Journal of Economic History*, 1947.

yields roughly comparable with the aggregates of the continents which they are meant to represent.

For the 1930s and earlier, much less information is available. The figures quoted in Table XXXVIII are compiled from the reports of FAO's predecessor, the International Institute of Agriculture, with two wheat figures for the 1880s from the Food Research Institute at Stanford.

The table shows a regrettable picture of stagnant or declining yields in many countries, with, in some cases but by no means all, signs of an upturn in recent years. In Latin America there are as yet no signs of an upturn. The aggregate for Central America is much influenced by Mexico. India has shown a gradual improvement in yields since 1950. Part of this may be spurious — in the years around 1950 compulsory government purchase of crops prevailed, and the farmer had every incentive to understate his yield. But the recent figures may be considered accurate; and they have only about brought yields back to where they were in 1909–13.

With persistent cropping by a dense population, and no input of any other than natural fertilizers, some decline in yields is to be expected. This had happened indeed, as pointed out above, in nineteenth-century Egypt, which was one of the first of the poor countries to begin using chemical fertilizer. Even in 1950 the yields were quite out of relation to those in other subsistence agricultural countries, and they have shown large further improvements. This is true even in sorghum and millet, which give such extraordinarily poor yields in most countries. Egypt of course benefits from completely reliable supplies of both water and sunlight.

Data are now becoming available on the effects of introducing high-yielding varieties into 'package scheme' areas.[1] It is interesting to find that in general participants set aside only a portion of their area under crop for experiments in planting high-yielding varieties; but expenditure on these has increased nearly fourfold for fertilizers and pesticides. Hired labour costs increase by 12–15 per cent. Significantly, those willing to participate tend to be the more prosperous cultivators in a better position to accept the higher-risk, higher-profit, higher-output combination characteristic of a modernized agriculture.

The large part played by fish in the output of Japan, and to a

[1] M. R. Haswell, 'Investment Priorities in Indian Agriculture for Economic Growth', Conference on Modern South Asian Studies, Cambridge, July 1968.

TABLE XXXVIII. CROP YIELDS IN METRIC TONS/HECTARE.

	Wheat							Rice (paddy)						Maize						Sorghum-millet		
	1885–9	1909–13	1925–9	1934–8	1948–52	1952–6	1964–6	1909–13	1925–9	1934–8	1948–52	1952–6	1964–6	1903–13	1925–9	1934–8	1948–52	1952–6	1964–6	1948–52	1952–6	1964–6
Mexico			0·57	0·76										0·85	0·64	0·56						
North and Central America (excl. U.S.A. and Canada)					0·87	1·07	2·36				1·54	1·60	1·65				0·79	0·81	1·09	0·88a	0·84a	0·82a
Colombia			0·70	0·80											0·89	0·90						
South America (excl. Argentine, Chile and Uruguay)					0·74	0·86	0·86			1·43b	1·68	1·57	1·64				1·22	1·19	1·23			
India	0·65	0·81	0·68	0·69	0·66	0·74	0·82	1·66	1·42	1·36	1·11	1·28	1·40		0·90	0·74	0·65	0·78	1·00	0·37	0·42	0·44
Indonesia								1·69	1·54	1·58	1·61	1·70	1·82			0·97	0·76	0·92	0·95			
Pakistan					0·87	0·75	0·81			1·48	1·38	1·37	1·63			1·11	0·98	1·00	1·04	0·41	0·42	0·47
Rest of Asia (excl. Japan)					0·88	0·91	0·93	1·36	1·36	1·45	1·49	1·55	1·83				1·11	1·04	1·28	0·63	0·71	0·77
Egypt	1·67	1·75		2·01	1·84	2·17	2·73	3·56	3·09	3·49	3·79	4·44	4·42				2·09	2·17	3·27	2·71	2·89	3·77
Rest of Africa (Excl. South Africa)				0·58	0·58	0·63	0·61	1·15	0·98	0·97	0·98	1·06	1·33				0·83	0·87	0·90	0·55	0·58	0·65

a Excludes Mexico.
b Brazil only.

lesser extent of the Philippines, has already been noticed. A representative seaside village in Malaya,[1] though part of its output was for sale to inland villages, had a fish output of 360 kg. (liveweight) per head of the whole village population. FAO have drawn attention[2] to the very high yields which can be obtained from cultivated ponds, ranging from 1 ton liveweight fish/ha./year in Indonesia to 1·65 in Israel and 2 in the Belgian Congo. (The highest recorded natural yield of fish was 0·8 in Lake Tempe, Indonesia: some lakes in Egypt yield 0·1 and 0·2; but most natural lakes are much lower yielding; for Lake Victoria the estimate is only ·002.) Cultivating fish in the rice fields at the time when they are under water, by introducing the fish fry, and feeding them, has been said to give a yield of 2·25 tons/ha./year in Japan. A pond at Jos in Nigeria[3] was said to yield 2½ tons, and a similar claim has been made by the Chinese, but it has been disputed.[4] A case has been quoted in Thailand, where perhaps the village refuse is particularly appetizing, of 3 tons.[5] Even if only half of these claims are accepted, it is clear that these densely populated countries have a means of obtaining high protein food at a very high rate per unit of area. At any rate in high rainfall countries, the amount of land which could be converted into fishponds is quite high — although they might not be so productive if the village drainage had to be divided among more of them. But it is clear that the capital requirement for constructing a pond, and the labour and pumping equipment for maintaining it, put it beyond the reach of a poor family. In Siam, in addition, a substantial tax is levied on each cubic m. of fishpond.

[1] Firth, *Malay Fishermen, Their Peasant Economy*, Institute of Pacific Relations, 1946.
[2] Schuster *et al.*, *Fish Farming and Inland Fishery Management*, F.A.O., 1954.
[3] F. J. Pedler, *The Economic Geography of West Africa*, London, 1955.
[4] Billings, *Annual Review of Plant Physiology*, Vol. VIII, p. 375, 1957.
[5] J. E. de Young, *Village Life in Modern Thailand*, 1955.

CHAPTER X

Rents and Prices of Agricultural Land

Early in the nineteenth century, David Ricardo, a successful stockbroker-economist, developed the Ricardian Theory of Rent, which has been ever since a basic proposition in the teaching of economics. Rent was not, as had hitherto been supposed, an element in the cost of production — this might appear to be true for the individual farmer, but the rent of land was not a cost which should be taken into account in estimating in general the costs of producing a commodity. Rents were not a cause, but a consequence, of the differences between costs of production on different farms. Surveying the rather simple agricultural institutions of his day, Ricardo concluded that these arose largely from differences in the fertility of the soil, and in transport costs. As demand increased, farms of worsening fertility had to be brought into cultivation — we can still see traces of what was going on in England at that time in districts like Dartmoor, when the high prices of the Napoleonic Wars pushed the margin of cultivation up the slopes on to cold acid lands, which were soon afterwards abandoned again. These lands at the limit of cultivation, Ricardo taught, received no rent. Every other piece of farm land tended to receive a rent, equivalent to the difference between its costs of production and those of the land at the limit of cultivation.

Though we must now regard this theory as excessively simplified, it was nevertheless a permanent contribution to economic knowledge. It was not universally accepted in Ricardo's time. Ricardo taught other doctrines, including the unpleasing idea that the rate of population growth among the labouring classes was so great that competition between them was always bound to drive their wages down to the very minimum of subsistence. William Cobbett referred to Ricardo as 'nothing but a stupid bothering stockbroker, with a head full of discount, scrip, omnium, percentages and shades'.

The Ricardian theory of rent may be regarded as a preliminary statement of the more exact proposition, stated later in the nineteenth century by Jevons and Marshall, that we should expect rent to be determined by the marginal productivity of land. This latter statement, in its turn, we may expect to see supplanted eventually by the use of production functions.

At present (although a more elaborate function may later be found necessary) the Cobb-Douglas function is the one generally used. This may be formulated as follows:

Let P be production, L the input of labour, A the area of land used.

$$\text{Then } P = L^a A^b$$

Even in the most primitive agriculture, however, it is not entirely true to say that land and labour are the sole factors of production. In the more advanced forms of agriculture, there will be very large inputs of equipment, fertilizers, and other commodities. It may be convenient for some purposes, therefore, to define P not as the gross product, but as the 'factor income' of agriculture, after debiting the cost of all these other inputs. In the simpler forms of agriculture, it is permissible to assume that expenditure on these inputs bears a small and fairly constant relation to the gross product; not so however in the advanced forms of agriculture.

A simple differentiation of the Cobb-Douglas function shows that a measures the marginal productivity of labour, b of land, as a proportion of the total product, if we assume that there are no general economies or dis-economies of scale, which is equivalent to assuming that $a + b = 1$, which is found to be approximately the case. According to the way in which P has been defined, therefore, b represents the proportion which the rent of land may be expected to bear either to the gross product or to the total factor income, according to the way in which the equation has been constructed.

A great deal of further research on this subject is needed, but there are some preliminary indications, at any rate for low-income agriculture, that the order of magnitude of b may be about $\frac{1}{2}$. In Nigeria[1] Cobb-Douglas functions were prepared showing a co-efficient for land of 0·6 in the case of cocoa and 0·5 in the case of food crops. From the data given in previous chapters, we conclude that marginal product of labour may sometimes be considerably less than half average product in India, is about half in Iraq, is almost nominal in Japan, and is rather over half in Yugoslavia.

[1] Galletti, Baldwin and Dina, *Nigerian Cocoa Farmers*, pp. 314, 328.

The results of a number of production functions worked out for India and elsewhere have been quoted in Chapter VI. They were designed to throw light on the marginal productivity of labour, using the Cobb-Douglas equation, but they also indicate marginal productivities of land, which appear to be highly variable.

A number of instances can be found in low-income agricultures in which rent may be expected to take nearly half of the gross product, but there are certain important qualifications to this proposition which will be discussed below.

Ricardo, having in mind no doubt what we would now call a very simplified model, conveyed the idea of rents being highest on the high-yielding land and low, coming down to zero, on the low-yielding land.[1] An important qualification to this simple principle was pointed out in the 1880s by the French economist Leroy-Beaulieu, whose work received little attention from his contemporaries — perhaps because he wrote in a language which was understood by ordinary men. Comparing (his figures are given in the large table following) rents in the highest yielding region of France (Departement Nord) and in the lowest yielding mountain regions, he showed that, while the absolute amount of rent was higher in the former, yet the proportion of the product taken by rent was higher in the poorer regions. For the marginal productivity of the land to represent half or any other specified proportion of the total product does not in itself suffice to bring rents up to that proportion of the total product. A further necessary condition is that, in respect of any area of land under consideration, the intending tenants should, as we might put it, have nowhere else to go; that is to say, that there is no great competition for their labour either from more fortunately situated agricultural lands, or from industry.

The classical Ricardian situation, in which labour (and managerial enterprise) had to compete for a limited supply of land, with few or no opportunities of being employed elsewhere, and therefore the rent of agricultural land rose as a function of rural population density, is strikingly exemplified by the experience of several countries now, and by our own eighteenth-century past. In England this relationship had completely disappeared by 1850. Nothing like it is to be expected in modern industrial countries, in

[1] There is a Cambridge legend concerning Fay, Marshall's disciple, travelling in northern Canada and, on reaching the furthermost point of agricultural settlement, promptly sending a postcard to Marshall to say that he had at last found the marginal farm.

which labour and enterprise can find employment in industry if they do not like the terms which agriculture offers.

The following diagrams indicate a relationship between agricultural rents or land prices, and rural population density, in Italy,[1] pre-Communist Roumania,[2] the Philippines,[3] Poland,[4] and

CHART XIII

LAND VALUES IN ITALY 1960

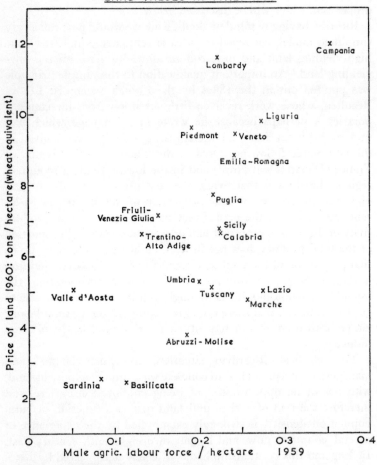

[1] *Annuario dell' Agricultura Italiana*, 1960, pp. 144–6.
[2] Warriner, *Economics of Peasant Farming*.
[3] Land price data from National Bank of the Philippines; employment data from 1960 census.
[4] *Statistical Yearbook* (in Polish). I am indebted to Mr. H. Frankel for translation and interpretation.

CHART XIV

LAND VALUES IN ROUMANIA 1923-27

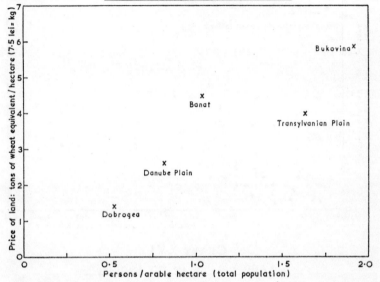

eighteenth-century England[1] — all countries in which, on the whole, agricultural labour 'had nowhere else to go', though the situation in Italy is now rapidly changing, and land prices are falling fast. It will be seen that in Lazio (the country surrounding Rome) and Marche (on the Adriatic coast where the gas-field has been discovered) land values are much below expected, probably because so much alternative employment is available.

Although Poland is a Communist country, land can be freely bought and sold by owner-occupiers (as it can also in Yugoslavia); and indeed the price of land in real terms is now higher than it was in the 1930s. Unlike Italy, proximity of industrial centres does not appear to lower the price of land, at a given rural density, and indeed proximity to the mining area of Katowice appears to raise it.

The objection has been raised that land values are not determined solely by agricultural population density but that the values

[1] Rents from Caird, *English Agriculture in 1850–51*, p. 474, quoting Arthur Young, converted to wheat. Area of agricultural land assumed to be the same as that shown by the first agricultural returns in 1867, excluding rough grazings. Agricultural population from Deane and Cole, *British Economic Growth*, p. 103. Male agricultural population assumed at 25 per cent, 20 per cent and 17½ per cent of total in counties classified as agricultural, mixed and industrial respectively.

CHART XV

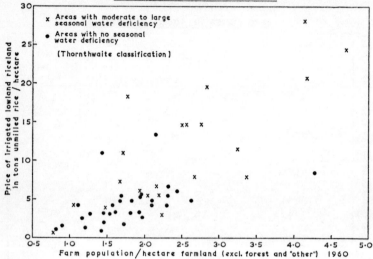

CHART XVI

LAND VALUES IN POLAND 1962

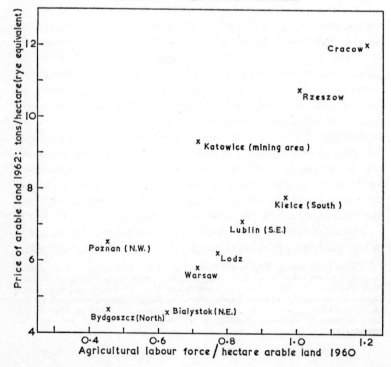

CHART XVII

RENTS AND AGRICULTURAL POPULATION DENSITY, ENGLAND 1770

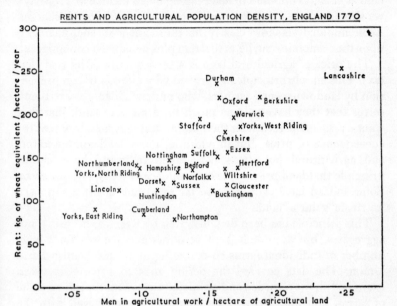

are the result of climate, soil and relief in a particular area. By this argument, it is the environmental factors which account for the land value, and the population density is the consequence. This objection does not appear to be valid if the diagrams such as that for eighteenth-century England are examined. A test has been made by examining the relationship between land values, population density and climate in the irrigated land of the Philippines. The 56 provinces were divided into two climatic zones on the basis of Thornthwaite's classification giving the region of moderate or large winter water deficiency and the region of small or no seasonal water deficiency. The resulting diagram indicates a relationship between price of irrigated land, and the population per hectare, irrespective of climatic zone.

The Roumanian diagram shows a slope of approximately 3, i.e. a rise in land value of 3 tons/ha. for each additional person/ha. It is very interesting that an exactly similar coefficient was estimated in 1897 for Chile,[1] namely that a density increase of 1 person/sq. km., i.e. 0·01 person/ha., raised land value by 0·03 tons wheat equivalent/ha. (i.e. 3 pesos/ha.).

[1] Kärger, *Landwirtschaft und Colonisation in Spanischen Amerika.*

When taxes, rates, tithes and similar charges are imposed upon land as such (as opposed to taxes falling on all income or property), we should where possible measure rents *inclusive* of such charges. Economic analysis shows clearly that the incidence of such charges is upon the economic rent, i.e. actual rent plus tax equals economic rent.

The price of agricultural land is a consequence of its rent (less tax). This simple principle has proved very difficult of comprehension by landowners and farmers, who understandably say to themselves that they have paid so much for a piece of land, that they want a reasonable return on their outlay and that therefore rent is a consequence of price. But in addition, many land administrators and agricultural politicians have failed to grasp the economic principle that land prices are a consequence of rents, not *vice versa*. Some indeed have even gone so far as to talk about a supposed 'intrinsic' value of land.

This principle has been demonstrated by Rasmussen[1] using, not aggregates, but accurately kept accounts and records for a large number of individual farms co-operating under the Danish Farm Union. The data covered the period 1925 to 1950. Rasmussen examined all the recorded and estimated changes of the selling value of farms, and found that these changes correlated well with the variable (net income from farm/price of farm at beginning of period). The equation indicated, however, that an annual net return of only 2·7 per cent on the market value of the farm was the point of equilibrium which kept the price of the farms stable. If the net return exceeded 2·7 per cent, buyers would begin to bid up the price of the farm.

The average rate of return on commercial investments in Denmark throughout this period was far higher. We are compelled to conclude therefore that the difference between these two returns must represent the advantages of land ownership other than the direct monetary return from farming in Denmark — the feeling of personal security, the sporting rights, the social position, possibly some taxation advantage. In a country like Britain, the social position and the sporting rights of land ownership count for a good deal more, and in addition there are very substantial death-duty concessions on agricultural estates; we should expect, therefore, the rate of return on agricultural land to be even lower than in Denmark, possibly approaching 1 per cent per annum only.

But hardly anybody seems to understand the position, judging

[1] Privately communicated.

from the persistency of the complaints, from so many countries, that landowners are not getting a fair return on their investment.

On the other hand, we must not assume that these non-monetary advantages of land ownership are constant at all times; nor that the ratio of the price of land to its rent is independent of commercial rates of interest. In some countries, the non-monetary advantages of holding land are small. At a given level of rent, moreover, and with the non-monetary advantages also given, the price of land will depend, not only upon changes in the rate of interest, but also upon the political outlook. Where landowners feel that their political future is quite secure, they may bid land up to very high prices; and conversely.

Converting all land prices into an equivalent in tons of wheat per ha., so as to make possible comparisons between very varied countries and times, the high figures shown at certain dates for Egypt, Japan and Belgium must be considered as an indication of this feeling of political security on the part of landowners, together with, of course, a high rural population density, and high rents of land.

Landowners can feel political stability in communist Yugoslavia where private ownership of small farms is permitted, and the price of land in the most densely populated region is about as high as anywhere in the world.

The rise in the price of agricultural land in the United States during the past decade probably represents a shrewd assessment of the increasing political security which American farmers now feel in their ability to go on extracting support from the U.S. Treasury.

In sparsely populated, newly settled countries, on the other hand, such as Brazil, the prices of land measured in real terms are low, and may indeed show a tendency to fall.

The comparatively low prices of land in pre-communist China probably measure the effect of political insecurity, largely counteracting the effects of high rural population density and lack of alternative employment, which would have been expected to raise prices. The nineteenth-century prices of land in the area devastated by the Taiping Rebellion provide probably the most striking example ever known of the effects of depopulation on land values.

The gradual upward trend of land values in India, with increasing population density, is of interest. In Japan, land values appear to have reached their maximum in the 1920s, and now to be falling, as more industrial employment becomes available.

TABLE XXXIX
RENTS AND PRICES OF AGRICULTURAL LAND

Country or Region	Date	Currency unit	Rent as % of		Rent/ha. land in		Price/ha. land in	
			gross product	factor income	money	tons grain equiv.	money	tons grain equiv.
AFRICA								
Egypt	1st c. A.D.		34			0·64		
	4th c. A.D.		21			0·40		
	1877	£E			7·5	0·75	125	12·
	1897	£E		57	8·6	1·35		
	1923-7			55	16·0	1·33		
	1935-9	£E		53	17·1	1·82		
	1947-8	£E			42·5	1·99	1062	47·
	1951	£E		35	59·5	2·79		
	1953	£E	32	45	49·4	2·31		
Ethiopia: barley land	1969						20	
superior land							30	
Ghana	1957		25-33			0·6-0·7		
AMERICA								
Barbados	1838	£					32	14·
	1911-13						19	14·
	1960-3						304	71·
Brazil:								
Matto Grosso 1st cl. land	1935	$US					5	0·
,, ,, ,, 2nd cl. land	1948	$US					45	0·
Sao Paulo	1948	$US					30	0·
	1944	$US			5	0·2		
Chile	1960		44			0·5-0·7		10·
Guatemala: sheep land	1947	$US	10					
potato land	1947	$US	10		7			
Jamaica	1959	£					86	3·
ASIA:								
China:								
Taiping War Area	1850	$C					480	16·
	1860	$C					12	0·
Chinese Turkestan	1940		50-80				28	1·
Ting Hsien wheat region:								
dry	1928	$C	35-40		65		645	5·
irrigated	1928	$C	35-40		116		1160	10·
Average: wheat	1933		32			0·35		4·
rice	1933		32			0·8		10·
India:	17th c. (tax)		33-50					
Punjab	1885	Rupee					74	1·
	1900	Rupee					190	2·
	1910	Rupee					306	3·
	1916	Rupee					560	5·
Deccan	1914	Rupee					198	2·
	1921-9	Rupee					277	1·
	1930-9	Rupee					347	4·
	1949-52	Rupee					830	2·
All	1950	Rupee					1420	4·
Median of districts	1957-8	Rupee					1635	3·
Lowest — Rajasthan	1957-8	Rupee					250	0·
Highest — Kerala	1957-8	Rupee					4700	10·
All India	1961	Rupee					1220	2·
Maharashtra — Bombay State	1940	Rupee			69	0·70	1085	11·
Maharashtra — Bombay State	1954-6	Rupee		67	870	2·27	3710	9·
Iraq: Northern	1930-40			25				
Southern	1930-40			70-80				
Israel	1933	Pruta		43				
Japan:	1873	Yen	50-60					
Upland (non-irrigated)	1886	Yen					407	20·
	1895	Yen					123	3·
	1914	Yen				0·45	280	3·
	1930	Yen			78	0·50	1480	10·
	1933	Yen				0·66		
	1938	Yen				0·75		
Irrigated rice land	1886	Yen					3040	13·
	1895	Yen					404	12·
	1908	Yen					870	11·
	1914	Yen					1820	18·
Japan	1919-21	Yen	38			0·86	2770	20·
	1924-6	Yen	51			0·88	5600	22·
	1927	Yen	47		311	1·49	6200	31·

Country or Region	Date	Currency unit	Rent as % of		Rent/ha. lnd in		Price/ha. land in	
			gross product	factor income	money	tons grain equiv.	money	tons grain equiv.
an (continued)	1930	Yen			281	1·82		
	1933	Yen				0·79		
	1936	Yen	46		312	1·25	4200	21·0
	1938	Yen			316	1·40	5190	23·1
ice land, Shiga Prefecture	1961	ooo yen					2410	31·3
laya	1958	$M	50		173	0·82		
aysia: Double-crop rice land	1966							7·6
istan	1961	Rs. 1000			0·53	0·66	16·0	20·4
ilippines	1955	Peso		55	368	1·08	2934	8·6
ia: irrigated	1930-40	£S	60		325			
non-irrigated	1930-40	£S	40-50		55-70			
	1964	£S			1550	0·69	1250	5·6
ailand			35					
ailand, N.E.								4·3
tnam	1899		50					4·4
	1930		50					8·5
	1958		25					8·0
	1967		20					4·0
ROPE								
gium: arable land	1830	Fr.			57	0·16		
	1846	Fr.			108	0·43		
	1866	Fr.					2630	8·3
	1880	Fr.					4250	16·5
gland:								
nd and buildings	1376-1460	Pence			20·5	0·15		
	1688	£		43				
nce:								
rable land	9th c.	Fr.	8				70	
	12th c.	Fr.					93	
heat land			6-14					
live land			9-25					
	1200-25	Fr.					135	
	1276-1300	Fr.					261	
	1301-25	Fr.	14		8	0·094	222	
	1325-50	Fr.	14					0·8
	1351-1400	Fr.	10			0·069	90	0·8
	1426-50	Fr.					68	
	1451-75	Fr.	10			0·064	48	
	1476-1500	Fr.	10			0·064	97	1·18
	1501-24	Fr.					95	1·49
	1576-1600	Fr.	10		17	0·065	317	
	1600-50	Fr.	13			0·085	292	1·22
	1650-1700	Fr.	11			0·072	428	2·25
	1700-50	Fr.	11		11		305	
	1788	Fr.	39	43	22·5	0·125	640	3·54
	1815	Fr.	45		35	0·134		
	1845	Fr.	26	33	31	0·103		
	1851	Fr.					1497	7·7
	1879	Fr.					2197	7·8
	1885	Fr.		41	73	0·32		
	1890	Fr.					1500	6·0
ational average	1885	Fr.	18		50	0·225		
Dept. Nord — highest	1885	Fr.	15			0·45		
Dept. Cantal, Aveyron — lowest	1885	Fr.	31			0·195		
rmany	1861	DM					525	2·3
	1889	DM					1500	7·7
eece	5th c. B.C.		8			0·075		
and	1884	£		19	1·36	0·18		
y:								
orth and central	8th-11th c.		15					
	12th c.		40					
ll	1930-9		26	35				
	1960	ooo lire			22·5	0·32	475	6·8
Campania: highest-priced land		ooo lire			50·5	0·72	816	11·6
Basilicata: lowest do.		ooo lire			7·8	0·11	164	2·3
umania:	1886	lei					33	0·13
	1905	lei				0·02	535	3·4
	1911-16	lei				0·03	988	5·5
owland	1929	ooo lei					32	0·9
rable	1932	ooo lei					16	
ain: dry land	1960	peseta					8000	1·9
irrigated land	1960	peseta					40000	9·5
goslavia:	1938	ooo din.					25	25
lovenia	1938	ooo din.					7	7
oivodina	1954	ooo din.					150	7·5
erbia: densely settled areas	1954	ooo din.				0·4	450	22·5
ll	1957	ooo din.					166	4·8
lovenia	1957	ooo din.					70	2·0

Sources and Notes to Table on Rents and Prices of Agricultural Land:

EGYPT: Early centuries: D'Avenel, *La Richesse Privée depuis Sept Siècles*. Hectolitre taken as 75 kg. Yield in ancient world as estimated by Michell, *The Economics of Ancient Greece*.

1877: Baer, *A History of Landownership in Modern Egypt*.

1897 Willcocks and 1923–7 Minos, communicated by Bent Hansen. Taxes took half the produce on medium- or low-quality land, the proportion having been raised from one-third in 1864 (except for a few favoured large landowners, whose tax was only £1·25/ha.). Baer agrees with Issawi that Egypt, at this time, was underpopulated rather than overpopulated — he records that taxation and fears of forced labour were causing land to be abandoned.

1935–9 and 1951: C. Issawi, *Egypt at Mid-Century*.

1947–8 and 1953: D. Warriner, *Land Reform and Development in the Middle East*.

1930s: Bresciani-Turroni, *Weltwirtschaftliches Archiv*, October 1933, estimates rent at only 38 per cent of factor income; Bonné, *Economic Development of the Middle East*, at 44 per cent. The latter considers that it had fallen to 42 per cent by 1950, *International Symposium on Desert Research*, Jerusalem, 1952.

ETHIOPIA: Oxford Expedition to the Gamu Highlands (privately communicated).

GHANA: Dr. Torto, Deputy Director of Agriculture, private communication. Maize growing on worn-out cocoa land, cropped twice a year.

BARBADOS: Janet Henshall, Institute of British Geographers 1966, and privately communicated. This appears to be the most valuable agricultural land in the world, and has been for a long time. In his despatch of 4 July 1676, the Governor wrote: 'There is not a foot of land in Barbados that is not employed even to the very seaside . . . so that whoever will have land in Barbados must pay dearer for it than for land in England.'

BRAZIL: Waibel, *Geographical Review*, October 1948; *Foreign Agriculture*, U.S. Department of Agriculture, June 1945, for São Paulo.

CHILE: Professor T. Davis, Cornell University, private communication.

GUATEMALA: Higbee, *Geographical Review*, April 1947.

JAMAICA: Edwards, *An Economic Study of Small Farming in Jamaica*.

CHINA: 1850 and 1860: Richtofen, quoted in Ping-ti Ho, *Studies in the Population of China, 1368–1953*, Harvard University Press. Grain prices were not available for this period. In the eighteenth century Chinese prices were rising steadily, but at the end of the century rose only to 10 silver dollars (7·2 oz. silver)/ton, much below European prices of that time. It is assumed that Chinese prices went on rising with the impact of world trade, and that in 1850 and 1860 they stood at two-thirds of prices in U.S. which at that time also used a dollar based on silver (i.e. $44/ton in 1850, $53/ton in 1860).

Chinese Turkestan: Chang Chih-yi, *Geographical Review*, 1939. In this case the landowner provides water and draught animals as well as land.

Gamble, *Ting Hsien*, Institute of Pacific Relations.

Shen-pao Nien-Chien, *Year Book*, Shanghai, 1933, gives rents and land prices in relation to yields. FAO figures of average yield used (rice expressed rough).

Very much lower prices are quoted by Buck, *Land Utilization in China*, p. 37. It appears that he is quoting some official value of the land rather than its real selling price.

INDIA: Habib, *Journal of Economic History*, Mar. 1969.

Punjab: Calvert, *Indian Journal of Agricultural Economics*, December 1918, prices of cultivated land. Wheat prices from Brij Narain, *Indian Economic Life*, p. 105.

Deccan: Diskalkar, *Resurvey of a Deccan Village*, Indian Society of Agricultural Economics, 1960.

All India: Datta and Pratash, *Conference on Research in National Income*, New Delhi, 1957.

The Reserve Bank of India's *Rural Credit Follow-up Survey; 1957-8*, gives data of land values in 1957–8 per farm, from which land values per ha. can be computed for 12 districts, scattered throughout India. The 1961 average estimated by the Reserve Bank was quoted in *Agricultural Situation in India*, August 1965, p. 360.

Maharashtra data from Ghatge and Patel, *Indian Journal of Economics*, 1942–3; and Institute of Agriculture, Anand, Bulletin No. 4, March 1958. Rent of land computed here as residual after imputing standard wages to family workers. Further data for villages in southern India, showing great variations between villages, were published by University of Madras in *Some South Indian Villages — a Resurvey*. 1961 data from M. R. Haswell, *Economics of Development in Village India*.

		Annual rent			Land price		
		1916	1936	1961	1916	1936	1961
	Tons paddy per hectare						
Dusi	wet area	1·68	1·44	1·20	53·8	38·3	17·3
Eruvellipet	wet area	0·88	0·79	0·99	n.a.	12·6	25·0
Gangaikondan	wet area	1·9	2·2	1·3	38·2	43·4	23·8
	dry area				6·0	7·3	1·0
Guruvayur	outlying land				4·2	9·1	
	village land		0·91		6·1	12·1	
Palakkurichi		0·82	1·57				
Vunagatla	black soil		0·52			16·9	
	sandy soil		0·36			9·1	
Watakancheri					4·2	3·3	
	Tons millet per hectare						
Vadamalaipuram	wet area		0·45		13·6	6·2	12·1
	dry area				2·7	1·2	2·8

Of the five villages re-surveyed in 1961, Dusi had the highest advantage in transport facilities and proximity to markets. Rents are higher near the village and sources of irrigation. Irrigated land is scarce in Gangaikondan; the high rents of the 1930s have been considerably reduced because of competition for labour in local industry. Palakkurichi had exceptionally high yields. The higher price paid for land within the village of Guruvayur as compared with outlying land was said to be due predominantly to the agricultural value of the animal and human manure accumulating in the inhabited region. In 1961 all the land in Vadamalaipuram was cultivated by peasant proprietors, a situation which existed at the time of the first survey.

IRAQ: D. Warriner, *Land and Poverty in the Middle East*, inclusive of taxes, 10 per cent in south Iraq.

ISRAEL: Bonné, *Archiv für Sozialwissenschaft*, 1933.

JAPAN: For 1873, *Journal of Economic History*, 1947. Included in the rents are: national land tax of 12·2 yen/ha. plus local tax of 4·1, or 16·3 yen in all, payable by the landowners, which represented 34 per cent of average gross production of rice land/ha., which was 2·4 tons, valued at 48 yen, measured apparently as brown rice of 80 per cent extraction. These taxes represented (see Dore, *Land Reform in Japan*) 4 per cent of the land value then assessed, giving 407 yen/ha. as the average assessment. In 1878 national and local taxes were reduced to $2\frac{1}{2}$ per cent and $\frac{1}{2}$ per cent of the assessed value respectively. The surveyed and assessed area was incomplete however, sometimes to the extent of 20 per cent.

Other land price data from Kurt Singer, *Economic Record*, Australia, December 1947. D'Avenel, *La Richesse Privée depuis Sept Siècles*, for 1895. *Industrial Bank Index* for 1908, and for rice prices from that date and for rents in 1919–21 and 1936; on double-cropped land an additional 4 per cent of gross product went to rent in each case, quoted Dore, *Land Reform in Japan*. Sale, *Journal of the Royal Statistical Society*, April 1911, for early rice prices. Rent in 1914 from Grajdanzeff, *Institute of Pacific Relations*, November 1941. Yagi, *Kyoto University Economic Review*, 1930, p. 101 for 1927; Shiomi, *Kyoto University Economic Review*, 1931, for 1930. Research Institute of Farm Accounting, Kyoto University, for 1961. Other land values quoted 000 yen/ha. were vegetable land in Osaka Prefecture 3050, mixed farm land Kinki Prefecture 2440, poultry farm land in Hyogo Prefecture 1910, dairy farm land in Kyoto Prefecture 526. An index number of real land values, Economic Research Institute of Economic Planning Agency, Economic Bulletin No. 9, shows a heavy fall in the inflation period, followed by recovery.

Index of Real Land Values, 1934–6 = 100

1950	1951	1952	1953	1954	1955	1956	1957
22	21	31	44	62	80	93	98

MALAYA: Wilson, *Economics of Paddy Production in Northern Malaya*, Malayan Department of Agriculture, 1958. Rents in milled rice. The Institute for Medical Research, Kuala Lumpur, Report No. 13, 1950, also quotes rent at approximately half the crop, though in this case the yield is much lower at 0·77 tons/hectare rough rice.

MALAYSIA: Purcal, Australian National University thesis (Province Wellesley).

PAKISTAN: Habibullah, *Pattern of Agricultural Unemployment*, Bureau of Economic Research, Dacca University. Results obtained from a complete survey of the village of Sabilpur in East Bengal. Prices in terms of milled rice.

PHILIPPINES: Central Experiment Station Bulletin No.1, 1957. Equivalents in milled rice. Figures refer to net rent — 80 per cent of gross rent, after certain seed harvesting and other customary charges have been met by the landowner — and refer to rice land only. In Mindanao and Cagayan, lower rainfall areas, average farm land prices fall to some 1·7 tons rice equivalent/ha. Taxes are only 20 pesos/ha./year.

SYRIA: D. Warriner, *Land and Poverty in the Middle East*. Landowner's share on irrigated land rises to 80 per cent when he provides draught animals and equipment. J. L. Simmons, private communication.

THAILAND: Usher, *Economica*, November 1966, p. 440 and private communications. Rent is customarily half the crop for rice, but other land is leased almost for nothing. The price of land is generally 12½ years purchase of the rent.

THAILAND, N.E.: Janlekha, *Saraphi, A Survey of Socio-Economic Conditions in N.E. Thailand*.

VIETNAM: Sansom, Oxford University thesis, 1969.

BELGIUM: Combe, *Niveau de Vie et Progrès Technique*. Leroy-Beaulieu, *La Repartition des Richesses*, for 1830 and 1866.

ENGLAND: Gregory King, *Political Observations*. Davenport, *The Economic Development of a Norfolk Manor* (1906). Prices from Beveridge, *Economic History Review*, 1936.

FRANCE: D'Avenel, *La Richesse Privée depuis Sept Siècles*. Mayer, International Association for Research in Income and Wealth, Series III, p. 74, for 1788, 1845, 1885 factor incomes. Assumed cultivated area 40 m. ha. in 1788 and 1845, and 48 m. in 1885. Rent includes 100, 200 and 500 m. fr. respectively for taxes. Chaptel, quoted in *Salaire*, Vol. III, p. 95, for rent in 1815. Leroy-Beaulieu, *La Repartition des Richesses*, regional data for 1895.

GERMANY: Combe, *Niveau de Vie de Progrès Technique*.

GREECE: Michell, *The Economics of Ancient Greece*.

IRELAND: Giffen, *Economic Enquiries and Studies*.

ITALY: Herlihy, *Agricultural History*, April 1959. Informazione Svimez, Gasparini. *Annuario dell'Agricultura Italiana*, 1960, pp. 144, 146. Istituto Centrale di Statistica, private communication, provincial data on agricultural labour force.

ROUMANIA: Mitrany, *The Land and the Peasant in Roumania*. Manoilesco, *Weltwirtschaftliches Archiv*, July 1935, for 1932.

SPAIN: Fr. Garravilla, Burgos; private communication.

YUGOSLAVIA: Vinski, International Association for Research in Income and Wealth, 1957 Conference. Mihailović, World Population Conference. Starc, Private communication. Rent shown for Voivodina includes 0·2 tons/ha./year tax. The rate of tax has recently been doubled.

CHAPTER XI

Consumption at Low Income Levels

So many people having believed, at any rate until recently, that the majority of the world's population was malnourished or starving, it naturally followed that they should conclude that any increment in the production or income of subsistence farming families would almost all be consumed in the form of additional food for the family; in other words, the income elasticity of demand for food, at their level of real income, must be almost one. Except for a few in the very poorest areas, this in fact is found not to be the case. If subsistence-agriculture families produce more, much of the increment is spent on other urgent needs, for clothes, housing, fuel and medicine, sometimes for education. The fact that additional income is spent in this way is in itself an important confirmation of the conclusions suggested by closer examination of the physiological evidence, namely that the diets of most subsistence cultivators in the world, while monotonous, distasteful, and often insecure, are not on the average inadequate physiologically.

It might indeed be thought that physiological urges would however cause food consumption to rise in a more or less determinate manner, as real income increased above the lowest levels. But even this is found not to be the case. Various low-income communities, at similar real income levels, have widely different consumptions of food. Urban communities in most cases have higher income elasticities of demand than rural. It seems that the consumption of food, as of other commodities, is subject to 'demonstration effect', whereby a desire to consume particular types of food is induced by seeing them consumed by wealthy families in the neighbourhood. English agricultural labourers in the late eighteenth century had low real income, but an exceptionally high income elasticity of demand for food, partly from what they saw going on around them, but perhaps also because they remembered better days in the past.

A good transport and marketing system, and an abundance of manufactured goods on offer at low prices, as in Japan, plays its part in inducing farmers both to produce more and to consume less food.

A low income elasticity of demand for food, as has been observed both in Japan and Nigeria, whether arising from any of the above causes, or from natural abstemiousness, nevertheless plays an important part in national economic development. The rate at which a subsistence-agriculture economy can be transformed depends upon the rate at which the industrial population can grow, which in turn is limited by the amount of food available for them; and by the rate at which the country can develop exports to pay for its imports. These exports, in most cases, will have to consist of agricultural products.

A study of the effect of improved marketing facilities in inducing increased sales by subsistence cultivators was made by Mandal in West Bengal.[1] Shastri[2] made a comparison over a period of six years of production and retention (i.e. amount not sold) of various crops. He found that the results could be precisely measured on the assumption of linear marginal propensity to consume, with slopes of 0·7 in the case of rice and arhar (a leguminous crop), of 0·87 in the case of gram (another leguminous crop) and only 0·37 in the case of potatoes. Marginal propensity to consume must not, of course, be confused with the income elasticity of demand, though if the proportion of the crop sold is high, they will not differ greatly over a moderate range.

Dayal[3] pointed out that a rise in cereal prices might be expected to have both income and price effects. The composite of these effects, for a 1 per cent rise in cereal prices, he put at rises in money expenditure of 0·75 for the rural population and 0·47 for the urban (i.e. reductions in real expenditure of 0·25 per cent and 0·35 per cent respectively).

We begin with some examples of very low real incomes.

Overseas Chinese in Sarawak on smallholdings growing rubber, and employing no hired labour, appeared to be living at a low level with an income of 283 kg. wheat equivalent/person/year, of which 231 kg., or 82 per cent, was spent on food.[4]

Budget data obtained by Gourou on the income and expenditure

[1] G. C. Mandal, 'The Marketable Surplus of Aman Paddy in East Indian Villages', *Indian Journal of Agricultural Economics*, Vol. XVI, January–March 1961.

[2] Shastri, *Agricultural Situation in India*, April 1963.

[3] *Indian Journal of Agricultural Economics*, July–September 1964.

[4] W. R. Geddes, *The Land Dayaks of Sarawak*, Colonial Research Study No. 14, 1954.

of a number of poor Tonkinese peasants and small peasant proprietors, have been converted into economic wheat equivalents.[1]

CHART XVIII

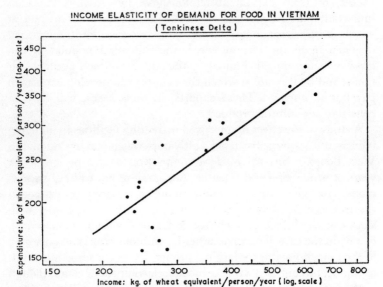

The high-income elasticity of demand for food is clearly seen in the diagram. Gourou emphasizes that the land here is supporting so dense a population at subsistence level only that no significant surplus is being produced for clothing, housing or other objects. He does, however, make the interesting comment that the mountains framing this plain are very lightly populated — three to four persons per sq. km. — and that apparently there is no lack of room for Tonkinese colonization; but fertile soils are rare, and malaria — non-existent in the Tonkinese Delta — is rampant in the mountains, causing widespread ill-health. Although in a normal year 60 per cent of the population are barely sustained, and require only slightly unfavourable conditions to suffer actual shortage of food, Gourou states that processions of starving people are not seen in Tonkin; this he attributes to the security they have in their family and village environment.

[1] P. Gourou, *The Standard of Living in the Delta of the Tonkin*, Institute of Pacific Relations, 9th Conference, French Paper No. 4.

It is an interesting sidelight on the difficulties encountered in persuading peasants from overcrowded Java to migrate to the less populated outer islands, that those who have a minimum of 218 kg. of economic wheat equivalent per head per year available for food consumption are not likely to migrate,[1] which suggests that at this low level of living causal inter-relationships include non-economic factors.

Information from China is very difficult to obtain. A study was made near Peking by Dittmer in 1918.[2] This study was interesting because it included a number of former Manchu aristocrats reduced to peasant status, who before the Revolution in 1911 lived on tribute money. They were living at a very low level, of 150–400 kg./person/year grain equivalent, as against 300–500 for the Chinese. Demonstration effect in their case seems to have reduced income elasticity of demand for food, but raised it for other commodities.

We have a useful review of consumption, measured in grain equivalent units, for low-income Indian families living at an average level, not far from subsistence, of 430 kg. grain equivalent/person/year.[3] These 430 units were consumed as follows: cereals 215, pulses 53, other food 51, clothes and bedding 76, all other goods and services 34. In this case 74 per cent of income was

Pakistan	Wheat equivalents kg./person/year	
	Purchased	Home-produced
Rice	112	95
Wheat	15	
Pulses	6	
Milk	2	
Fish	10	5
Meat and eggs	3	2
Fruit, vegetables and spices	32	10
Salt	4	
Lighting	6	
Firewood		41
Clothing	15	
Tobacco	5	
Other non-food	15	
Rent	2	
Total	227	153

[1] Pelzer, *Pioneer Settlement in the Asiatic Tropics*, New York, 1954.
[2] C. G. Dittmer, 'An Estimate of the Standard of Living in China', *Quarterly Journal of Economics*, Vol. XXXIII, November 1918, No. 1.
[3] Agrawal, *Indian Journal of Agricultural Economics*, March, 1950, p. 106.

consumed as food. A similar budget is available for Pakistan, for a rural labourer's family.[1] (See previous page.)

The farm labourers whose budgets were available in eighteenth-century England[2] were living over the range 300–700 kg./person/ year which puts the lowest of them nearer to subsistence level than most Asian families. Enclosure had deprived the agricultural labourer of various sources by which he could supplement his wages — his fuel from waste land, his cow and pig on the common pasture, a strip under a crop in the common fields; and an industrial revolution had swept away the earnings of his family from village crafts. He had become merely a wage-earner. Many families were frequently in great distress, often in debt, and sometimes without bread, living almost entirely upon barley and water, and a few potatoes. The high-income elasticity of demand for food and drink includes, however, a relatively high expenditure on beer and meat on the part of families who could afford them. We may see here some 'demonstration effect' from the example of wealthier families; and also perhaps, in contrast to modern Japan, the effect of the scarcity and high prices of industrially produced consumption goods. Japanese agricultural families[3] show a low income elasticity of demand for food of about 0·25 throughout the whole range of incomes from 300–3000 kg./person/year grain equivalents. Urban income elasticities have been summarized by Misawa.[4]

TABLE XL. JAPAN — URBAN INCOME ELASTICITIES

	1930s	1954–6
All food	0·3–0·4	
Rice	−0·1–0	0·1
Barley		−0·4 to −0·8
Vegetable	0·3–0·4	0·3
Fish	0·3–0·5	0·3
Milk	1·0–1·7	
All livestock products		0·7–0·8

Even if both rural and urban elasticities are low and stable, the national aggregate may be higher and rising, if an increasing proportion of the population is transferring to urban employments,

[1] Bose, *Pakistan Development Review*, autumn 1968. Converted from rupees into wheat equivalent on the assumption of 5 persons/family and wheat price of 445 Rs./ton.
[2] F. Morton Eden, *The State of the Poor*, 1797.
[3] Kyoto University, Research Institute of Farm Accounting, No. 1, *The Report of Investigation of Family Farm Economy in 1956, Kinki District*, Japan, 1959.
[4] International Conference of Agricultural Economists, 1958.

where food consumption is at a higher level. Noda[1] from time series analysis estimated an income elasticity of demand for food for the whole country of 0·6 up to 1921. After that date, however, it fell to 0·2.

Some claims have been made that income elasticity of demand for food in India may be as high as 0·9. Most of these results are vitiated by a rather subtle fallacy. Most of these budget studies state income and expenditure per family. But an Indian who is able to increase his income somewhat above minimum level finds — as do Hollywood stars in our community — that a number of his more distant relatives offer to come and share his home with him. This increasing number of persons in wealthier families is bound to distort the results. Not many data are available on a per consumption unit basis. Khan, of Lucknow University,[2] has been able to do this for a number of civil servants' budgets in different cities, and also for steel workers at Jamshedupur; and in each case found an average income elasticity of 0·7.

G. T. Jones[3] studied the influence of income and family structure on the family diet, analysing food budgets for Maharashtra, one of the wealthier States of India. Measured in physiological components, income elasticities for both total calories and total protein were higher in rural than in urban households, namely 0·59 as against 0·29 for calories, 0·53 as against 0·19 for protein. This implies that the proportion of protein as well as of calories falls with income, high income elasticities for milk and pulses not being quite sufficient to balance high elasticities for sugar and oils. Absolute scarcity of protein may nevertheless be felt by low income groups.

The comparative proximity of Bombay may be reflected in the higher elasticities for Maharashtra compared with farmers in Punjab.[4] Budget studies of peasant proprietors working in the hill and sub-montane regions and in the plains of the Punjab, where all the chief means of irrigation are to be found, showed that an average of 41 per cent of total expenditure was for purchased goods and services, including education in the higher income groups; the relatively wide range of consumer goods and services available to these people is reflected in the low-income elasticity

[1] Quoted by Johnston and Mellor, Food Research Institute Studies, November 1960, in Japanese 1959.
[2] N. A. Khan, Lucknow University, private communication.
[3] Farm Economist, 1965, Vol. X, No. 11.
[4] Punjab Board of Economic Enquiry, Publication No. 39, Family Budgets of Nineteen Cultivators in the Punjab, 1953–4.

of demand for food. Nevertheless, in an economy based on peasant proprietorship of settled holdings in which ploughs and work animals are employed and financial resources are required, productivity may remain low, and the moneylender fulfil a major role. We have another curious example in which Slater and Thomas[1] found in Vunagatla, an upland village in West Godavari District in India, that the average consumption of food in the village was no higher than 250 kg. wheat equivalent/person/year with an average income as high as 974 kg. The latter, however, included the earnings of toddy tappers, who derived a considerable income from this source.

When data are insufficient to give a significant estimate of income elasticity of demand, single measurements of inter-village differences may still be usefully compared with the chart. The unweighted mean of six villages in Thailand in 1930–1[2] showed that at an income level of 542 kg. wheat equivalent/person/year, the equivalent of 292 kg., or 54 per cent, was spent on food. Analysis of the available data suggests a higher level of food consumption, and income elasticity of demand for food higher than might have been expected, probably because Thailand includes areas in which communication is almost non-existent, market opportunities are poor, and incentives to exchange food for other goods lacking.

An income elasticity of demand for food as high as 0·64 is quoted by the Ivory Coast Government dealing with high-paid men in Abidjan,[3] with income levels ranging from 600 kg. wheat equivalent/person/year and upwards. Here, however, we may have a contrast between the French and English traditions. In East Africa, low paid industrial workers in Mbale[4] at an income level of 5–600 kg./person/year grain equivalent, had an income elasticity of demand for food of 0·77. But higher paid workers,[5] with incomes in the range of 2000–5000 kg./person/year grain equivalent, show a virtual flattening-out of demand for food. Food consumption tends to stabilize when it has reached a level of about 28£/person/year, a little over 1000 kg. grain equivalent.

[1] University of Madras Economic Series, No. 1, *Some South Indian Villages*, ed. G. Slater, 1918; No. 4, *Some South Indian Villages, a Resurvey*, ed. P. J. Thomas, 1940.
[2] C. C. Zimmerman, *Siam Rural Economic Survey, 1930–31*.
[3] *Les Budgets Familiaux des Salariés Africains en Abidjan*, Côte d'Ivoire, August–September 1956, p. 83.
[4] East African Statistical Department, *Patterns of Income Expenditure and Consumption*.
[5] Government of Kenya, *Pattern of Income, Expenditure and Consumption of Middle Income Workers*, July 1963.

Thomson's study of an urban community in Zambia[1] also indicates the low income elasticity of demand for food; she found that the money spent on food tends to be a residual after meeting other requirements such as clothes, furniture or household utensils, indicating a decided preference for non-food items. She also noted a tendency for increased consumption of 'luxury' foods such as tea, sugar, cooking oil and tinned milk, in the higher-income households.

Some interesting effects are shown in a study from Senegal.

TABLE XLI. INCOME ELASTICITIES IN SENEGAL

	Isolated village	Commercial agriculture village	Mining village
Real income kg./person/year			
millet equivalent	620	975	1400
Food consumption do.	266	392	563
Income elasticity — all food	0·40	0·66	0·55
Rice and millet	0·95	0·7	0·35
Vegetable oil	0·95	1·3	1·4
Sugar	0·8	1·2	1·45
Meat	0·8	0·9	1·4
Milk (preserved)	0·9	1·1	1·3
Fish, fresh	1·4	0·8	1·25
Fish, dried	0·7	1·1	1·2

Institut de Science Économique Appliqué, *Besoins Nutritionnels et Politique Économique*, 1965.

Except for the cereals, income elasticity rises with income. It is, however, still difficult to say whether the lower elasticities in the first village are due to low income, or to isolation.

The following tables give values where not already mentioned in the text.

TABLE XLII. INCOME ELASTICITY OF DEMAND FOR FOOD

Rural communities	Year of survey		
England[a]	1795	Agricultural wage labour	0·92
Vietnam[a]	1938	Poor Tonkinese peasants	0·69
China (north)[b]	1914–18	Chinese peasants	0·77
China (north)[b]	1914–18	Manchu peasants	0·63

[1] B. P. Thomson, *Two Studies in African Nutrition: an urban and a rural community in Northern Rhodesia*, Rhodes-Livingstone Paper No. 24, 1954.

G

TABLE XLII. *continued.*

Rural communities   *Year of survey*

Iraq[b]	1958	Settlers: Kirkuk irrigation project	0·40
India — Punjab[a]	1953–54	Peasant proprietors	0·44
Japan — Kinki[a]	1956	Family farms	0·25

Urban communities

India — Faridabad[b]	1954	Indian National Sample Survey	0·74
India — Madras[b]	1935–36	Working-class (cotton mill) families	0·73
Africa — Zambia[a]	1947	Lusaka: urban African wage-earners	0·27
Africa — Nigeria	1959	Ilorin: Urban Consumer Survey	0·65

[a] Based on individual family budget data   [b] Based on income groups

TABLE XLIII. INCOME ELASTICITY OF DEMAND FOR NON-FOOD PRODUCTS

Country	Year	Clothing	Fuel	Housing	Taxes	Other
England	1795	1·84	1·35			
Vietnam	1938	0·65			0·86	
China (north) — Chinese	1914–18	2·56	0·90	0·45		3·69
China (north) — Manchu	1914–18	3·76	1·55	0·20		4·04
India — Punjab	1953–4	0·60		0·73		
India — Madras	1935–6	1·07	0·31	0·73		2·07
Japan — Kinki	1956	0·69		0·51		

Using data from 171 families interviewed in an urban consumer survey at Ilorin,[1] Heads set out to demonstrate how the interaction between a rise in agricultural productivity, and the low income elasticity of demand for food, has allowed the growth of secondary and tertiary industry and increased urbanization in Nigeria. He found also that, at high-income levels, imported foods tended to become relatively more important in food budgets, and the income elasticity of demand for home-produced foodstuffs is even less than the total income elasticity of demand for food.

Urban income elasticities were found to be in nearly every case higher than rural in the Philippines.[2]

[1] J. Heads, 'Urbanization and Economic Progress in Nigeria', *South African Journal of Economics*, Vol. 27, No. 3, September 1959.
[2] *The Philippines: Long-term Projection of Supply and of Demand for Selected Agricultural Products*, ERS-Foreign-34, United States Department of Agriculture.

TABLE XLIV. PHILIPPINES: INCOME ELASTICITIES
BETWEEN COMMODITIES

Products	Manila	Other urban	Rural
Rice	·00	·12	− ·15
Maize	− ·05	·10	·01
Bakery products	·37	·40	·60
Fresh milk and milk products	·65	·90	− ·02
Canned whole milk	1·59	1·28	·41
Pork	·38	·41	·21
Fresh beef	·56	·39	·12
Poultry	·18	·39	·26
Fish and fish products	·15	·27	·33
Cotton yarn	·01	·28	·18
Other fibres	·62	·21	·32

The survey quoted for industrial workers in Madras showed high income elasticities for non-cereal food, 1·1 for fish and meat, 1·4 for sugar, 2·2 for tea and coffee, and 2·2 also for milk and butter.

Calculations of income elasticities so far have been made by the orthodox method of drawing a double logarithmic diagram for income and consumption and estimating the slope of the data, which should lie along a straight line if income elasticity is constant. This method appears valid at low income levels, but not at higher.

Studying the relationship between real income and food consumption in a large number of economically advanced, and also middle- and low-income countries, Jones and Basu,[1] after testing hyperbolae and a number of other possible mathematical relationships, concluded that the best fit to the data was obtained by a function which made food consumption vary with the logarithm of real income. (Consumption of cereal was best expressed by an equation containing a negative exponential, i.e. rising to a maximum at a certain specified income level, and falling beyond that point.) This relationship necessarily implies that income elasticity must fall steadily, in inverse proportion to the quantity of food consumption, as real incomes increase.

All measurements so far have been made in terms of family income per head. But some examination should be made of the question whether, at a given level of family income per head, consumption of any commodity may be affected by the number of persons in the family; or to put it another way, whether there are

[1] 'International Pattern of Demand for Foodstuffs in 1954', *Farm Economist*, Oxford, 1957.

any 'economies of scale' in various forms of consumption. Some of the information analysed could be tested in this respect. The most striking result found was in respect of expenditure on education in Japan, where, at a given level of real income per head, expenditure rose with the numbers in the family.

Unlike peasant families in Europe, which tend to spend less on education when they have several children to support, in the larger peasant families in Japan, apparently, the working members of the family are willing to make more effort than the smaller families to secure additional education for one of the family members. There were slight indications that the same thing was happening in India, though the results were hardly statistically significant.

Significant negative results were shown (i.e. capacity of large families to make *economies* in per head expenditure, not open to smaller families) for food consumption in both Japan and India, likewise for clothing in both countries.

A most important element in the economics of the life of the subsistence cultivator, which has received far too little study, is his housing. We may examine the available data in sq. m. (10·8 sq. ft.)/ person.

For China, Buck found a much higher figure than might have been expected, of 8·5 sq. m./person (9·3 in the richer rice-growing region in the south, 7·4 in the north).

Surprisingly, almost the same figure (8·4) is found for Yugoslavia.[1] The figures range from 6–7 in Bosnia, Montenegro and Macedonia to 10·9 in Slovenia and 12·4 in Voivodina, the richest areas. The houses in Yugoslavia, however, are more substantially built.

Of the farm population of Jamaica[2] about one-third lives with less than 4 sq. m./person, half between 4 and 8.

Very low standards seem to prevail in India. In a small town[3] the median family had about 4·5 sq. m./person, a fifth of the families less than 2·3. In the rapidly growing city of Poona,[4] in 1953, the median was only 2·8, and nearly a third of all the people were below 2·3. In the worst districts of Singapore the average net dwelling space per person falls to 1·8 sq .m.[5] and even worse crowding pre-

[1] Vinski, International Association for Research in Income and Wealth, 1957 Conference.
[2] D. Edwards, *An Economic Study of Small Farming in Jamaica*, 1961.
[3] Dhekney, *Hubli City*, Karnatak University, Dharwar.
[4] *Poona, A Resurvey*, Gokhale Institute, 1953.
[5] 'The Character of Cities', J. M. Fraser, *Town and Country Planning*, November 1955.

vails in Hong Kong. What evidence we have indicates that crowding in mainland China is worse still. Table XLIII shows the high income elasticity of demand for housing both among the peasant proprietors of the Punjab, and the Madras mill workers.

In the cold north China climate, however, consumption of clothing is substantial even at very low levels of income; conversely, Vietnam peasants, also living near the margin for subsistence, show a much lower income elasticity of demand for clothing since this community live in tropical south-east Asia. In eighteenth-century England income elasticity of demand was relatively high both for clothing and fuel; rent on the other hand was non-significant.

Fraenkel[1] has found income elasticity of demand for clothing in Europe to range from 0·8 for high-income families to 1·6 for the lowest. We need not, however, expect African or Asian income elasticities necessarily to be higher than 1·6 — after all, the poorer families in European countries suffer a considerable 'demonstration effect', causing them to desire to spend more on clothing than fairly they can. The relatively high income elasticity of demand for clothing in the Japanese sample in Table XLIII is characteristic of a country in which consumption of clothing fibres has always tended to be above that of most Asian countries. Data from 1926–7 family expenditure studies showed an income elasticity of demand for clothing of 1·1.

Some high non-food income elasticities were found in Ivory Coast[2] namely 0·5 for rent, 0·7 for tobacco, 1·1 for travel and personal services, 1·1 for drink, 1·1 for urban transport, 2·1 for clothing, and 2·7 for consumer durables.

A comprehensive set of estimates for India has recently been prepared (Table XLV).[3]

The studies in Mbale indicated an income elasticity demand for drink and tobacco of 2·8 at the lowest income levels of 60–90 shillings/family/month, but at only 0·7 above that level.

The income elasticity of demand, we have seen, is the best measure to use when we are examining consumption of such objects as food and clothing, which are consumed in substantial quantities at every level of income. When, however, we are dealing with such an object as savings, which may be zero or even negative, or even if we are dealing with a commodity whose consump-

[1] Centraal Planbureau, The Hague, Overdrukken 62.
[2] *Les Budgets Familiaux des Salariés Africains en Abidjan*, Côte d'Ivoire, Aug.–Sept. 1956.
[3] Indian Statistical Institute, *Studies on Consumer Behaviour*, 1960.

TABLE XLV. INCOME ELASTICITIES IN INDIA

	Rural	Urban
Food grains	0·75	0·52
Pulses	0·76	0·75
Edible oil	0·90	0·85
Vegetables	0·90	0·75
Milk and products	1·37	1·35
Meat, eggs, fish	0·90	1·02
Fruit	0·97	1·49
Restaurant	0·91	0·88
Salt	0·55	0·48
Spices	0·67	0·62
Sugar	1·08	0·93
Pan	0·89	0·70
Tobacco	0·88	0·77
Intoxicants	1·11	1·18
Fuel, light	0·67	0·73
Clothing, cotton	0·80	0·89
silk	2·03	2·07
wool	1·81	1·83
Bedding	1·31	1·27
Amusement	1·34	1·24
Education	1·82	1·63
Medicine	1·53	1·52
Toilet	0·90	1·06
Petty Art	0·97	0·84
Transport	1·24	1·20
Services	1·72	1·44
Furniture	1·51	1·67
Equipment	1·93	1·91
Musical instruments	0·81	2·00
Ornaments	2·04	2·25
Footwear	1·13	1·08
Utensils	1·04	1·23
Ceremonials	1·50	1·49
Rent	1·31	1·15
Taxes	1·29	2·03

tion is very small at the lower income levels, the method of logarithmic plotting becomes impracticable. When the income and consumption (or saving) are plotted on natural scales, and a straight line can be approximately drawn through the points, the slope of this line is defined as the 'marginal propensity to consume' (either for consumption or saving in the aggregate, or for consumption of individual commodities). This was the method of analysis which was applied by Keynes. It is very important not to confuse *marginal propensity to consume* with *income elasticity of demand*. The marginal propensity to consume a commodity which plays a relatively small part in total consumption, for instance, must inevitably be small, even if its income elasticity of demand is very high. On the other hand, this method of analysis by marginal propensities is very useful, as Keynes found, to anyone who is trying to consider what the effects of an income change may be. It has been used for analysing both savings and imports.

As Keynes's idea got into circulation in the 1930s, many of his followers, particularly in the United States, set out to measure marginal propensity to save by simple comparisons, over a limited number of years, of income and savings data. This method gives estimates of the marginal propensity to save which, in fact, for a reason which we shall see in a moment, are far too high. Many of its practitioners were led by it to make quite unrealistic predictions of what was likely to happen in the 1940s, when wartime expenditure was reduced. Other economists, vaguely suspicious of this simple analysis of time series, set out to compare savings by families at widely different income levels.

The defect in both these methods of analysis was shown by Friedman.[1] People do not immediately adjust their expenditure, either upwards or downwards, in responses to changes in income. They tend to spend in accordance with what they regard as their probable average income. Friedman went on to show that, in fact, a weighted average of their incomes in recent past years, with weights exponentially diminishing as we go further back into the past, gives a good approximation to their estimate of their 'permanent' income, in accordance with which they control their spending.

It thus follows that any sudden rise or fall in income must of necessity lead temporarily to a much greater rise or fall in savings than that which is to be expected after people have had time to adjust their expenditure to any 'permanent' rise or fall of income. Conversely, where we use a set of data of family expenditures *at any given time* to estimate income elasticity, we are liable to include, in both the highest and the lowest income groups, families who have only recently entered these groups, and have not yet adjusted their expenditure upwards or downwards to them. In this way we tend to *underestimate* income elasticities of demand for commodities.

There has not yet been much application of Friedman's principle to data on consumption and savings among subsistence cultivators,

[1] M. Friedman, *The Theory of the Consumption Function*, Princeton, 1957.

which data are scanty enough in any case. Some work has been done in Japan by Shinohara.[1] Marginal propensity to save among Japanese peasants, which appeared to be as high as 0·46 (i.e. 46 per cent of any increase in income saved) on a crude time-series analysis, was examined by inter-family comparisons in single years; for two years of good harvest (1951 and 1955) it averaged 0·38, and for a year of general bad harvest (1953) it averaged 0·31. This decline in the figure is as Friedman's theory would predict. Even if the true long period propensity to save on the part of Japanese peasants is only 0·25, this is still, however, a very high figure.

Japanese urban family expenditure data[2] show a marginal propensity to save of about 0·2, even at the lowest income levels, rising with ascending income, as might be expected. For the higher incomes, an income elasticity of demand for saving of 2·2 was concluded.

Some data for Indian industrial workers at Cawnpore[3] indicated a marginal propensity to save as high as 0·16.

Newman[4] made one of the few available studies of marginal propensity to import, based on family expenditure data, for a low-income economy. For the greater part of the people of Ceylon, up to an income level corresponding to 800 kg. grain/person/year, the marginal propensity to import was as high as 0·41, of which 0·28 represented imports of food. It was definitely only the wealthier people in Ceylon who had a higher marginal propensity to spend upon locally produced goods and services. It is rare to find a low-income country so dependent upon imports to meet the necessities of life as is Ceylon; but it is not unknown.

A really important advance in the technique of consumption studies in low income countries has been made by Mostafa and Mahmoud.[5] They classified the Egyptian population into consumption units (children under 13 0·6, males 13–50, 1·0 then 0·8, females 13–50 0·7, then 0·5. They derive consumption functions in terms of their principal variable x, namely *total consumption* (no

[1] Of Hitotsubashi University, privately communicated.
[2] *Proceedings of the International Institute of Statistics*, Tokyo Session, 1930, for 1926–7 results. *Monthly Labour Review*, Washington, October 1938, for 1936–7 results.
[3] Royal Commission on Indian Labour, 1928.
[4] *Studies in the Import Structure of Ceylon*, Ceylon Planning Secretariat, October 1958.
[5] United Arab Republic Institution of National Planning, Memo. 497, October 1964.

attempt was made to measure savings) in Egyptian £/consumption unit/year, measuring x over a range from 18–84 in rural, 24–180 in urban areas (the rural and urban functions were found to be different in almost every case). Analysed in this way, of course, many commodities represent at lower levels a rising, at higher levels a falling proportion of total consumption. This requires parabolic fitting; but the fits were remarkably good in all cases. This method of fitting renders possible a precise calculation of the point of inflection, above which the relative consumption of the commodity in question begins to decline. The fittings in most cases were to log x, but occasionally to x direct. In Table XLVI the fittings are logarithmic except for the following, where the coefficients apply to x and x^2 direct, namely fruit and vegetables, rural only, miscellaneous foods, rural only, tobacco and alcohol, rural only, clothing and linen, rural only, furniture and utensils, urban only, medical services, transport and communications, miscellaneous services, urban only, other consumption, rural only.

These figures cover approximately a tenfold range of income increase. The poorest family, as was stated, has an income of £18/ consumption unit/year. Converted into grain units and income per head, this represents approximately 500 kg. grain equivalent/ person/year.

An interesting set of figures is available for Madagascar.[1] The diagram covers more than a 15-fold range of incomes. The high income elasticity of demand for sugar, of approximately 0·6, ought to be good news for otherwise discouraged sugar producers.

It is interesting to see that the demand for rice still shows an income elasticity of approximately 0·2 until an income level of 1900 kg. paddy/person/year has been attained, after which rice consumption becomes practically stabilized. The principal reduction of consumption, with rising income, is in tubers; these have been replaced by foods with a high protein content. Pulses show a more moderate decline, tending to be the least preferred of the protein-rich foods. The demand for milk shows no significant rising trend with income and in no group does it exceed 10 litres/person/year.

While milk and milk products are readily consumed in India and Pakistan, and are now enjoying a rapidly increasing sale in Japan, they appear to be little in demand in other countries in the

[1] Patrick J. François, *Budgets et Alimentation des Ménages Ruraux en 1962*, République Malgache, Ministère des Finances et du Commerce.

TABLE XLVI. EGYPTIAN CONSUMPTION FUNCTIONS

Percentage of total expenditure on specified commodity $= a + b \log_{10} x + c(\log_{10} x)^2$

	Urban				Rural			
	a	b	c	x at point of inflexion	a	b	c	x at point of inflexion
Cereals and starches	63·9	−26·39			75·6	−30·01		
Dry beans	5·3	− 2·106			2·3	7·623	−2·738	24·7
Meat, fish and eggs	−17·4	+29·20	−7·523	65·3	− 6·2	19·356	−5·295	67·3
Oils and fats	6·1	− 2·245			0	2·615	−0·994	20·7
Milk and products	−15·1	23·108	−6·089	79·1	−17·5	31·48	−9·52	45·0
Vegetables	1·4	4·327	−1·611	22·0	3·3	·008	−0·0001	38·5
Fruit	− 9·4	11·503	−2·56	176·2	0·7	·041	−0·0002	101·2
Sugar and confectionery	6·7	− 1·837			12·1	8·146	1·982	113·3
Other food	16·6	−11·545	+2·222	concave	1·0	0·0116	−0·0001	58·0
Beverages	0·1	4·533	−1·474	34·5	4·9	0·920		
Tobacco and Alcohol	3·2	12·216	−3·909	36·6	7·0	0·011		
Fuel and light	5·7	− 1·214			4·8	0·853		
Personal cleaning and cosmetics	1·1	1·717	−0·367	216·9	0·3	0·416		
Domestic cleansers	3·0	− 0·784			2·0	0·461		
Clothing and linen	−25·2	31·258	−7·152	133·2	3·2	0·146	−0·0008	91·5
Furniture, utensils and consumer durables	0·2	0·017			1·3	1·27		
Education and sport	− 6·3	5·056			2·5	1·902		
Medical and therapy	0·1	0·043	−0·0001	215·5	0·6	0·070	−0·0002	175·7
Transport and communications	0·8	0·027			0·2	0·041		
Other services	2·4	0·022			13·4	−15·236	5·544	concave min. at 23·7
Other consumption	2·8	4·452			2·5	·027		

CHART XIX

FOOD CONSUMPTION IN RURAL MADAGASCAR

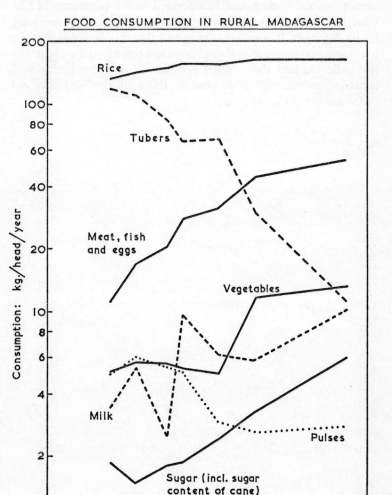

Far East, or in Africa. This may be a question which only physiologists can answer; there may be something in the theory that some sections of the human race lack (except in the beginning of life, when they are consuming their mother's milk) an enzyme necessary for its digestion. It is universally agreed that it is desirable that the low-income communities should consume more protein, especially the children, and that animal protein has a better amino-acid composition than vegetable protein. But milk products may not be the answer to the problem.

CHAPTER XII

Transport

The material development of Africa may be summed up in one word — transport.'

So wrote Lord Lugard,[1] who brought peace and order to vast regions of Africa which were then living in the chaos of slave trading and tribal war.

It cannot be emphasized too strongly that the first requisite for the improvement of the production of a subsistence economy is the provision of transport. Fertilizers, improved strains of seed, education and other objects are all of the greatest importance. But the need for transport is prior to all these. It follows from the nature of the case. If there is to be any improvement in an agriculture which at present only provides for subsistence, crops must be grown which can be sold. Selling implies transport to market. The methods of transport available to subsistence agricultural populations, as will be seen below, are so costly that produce only has to be carried a limited distance before most of its value, from the point of view of net returns from the sale, has gone.

The customary unit for measuring transport performance is a ton km., the carrying of one ton for a distance of a kilometre. As with production and consumption, we measure the cost of performing transport in terms of kg. grain equivalent/ton km. When, as in extreme cases, over 30 kg. of grain equivalent have to be expended in order to get one ton km. of transport performed, it is clear that transporting grain to market, even over a distance as short as 20 km., is economically out of the question — the costs of transport would have taken three-fifths of its value. Some Japanese settlers who went to Ecuador and the Upper Amazon Valley to produce rice found that the transport costs were so high they had to give up their farms.[2] In Tanganyika, before the building of the railway (1902) long distance transport costs were estimated as high as 6 shillings/ton mile. Under these conditions ivory was about the

---

[1] *The Dual Mandate in Tropical Africa*, Edinburgh, 1922, p. 5.
[2] Sasaki, Eichi University, Osaka, private communication.

only export.[1] In the eighteenth century Cantillon[2] took it for granted that food would not normally be transported more than 15 km. from its place of origin. The corresponding figures for the supply of food to Paris[3] were 50 km. in 1830 with the improvement of roads and canals, and 250 km. in 1855, with the coming of the railways.

The cultivator may mitigate such a situation by growing for sale a crop which has a higher value per unit of weight, such as coffee (value of 1 kg. in grain units 5·6) or tobacco (value 8) — if his own skill, the productive possibilities of the soil and climate, and the availability of markets permit it. Thus in some of the more isolated mountainous regions of Macedonia the principal crop produced for sale is tobacco, because the burden of transport costs on it is relatively less; and many African cultivators have a preference for coffee for the same reason. It has been said in defence of the dwellers in the remote mountain regions of Kentucky, that their persistent tendency to produce 'moonshine', in face of all the efforts of excise officers, is explainable in terms of high transport costs in those regions, and the need to earn cash income and to produce for sale something which has a higher value per unit of weight than simple grain.

The situation is vividly described in Madagascar.[4] In the plateau region, communications are often suspended altogether for a substantial part of the year. It is quite clear that transport difficulties are checking economic development, and also leading to concentration on high-value crops such as coffee, pyrethrum and vanilla. The latter is so high-valued that it can stand the cost of porterage for a considerable distance. But even where roads and motor vehicles are available, the costs are exceptionally high. Where the route is broken by frequent ferry crossings, the costs are such as to double the price of rice for a journey of only 80 km. An extreme case is quoted of one village where even the foot track is only open during the short dry season of two months a year. Its only saleable crop is coffee, which has to be carried for a distance of 56 km. by porters massed for the occasion, whose charge is 25 per cent higher even than the high average given in the table, and

---

[1] International Economic Association, *Economic Development of Africa south of the Sahara*, p. 97.
[2] Spengler, *Journal of Political Economy*, 1954, pp. 289–93.
[3] Renouard, *Le Transport de la Marchandise*, 1960.
[4] *Analyse de la Structure des Prix et des Circuits Commerciaux Internes*, Madagascar, Ministry of National Economy.

transport for this distance absorbs 25 per cent of the value even of
a high-priced crop such as coffee.

The authors go on to point out further undesirable effects of the
lack of transport, in requiring traders to carry exceptionally large
stocks, and also encouraging speculation in the necessities of life,
whose price may under certain circumstances suddenly double or
treble, driving poor farmers deeply into debt, and to the pledging
of future crops, which are often taken at 'derisory' prices.

One of the authors has found even higher charges prevailing in
Malawi, which effectively compel the remoter villages to live
entirely by subsistence agriculture. Charges for ox-wagon transport increase with distance.

Usher[1] has pointed out the interesting possibility of what he
calls 'transport bias'. When a country with high internal transport
costs is exporting to the world market, prices in the interior of the
country will be low for this reason, and the further from the commercial centre, the lower. This is accentuated when the country
also imposes taxation upon exports at a substantial level, as does
Thailand.

One of the most striking examples of this was in mid-nineteenth-
century Ghana,[2] which was at that time almost entirely out of
contact with world commerce. The local currency was a string of
cowries, comparatively rare sea shells, 4 or 5 of which exchanged
for a penny. At this rate of exchange, a ton of maize in Ghana cost
112 pence, at a time when its world price was about £7.

An equally striking example comes from Basutoland,[3] where in
1839 sorghum was selling at 1 shilling/bushel, and at 6 or 7 times
that price at Carlsberg, 200 miles away.

A little less extreme was the situation in the northernmost part of
Malaya,[4] which had no road communications until 1920. About
1880, when the only communications were by small boats, and
probably subject to piracy, the local price of rough rice was about
1·7 £/ton, when its world price was over £7. By 1890 however,
with improved communications, the price had risen about 70 per
cent.

Sweet potatoes are admittedly a cheap form of food. But in rural

---

[1] *Economica*, May 1963 and November 1966.
[2] Reindorf, *History of the Gold Coast and Asante* (1895) quoted Anyane,
Ghana Agriculture.
[3] Backhouse, *Basutoland*. I am indebted to Mr. Peter Stutley for this quota-
tion.
[4] Firth, *Malay Fishermen*.

Indonesia in the 1920s[1] they were selling at 4 Dutch guilders (1·6 dollars)/ton. The internal price of maize in East Africa in the 1930s[2] was only 3·3 £/ton, a little over half the world price. A very clear example of transport bias is provided by the history of rice prices in India[3] which were very low in relation to European prices in the eighteenth and early nineteenth centuries, and were raised by the gradual increase in commerce, the coming of steamships, and the Suez Canal (opened 1869).

Price Indexes 1899–1901 base

	1861–9	1841–53	1760–85	1704–49
Wheat (U.K.)	176	192	176	112
Rice (India)	66	25	38	19

Chisholm[4] quotes an interesting example from the Kasai region of the Congo in 1951, where manioc (cassava), which is transported for sale in the mining towns, sold at 1·5 Bfr/kg. (30 $/ton) within 15 km. from the railway, and at prices progressively descending to 1·0 at 150 km. distance. This implies 3·3 kg. manioc or only 0·8 kg. wheat equivalent/ton km. of transport — presumably on fairly good roads.

But we get also some examples of the opposite phenomenon from some low-income agricultural areas which import staple cereals, or at any rate produce only just enough for their own requirements, depending mainly on cotton, cocoa, or other export crops. Thus, at the time when Fuggles Couchman found maize prices so low in East Africa, Beckett[5] found the internal price of maize in a cocoa-growing district in Ghana over 9£/ton. In the studies previously quoted for Cameroun, Senegal and Uganda, internal prices for sorghum in Cameroun and for millet in the other two countries were found to be 96, 104 and 124 dollars/ton respectively, far higher than the world price.

Transport in its simplest form — and there are many places where this is still the only possible form of transport — requires the direct carrying of goods by men or women in packs on their

---

[1] Boeke, Economics and Economic Policy of Dual Societies, p. 191.
[2] Couchman, East African Journal of Agriculture, March 1939.
[3] Back to 1841 from Dharma Kumar, Land & Caste in South India (Cambridge Studies in Economic History). Earlier from Brij Narain, Indian Economic Life, Lahore, 1929.
[4] M. Chisholm, Rural Settlement and Land Use, p. 84.
[5] London School of Economics Monograph in Social Anthropology, No. 10.

backs or, more usually in Africa or Asia, in loads balanced grace-
fully on their heads. Holmberg[1] has seen hunters in Bolivia return
from the forest carrying up to 90 kg. game on their backs for a
distance of 16 km. without exhibiting a great deal of fatigue. He
found the average pack for a man or a woman to be about 30 kg.
These Siriono hunters sometimes travel as many as 64 km. a day
in their quest for game, and when nuclear families are away on
hunting and gathering expeditions, men, women and children
may walk 40 km. within a single day.

Even in the poorest and most primitive subsistence economy, a
man must at least be well fed for the arduous task of carrying a
heavy load all day — and also fed for the return journey. These
requirements alone create a fairly high minimum cost, measured
in kg. grain equivalent/ton km. In more advanced communities, as
in those parts of southern Italy where some transport is still by
porterage, where a man, however poor, nevertheless expects to be
paid considerably more than the mere grain ration for a day's hard
work, the grain equivalent of porterage costs becomes very high
indeed.

The Chinese long ago invented the wheelbarrow (the Japanese
shared this knowledge), which considerably reduced the cost of
carrying heavy loads — though by no means everyone can afford
to own one. (That they fitted their wheelbarrows with sails to
catch the wind when it was favourable in order to help them on
their journeys may be a fact, or merely an entertaining legend.)
The simple but useful device of the wheelbarrow appears still to be
unknown in many parts of the world. (Sidney Webb, travelling in
Soviet Russia in the 1930s, supplemented his published account
by remarking in private that the wheelbarrow and the mop
appeared still to be unknown there, and that many heavy goods
were still head-loaded, just as many floors were left uncleaned.)
When most transport in Japan was still by wheelbarrow along
narrow paths[2] the maximum radius over which vegetables (less
valuable per unit of weight than grain) could be supplied to towns
was 12 km. With the advent of better roads and waggons this
became 20 km., with motor trucks 40 km. These radii must not,
however, be regarded as measuring the comparative costs of the
different forms of transport. The ratio of motor transport cost to

[1] A. R. Holmberg, *Nomads of the Long Bow: the Siriono of Eastern Bolivia*,
Smithsonian Institute of Social Anthropology, Publication No. 10, 1950.
[2] Lockwood, writing in the Symposium by Kuznets and others, *Economic
Growth — Brazil, India, Japan*.

TABLE XLVII. COMPARISON OF THE COST OF DIFFERENT METHODS OF TRANSPORT

Country or Region	Date	Length of journey (if specified) km.	Transport costs (original measure)	Grain equivalent used (if not wheat)	Transport cost expressed as kg. grain equivalent/ ton km.	Source
PORTERAGE						
Central America	1946		$0·88/ton mile		7·4	M
China	1929				7·4	N
„	1930			millet	4·5	A
„	1938	11	0·71 yuan/ton mile	varied	2·0	P
East Africa	1953		10 shillings/ton mile	milled rice	12·4	AA
France	1880		3·33 franc/ton km.		12·0	L
Ghana	1900		4 shillings/60 lbs.		4·6	MM
India and Pakistan	1937	40	7-12 pies/maund mile	maize	8·2	B
Italy	1953		700 lire/ton km.		9·3	C
Kenya	1953		$1-1½/ton mile		11·4	O
Madagascar	1961				12·2	YY
Malawi	1968	8	2·5 shillings/32 kg.	maize	37·2	ZZ
Nigeria	1926		30 pence/ton mile		6·5	LL
Northern Rhodesia	1930s	25-30		milled rice	37·1	O
East Pakistan	1958		4 annas/maund mile		5·5	R
West Pakistan	1958		3 annas/maund mile		9·0	R
Turkey	1951		$1/ton mile		10·0	U
WHEELBARROW						
China	1929				4·4	N
„	1930		0·30 yuan/ton mile		1·9	A
PACK ANIMALS						
Camel: China	1929			millet	3·3	N
„	1930			varied	2·3	A
Middle East	1880				1·7	L
Niger	1961	25	0·87 francs/ton km.	paddy	4·8	AAA
Nigeria	1926		82 fr.CFA/ton km.		2·1	LL
Pakistan	1958		10 pence/ton mile		4·5	R
Sudan	1937	140	1¼ annas/maund mile		2·1	Z
			£16·7/000 ton km.			
Donkey: China	1929		0·56 yuan/ton mile	millet	4·7	N
East Africa	1930				3·5	A
Kenya	1953		9·5 shillings/ton mile		11·8	AA
„	1953				11·4	Q
Niger	1961	25	89 fr. CFA/ton km.	paddy	5·2	AAA
Pakistan	1958				6·0	R
Horse	Central America	1946		millet	5·2	M
China	1929				6·3	N
„	1930				3·4	A
„	1938	11		milled rice	2·3	P

Region	Year	No.	Price	Commodity	Value	Code
England	1655	190	8 pence/ton mile		4·1	T
	1754		12 pence/ton mile		6·2	T
India and Pakistan	1937		2·4–5·6 pies/maund mile		2·1–4·9	B
Italy	1953		440 lire/ton km.		5·9	C
Pakistan	1958				6·0	R
Turkey	1951		$1/ton mile		10·0	U
United States	1790		5½ shillings/ton mile		7·5	X
Llama: Chile	1937		56 pesos/ton mile		3·3	s
Mule: Basutoland	1950	55	15 shillings/200 lb. grain		6·8	NN
	1950	55	15 shillings/140 lb. wool		9·8	NN
,, China	1929			millet	3·4	N
,,	1930				3·0	N
,, France	1880				3·1	L
CARTS AND WAGONS						
Australia	1795	58	20 pence/ton mile		2·8	I
,,	1839		8 pence/ton mile		1·4	I
,,	1854	225	24 pence/ton mile		3·4	I
,,	1860		42–66 pence/ton mile		3·6–5·6	I
China	11th c.		24 pence/ton mile	millet	2·6	N
,,	1929		0·022 cash/lb. mile	milled rice	1·2	RR
England: long journeys	1930		3¼ pence/ton mile		2·3	A
,,	13th c.		1 penny/ton mile		8·0	F
,, short journeys	13th c.		13 pence/ton mile		2·3	
,, France	Early 19th c.	30	6 pence/gall. milk	rye	5·7	SS
,,	1864				16·4	PP
,, Estimate for 17th c. wagon design					5·4	L
France	Early 19th c.		3 pence/ton mile		1·7	SS
,,	1912	short	0·6 francs/ton km. (firewood)	rye	2·2	V
Germany	1815	37	(rye)	rye	3·1	OO
,,	1815	166	(butter)	rye	2·7	OO
India (Nagpur-Mirzapore)	1848	800	£17.10.0/ton		7·5	G
India and Pakistan	1937	13			2·4	B
South India	1936	6			2·3	H
	1953				3·3	C
Italy ,,	1968		270 lire/ton km.		1·8–5·5	ZZ
Malawi	1968	8	10 shillings/800 kg.	maize	3·6	ZZ
Nigeria	1020		22·5 shillings/410 kg.	maize	6·8	Q
Pakistan	1958	21			11·3	R
,, urban areas	1958		40 pence/ton mile		5·5	R
,, short journeys	1961				4·5	J
Roman Empire	3rd c. A.D.		37 denarii/ton mile		2·2	J
					3·2	E

Country or Region	Date	Length of journey (if specified) km.	Transport costs (original measure)	Grain equivalent used (if not wheat)	Transport cost expressed as kg. grain equivalent/ton km.	Source
Roman Empire Eastern Provinces	3rd c. A.D.		20 denarii/1200 lb./mile		4·4	W
Thailand	1900		21 cents/ton km.	rough rice	2·5	KK
United States	1790–1818	Over 300	13 cents/ton km.		3·5	X
"	1790–1818	Under 300	15 cents/ton mile		1·6	Y
"	1800		20 cents/ton mile		4·9	K
TELEFERICHE						
Italy	1953		175 lire/ton km.		2·3	C
BOATS						
China	11th c.		0·0038 cash/lb. mile	millet	2·3	N
"	1928		0·14 yuan/ton mile		0·2	RR
Egypt: canal	1930		1 drachma/ton mile		0·9	A
" River Nile	3rd c. A.D.				1·1	D
England: Mersey and Irwell	3rd c. A.D.				0·3	D
"	17th c.	150	1 penny/ton mile (wool)		0·5	T
"	14th c.	500	(coal)		1·3	F
"	14th c.	River Bure 360	⅓ pence/ton mile		0·8	F
"	16th c.		6 shillings/ton		0·4	QQ
"	Early 19th c.				0·55	QQ
" Thames	17th c.		4 pence/ton mile (water route)		1·8	SS
" Thames	17th c.		2 pence/ton mile (water route)			
" Thames	1790		2·4 pence/ton mile (water route)			
France	Early 19th c.		1½ pence/ton mile		0·8	SS
Germany	14th c.	1700			0·3	XX
Ghana	1900	43		maize	5·8	MM
Pakistan	1958	5		milled rice	2·1	R
"	1958	30		milled rice	0·7	R
" short journey	1961		1¼ anna/maund mile		1·9	JJ
" long journey	1961	80	½ anna/maund mile		0·6	JJ
United States: canal	1810	450			2·2	U
" New Orleans–Louisville	1810	30			0·4	X
" "	1810				4·8	X
" " downstream	1810				0·9	X

Item	Date		Cost	Commodity	Index	Ref
STEAMBOATS						
Central America	1946				0·6	M
China	1928	850	0·08 yuan/ton mile	millet	4·1	N
Nigeria	1930				0·5	A
Thailand	1960	400	2·34 pence/ton mile	rough rice	0·1	BB
EARLY RAILWAY SYSTEMS						
Australia	1850s		6 pence/ton mile		1·4	J
" Wheat	1870s	250	2 pence/ton mile		1·2	J
" Machinery	1870s	250	7 pence/ton mile		4·1	J
Central America	1946		8·3 cents/ton mile		1·2	M
Chile	1937		1·5 pesos/ton mile		0·1	S
China	1930		0·09 yuan/ton mile		0·57	A
England: Birmingham-Liverpool	1830s		4 pence/ton mile		1·3	T
" London-Manchester	1830s		2·3 pence/ton mile		0·74	T
France	1830s		0·25 francs/ton km.		1·1	L
"	1870s		0·06 francs/ton km.		0·22	L
Ghana	1955	160	3·65 pence/ton mile		0·61	BB
Nigeria	1955	760	2·73 pence/ton mile		0·45	BB
"	1926		2 pence/ton mile		0·43	LL
Sudan	1910	1700	1·8 £/ton wheat		0·17	VV
"	1910	1700	3·8 £/ton cotton		0·34	VV
Syria	1953	650	45 £S harvest season	barley	0·46	TT
"	1953	650	22½ £S off season	barley	0·23	TT
"	1965	650	30 £S harvest season	barley	0·31	TT
Tanzania	1957		2·4 pence/ton mile		0·4	HH
"	1965		0·18 shillings/ton mile		0·36	WW
Thailand	1960	4–700		rough rice	0·15	KK
MOTOR VEHICLES						
Basutoland Mountain tracks	1950		1·6 pence/lb.		12·5	NN
" main road	1950	54	13 pence/ton		1·5	NN
Borneo (assuming 50% average only) ¾ ton jeeps	1960		43 cents/vehicle mile		3·3	II
" 3 ton trucks	1960		83 cents/vehicle mile		1·6	II
" 5 ton trucks	1960		96 cents/vehicle mile		1·1	II
Central America	1946		32 cents/ton mile		1·3	M
Ceylon: lowlands	1952	10	23½ cents/ton mile	rough rice	0·34	FF
" lowlands	1952	240	60 cents/ton mile	rough rice	0·25	FF
" highlands	1952	10	32½ cents/ton mile	rough rice	0·64	FF
" highlands	1952	240	15 pesos/ton mile	rough rice	0·35	FF
Chile	1937				1·1	S
China	1928		0·08 yuan/ton mile	millet	13·9	A
"	1930				7·2	A
Congo	1951	150	0·5 francs/kg.		0·8	UU

Country or Region	Date	Length of journey (if specified) km.	Transport costs (original measure)	Grain equivalent used (if not wheat)	Transport cost expressed as kg. grain equivalent/ ton km.	Source
MOTOR VEHICLES (contd.)						
Dahomey	1953	50	22 fr. CFA/ton km.	maize	0·93	BBB
"		200	11 fr. CFA/ton km.	maize	0·43	LBB
"		500	8 fr. CFA/ton km.	maize	0·35	B..B
East Africa			4½ shillings/ton mile		5·3	AA
India (Delhi-Rajasthan) lowest rate on agricultural goods	1960	30	26 NP/ton mile		0·65	GG
" " "	1960	150	12 NP/ton mile		0·30	GG
" " highest rate on industrial goods	1960		70 NP/ton mile		1·75	GG
" " "	1960		20 NP/ton mile		0·50	GG
Madagascar	1961	300		maize	5·2	YY
Malawi	1968	96	2·5 shillings/90 kg.		1·3	ZZ
Nigeria (Lagos and south)	1954		3·5 pence/ton mile		0·36	CC
"	1926		12 pence/ton mile		2·6	LL
" average	1955	70	7·25 pence/ton mile		0·75	BB
Pakistan (Punjab)	1950		3 pies/maund mile		1·25	EE
Senegal: near Dakar	1937				0·4	CCC
" remote region	1965	100-300	7£S/ton	barley	1·7	CCC
Sudan	1965		0·25 shillings/ton mile		1·2	Z
Syria	1960				1·0	TT
Tanzania	1950s	4-700			0·5	WW
Thailand	1950s		9·6 pence/ton mile		0·15	KK
Uganda			7·5 pence/ton mile		1·00	DD
" regular traffic					0·78	DD

Sources to Table on Comparison of the Cost of Different Methods of Transport:

A Buck, Land Utilization in China, p. 354.
B Report on Marketing of Jute in India, 1940.
C Ugo Sorbi, Borgo e Mozzano, Instituto di Economica, University of Florence.
D Johnson, Economic Survey of the Roman Empire, and
E Walbank, Cambridge Economic History of Europe, and
F Postan, Economic History of Europe.
G Bourne, Railways in India.
H University of Madras, Resurvey of some South Indian Villages, 1936–7.
I Dunsdorf, The Australian Wheat Growing Industry.
J Shann, Economic History of Australia.
K A. D. Welk, Recent Economic Changes, 1889.
L De Foville, La Transformation des Moyens de Transport.
M U.S. Department of Commerce, International Reference Service, 1949.
N Gamble, Ting-Hsien, A North China Rural Community.
O Audrey Richards, Land, Labour and Diet in Northern Rhodesia.
P Fei and Chang, Earthbound China, p. 187.
Q Hance, African Economic Development.
R Report on Marketing of Fresh Fruit in Pakistan.
S Rudolph, Geographical Review, September 1952.
T Jackman, Development of Transport in Modern England, 1916.
U Renshaw, University of Chicago Journal of Business, October 1960.
V Bernard, Le Progrès Agricole.
W Jasny, Wheat Studies (Stanford), March 1944.
X Carnegie Institute, History of Transport in U.S. before 1860, 1917.
Y Cochran and Millar, The Age of Enterprise.
Z Tothill, Agriculture in the Sudan, Oxford University Press, 1948.
AA East African Royal Commission, 1953–55.
BB United Africa Company, Statistical and Economic Review, March 1957.
CC Hawkins, Road Transport in Nigeria.
DD Hawkins, Colonial Office Research Study No. 32.
EE Yasin, Punjab Board of Economic Enquiry, Bulletin No. 114.
FF International Bank, Economic Development of Ceylon.
GG National Council of Applied Economic Research, New Delhi Occasional Paper No. 2.

HH International Bank, Economic Development of Tanganyika.
II Report on Transport Requirements in the Light of Economic Developments in North Borneo, Colonial Office 1960.
JJ Report on the Marketing of Jute in East Pakistan, University of Dacca.
KK Usher, Economica, Nov. 1966.
LL Neumark, Foreign Trade & Economic Development in Africa (Stanford), 1964.
MM Anyane, Ghana Agriculture.
NN Stutley, University of Reading thesis.
OO Von Thünen, The Isolated State (P. Hall's translation).
PP Gasson, Geography, 1966.
QQ Bowden (Finberg, Editor), The Agrarian History of England & Wales, Vol. IV, p. 612.
RR Hartwell, Journal of Economic History, March 1966, pp. 35–7.
SS Baxter, Journal of the Royal Statistical Society, 1866.
TT J. L. Simmons, private communication.
UU Nicolai & Jacques, Memoires de l'Institut Royal du Congo Belge, 1954, quoted Chisholm, Rural Settlement & Land Use, p. 84.
VV D. J. Shaw, private communication.
WW Tanganyika, Annual Report of Transport Licensing Authority.
XX Hay, Europe in the 14th and 15th Centuries.
YY Ministère d'Etat Chargé d'Economie Nationale (Malgache), Analyse de la Structure des Prix et des Circuits Commerciaux Internes, Tananarive, Dec. 1968.
ZZ Measurements made by one of the authors during a recent field study. A cost of 173·6 kg. maize/ton km. was found for porterage in the Northern Region of Malawi, a precipitous area where head-loading is the only means of transport.
AAA Société d'Etudes pour le Développement Économique et Social, Les Produits Vivriers au Niger, Paris, 1963.
BBB Ministère des Finances, des Affaires Économiques et du Plan (Dahomey), Circuits Commerciaux de Produits et Biens Essentiels, Note de Synthèse.
CCC Compagnie d'Etudes Industrielles et d'Aménagement du Territoire, Les Flux de Transport dans la République du Sénégal, Vol. II.

wheelbarrow cost is less than 12:40. Commerce became more competitive in the horse age, still more in the motor age, and consumers would not tolerate so large a proportion of the final cost of their purchases going to transport costs as they had at an earlier date.

In the newly settled areas in Mindanao,[1] where presumably roads are lacking, and transport has to be by porterage, the economic effect of high transport costs shows itself in the price of land. Near the markets a hectare of land sells at the equivalent of 3·3 tons of rough rice; at the equivalent of only 1·9 tons when distant 6 km. or more from market. If we assume that the buyers of land have on the average capitalized net income at ten years' purchase, this means that the transport disadvantage of the outlying areas is, in effect, about one-tenth of the difference in land price, i.e. 140 kg. rice/ha./year, or 13 per cent of the gross product. If we take the average additional distance over which the rice has to be transported at 7 km., this implies a transport charge of 20 kg. rough rice, or 14 kg. milled rice/ton km., comparable with some of the highest figures given in the table. The Philippines is a comparatively high income country, and porters presumably have to be fairly well paid. However, the statement made by the Central Experiment Station, that in some cases the transportation agent charged as much as one unit of rice for every two units carried to market, cannot apparently be substantiated, except in a few isolated cases.

Conflicting statements have been made (see table for sources) regarding loads and distances covered by head porters. For Japan, the load was estimated at 45 kg. and the average journey 30 km./day. Gourou[2] gave 50 km./day at an average load of 40 kg. For Pakistan the figures are given as 20–40 kg. for head loads, 75–100 for shoulder baskets. Fei and Chang give for China the high figure of a 59 kg. load, and also imply that distances up to 50 km. may be covered daily. However, even the strongest men can only do such work for twelve days a month, and receive two or three times the wages of an ordinary agricultural worker. Another estimate for China[3] gives 47 kg. carried for 32 km./day. The Rhodesian figures, on the other hand, are for only 23 kg. carried 25–30 km. A general estimate has been made of 27 kg. carried 24 kilometres daily.[4] These lower standards of effort, and higher real

[1] Philippines Central Experiment Station, Bulletin No. 1, 1957, p. 45.
[2] In his book, *The Tropical World*, 1961.
[3] Winfield, *China, the Land and the People*, 1948.
[4] Owen, *Strategy for Mobility*, Brookings Institution, p. 7.

TRANSPORT COSTS IN DEVELOPING COUNTRIES

Expressed as kilograms grain equivalent/ton-kilometre transported.

	Maximum	Median	Minimum
Porterage	37·2 (Malawi 1968)	9·0	2·0 (China 1938)
Wheelbarrow		3·2	
Pack animals	11·8 (East Africa, donkey)	4·6	1·7 (Middle East, camel)
Wagons	16·4 (England, 1864, milk collection)	3·4	1·2 (China, 11th century)
Boats	5·8 (Ghana 1900)	0·9	0·2 (China, 11th century)
Steamboats		0·5	
Railways	4·1 (Australia 1870)	0·5	0·1 (Chile 1937)
Motor vehicles	13·9 (China 1928)	1·0	0·15 (Thailand 1960)

wages, explain the very high cost. When jute is head-loaded in India and Pakistan, the average load is stated to be about 40 kg.

There are indications that these very heavy loads call for a quite disproportionate effort. Phillips[1] found that for head-load carrying total energy expenditure increases linearly with the weight of head load carried up to a certain optimum level, which would appear to be at 20 kg., and that any further increase in the weight of head loads leads to a disproportionate increase in energy cost.

In assessing the physiologically optimum head load, three factors should be taken into account: (a) the distance of carry; (b) the rate of carry; and (c) the period of rest. He argues that a head load of 20 kg. would be considered the upper limit if the carrier were walking for some time without rest, but that a load of 30 or 35 kg. would not be excessive, and would ensure a high degree of efficiency, provided that the distance of carry was short, or that the carrier returned unloaded (equivalent to a normal rest period). This, he notes, is in fact the custom in Africa. For long marches a carrier's load rarely exceeds 22 kg., and is normally not more than 14 kg., but in the tin mines, where the carries are short, the load is often more than 27 kg.; and in agricultural centres, sacks of groundnuts or cocoa beans weighing up to 100 kg. are often humped short distances. An important point is the position of the centre of gravity of the load relative to that of the body, which favours the carriage of loads on the head, since complete control and a stable centre of gravity is maintained throughout.

Another method of transport, without the use of animal power, is by bicycle. A cost of 15·9 kg. maize/ton km. was observed in

[1] P. G. Phillips, 'The Metabolic Cost of Common West African Agricultural Activities', Journal of Tropical Medicine and Hygiene, London, 1954, Vol. 57, No. 12.

Malawi during a recent survey by one of the authors. Malayan data[1] have shown costs of over 30 kg. grain/ton km., and these high figures have been confirmed by other observers. Again, however, Malaya is a relatively high-wage country.

For the very poor countries, pack animals do not represent any great saving over human porterage — the cost of maintaining the animal is high, in relation to the price of labour. The horse is the most expensive animal to maintain, and costs correspondingly high. The rise in pack-horse costs in England between the seventeenth and eighteenth centuries, shown in the table, is probably explainable in terms of rising real wages.

Direct comparisons of the cost of pack-horse and human transport were made in the Chinese village study by Fei and Chang, and the horse found to be more costly. The average pack horse only carries 90 kg., as against the man's 60 kg., and travels about half as fast again, requires one day's rest in five, and in this particular district only works nine months of the year because of the climate. With the work it did, and the keep it received, the average life of a pack horse was found to be only about one year. In mediaeval Europe[2] the different forms of transport were in interesting economic equilibrium. Wagons were used for local transport to fairs and for medium-distance transport. 'Continental commerce was carried on pack animals or, where the routes were steep, as on the Alpine passes, on the backs of porters.' In Hong Kong, to this day, where most of the transport is by motor vehicles, on the steep unroaded slopes of Lan Ta Island, the heavy loads are still carried by porters. In East Africa, comparatively high rates of wages show themselves in the very high charges for transport both by porter and by pack donkey.

A number of data are available for the cost of cart and wagon transport, for a great variety of times and places. The costs of long journeys seem to have been much higher than of short journeys, probably owing to the greater risk of having to return without a load. Nearly all the data referred to ox wagons; it was not until the nineteenth century, and then only in some countries, that the use of the horse wagon became widespread. De Foville's figures for France show that improvements in wagon design played an important part in reducing costs; these in their turn are only made possible by an improvement in roads. However, the Indian report

---

[1] Wilson, *Economics of Paddy Production in Northern Malaya.*
[2] Hay, *Europe in the 14th and 15th Centuries*, pp. 360–3.

on the marketing of jute indicated that transport costs by ox wagon on metalled roads were no lower than on unmetalled.

In Australia, the great rise in money costs in 1854 (the rise in real costs was less) was the consequence of the Gold Rush. The rates shown prevailed only in the summer, when the roads in Victoria were dry. In winter, when the roads were muddy, and the oxen needed for ploughing, rates might be five times as high. After the Gold Rush real costs settled down at a considerably higher figure than before the Gold Rush, owing to higher real wages.

A similar rise in the United States is noticeable. In the decades just before the arrival of motor transport, it was reckoned in the United States that it was quite uneconomic for anyone much more than 100 km. from the railway to attempt to produce wheat. This would indeed be the case, if transport costs were of the order of magnitude of $3\frac{1}{2}$ kg. wheat/ton km., which transport costs would, in effect, use up a third of the crop in transporting it to the railway. Thorn[1] pointed out that there were 1·3 million hectares of good land in the American Great Plains which in 1920 were still more than 130 kilometres from the railway, entailing, quite apart from the question of cost, 4 to 6 days' time to make a round trip by horse wagon to the railway line. This area was, in effect, made cultivable by the advent of motor transport. In Australia, the economic limit was generally adjudged at a shorter distance. When the West Australian Railways were constructed, a reasonable distance over which a settler could be expected to carry his produce, particularly wheat, was considered to be about $12\frac{1}{2}$ miles.[2] The consequence, in both countries, was a close network of railway branches (many of which have since been abandoned, but clearly discernible on contemporary maps) demarcating the 'wheat belt'.

Renshaw describes the average Turkish ox cart as carrying a quarter ton and only travelling 8 km./day. The University of Madras however reports wagons carrying over half a ton for short distances.

In England, between the 1780s and the 1830s, there was a substantial reduction in real transport costs, which Jackman attributes to the macadamizing of the roads. On routes where rail competition was beginning to make itself felt in the 1830s, he states that road charges were reduced to 5d./ton mile.

---

[1] *World Population Conference*, 1954.
[2] *Royal Commission on West Australian Government Railways*, p. 4, quoted *Economic Record*, December 1963, p. 474.

Transport costs can be substantially reduced by using boats. The high cost of land transport explains why so many ancient and mediaeval cities were built on the sea or on navigable rivers. The Aztecs, whose only land transport was by head-loading, built their capital city by a large lake, thereby facilitating the collecting of supplies over a greater distance than would have been possible otherwise.

We find rather similar real costs of water transport prevailing in ancient Rome and Egypt, in seventeenth-century England, and in modern China. On the River Nile, boats of $5\frac{1}{2}$ tons capacity were used, which greatly reduced costs, as compared with smaller boats, but larger boats were used in Roman sea transport. Jasny estimated that Roman sea transport costs, expressed as wheat equivalent/ton km., were only about three times those of modern shipping. Relative to agricultural and industrial production costs, sea transport was cheap in the ancient world, and the carriage of goods over comparatively long distances was therefore quite economic.

In England, navigation on the Mersey and Irwell was fairly straightforward, but the Thames was considerably obstructed by weirs. Moreover the river journey from London to Oxford was 2·1 times the length of the road journey. The figures in the table are per river mile, and upstream; downstream rates were about 25 per cent lower. On the canals, the water routes also generally worked out at almost twice the length of the road routes. Costs by canal were comparable with those on the Thames, because the locks imposed considerable costs and delays.

The figures for United States water transport, on the other hand, are computed per km. of *direct* route.

As wages rose and wagon transport became more expensive, the economic advantages of the canals and rivers, with the possibility of putting a much greater load under the charge of one man (at the cost of much greater capital outlay) became more apparent. The use of steam boats brought much further advantage. In the United States they were already in use in the 1820s; and the whole development of the Continent would have been far slower without them. Where rivers and canals are comparatively broad and unobstructed, they have been able to remain in active competition with railways as a means of transport to this day.

As might have been expected, costs on the early railway systems were high, and in Australia were still high in the 1870s. But as the techniques of railway operations improved, costs could be brought down, even on the smaller and more isolated systems.

When goods transport by road motor vehicle first made its appearance, for example in China, its costs were inordinately high. In the 1920s road motor transport was still a comparatively high cost form of transport in Europe, used only for fairly short distances to save the extra loading and unloading required for a railway journey. In recent years it has still been very costly in some of the remoter parts of East Africa (although the very high figure quoted by the Royal Commission appears to be exaggerated). In very sparsely populated mountain country, where the tracks are rough and the jeep is the only possible motor vehicle, costs are very high, as seen in Basutoland. Indeed under these circumstances air transport of goods costs almost exactly the same as jeep transport. Naturally, the costs go down as the roads improve — see for instance the difference between the northern Nigerian average, and the costs for the more developed southern regions. In areas with good roads, such as Ceylon and the Delhi region in India, costs have been brought right down, and are now comparable with those of the railways. Railway charges have to be much lower than road charges if they are to offset road transport's greater quickness and convenience, and its avoidance of double handling.

Some African countries, it will be seen, do already enjoy a fairly good road system and low costs. A report on Senegal[1] includes an interesting diagram showing how costs of motor transport rise with distance from Dakar; but even in the remotest part of the country they are still only 1·7 kg. paddy/ton km. Data on retail prices of the principal commodities purchased by rural families show a price difference between Dakar and the remotest regions of only 36 per cent — less than might have been expected. Figures for Dahomey show a heavy fall in charges as the length of the journey increases from 50 to 200 km., but with little further fall for greater distances. They also show an undesirable feature, namely that the transport operators, who are presumably organized in a cartel, are discriminating against the high-value products, a practice which has been traditional in fixing railway rates. The figures quoted in the table are for maize and millet. But the charges for the most valuable product, palm oil, are 2·4 times as high, while for sweet potato they are 25–50 per cent lower.

Sargent[2] ascertains the costs of a 5-ton vehicle at 17 pence/

[1] *Les Flux de Transport dans la République du Sénégal*, Compagne d'Études Industrielles et d'Aménagement du Territoire.

[2] *Report on Transport Requirements in the Light of Economic Developments in North Borneo*, 1960. Exchange converted at $8·4 Borneo/£.

vehicle km. in Borneo, and estimates that a third of these costs could be saved by the use of bituminized roads as compared with 'improved earth'. Hawkins[1] is considering cheaper transport in Africa, at costs which we may assume at 12 pence/vehicle km. for a 5-ton vehicle, of which he considers only 15 per cent could be saved by providing a bituminized surface as compared with gravel (two-fifths of this saving is on the depreciation of the vehicle). An alternative estimate, however,[2] makes the relative saving twice as high. In West Africa, where road transport costs in general are considerably lower, Pedler[3] puts the savings from bituminization at 18 per cent. Conversion from an unmade road to an 'earth track capable of carrying 15-ton lorries', according to Pedler, saved 25 per cent of transport costs. The costs recorded for short-distance road transport in Syria had recently been reduced by 30 per cent through the surfacing of the first 8 km. of earth road leading to the main road.

CHART XX

OPTIMAL ROAD SYSTEMS IN VENEZUELA

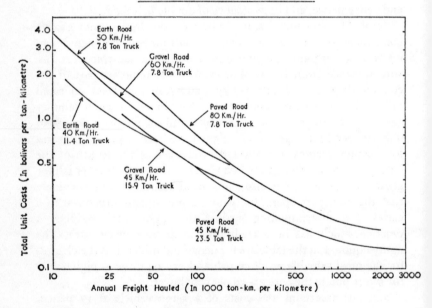

---

[1] E. K. Hawkins, *Road Transport in Nigeria*, O.U.P., 1958.
[2] R. S. Millard, 'Road Development in the Overseas Territories', *Journal of the Royal Society of Arts*, Vol. 107, p. 5032, March 1959.
[3] F. J. Pedler, *Economic Geography of West Africa*, London, 1955.

Reviewing the available evidence, Hawkins suggests that when traffic reaches 300 vehicles/day, bituminization becomes worth while.

A much lower estimate of only 100,000 tons of freight annually was made[1] for the point at which it became economical to construct a paved road, on the assumption that large trucks were used; but the equilibrium point was probably only about 200,000 tons/year with medium-size trucks. The calculations were made at costs of 1961, and assumed a 10 per cent interest rate. The bolivar is worth 21·8 American cents or 3·1 kg. of grain.

In India Healey, with smaller vehicles and lower wages, estimates much lower operating costs, and at the same time much higher numbers of vehicles/day required to justify conversion.

TABLE XLVIII. ROADS IN INDIA

	Operating costs kg. grain equivalent/ vehicle-km.	Estimated number of vehicles/day required to justify conversion
Unmetalled road — Earth	0·51	
do. — Gravel	0·45	
Waterbound Macadam	0·41	315
Bitumen	0·25	410
Concrete	0·22	1820

Each km. of road built, Sargent estimates, has the effect of opening some 60 ha. of new agricultural land. He estimates further that each pound spent on road building has the effect of permanently raising gross agricultural production in Borneo by as much as £4/year. This result, however, he points out, must not be taken at its face value. It is true that road building attracts new settlers into an area, who immediately become productive; but population and labour are scarce factors in Borneo, and the growth of production following upon the construction of a new road may be at the expense of production elsewhere.

It has been estimated[2] that a traffic of 500,000 tons/year will justify building a railway, even under North American conditions; a traffic less than 250,000 tons/year, on the other hand, will justify the abandonment of an existing railway. Under European conditions it is estimated to be worth while building a railway for a traffic of 350,000 tons/year.

[1] Soberman, *The Cost of Road Transportation in Venezuela*, Corporación Venezolana de Guayana, 1963, quoted Fromm and others, *Transportation Investment and Economic Development*.
[2] Owen, *Strategy for Mobility*, Brookings Institution, p. 7.

TABLE XLIX. ESTIMATES OF COST OF ROADS

	Construction Costs				Maintenance Cost: Borneo £/km./year
	Pakistan[1]	Borneo £/km.	East Africa[2]	India[3]	
Original earth road or jeep track	1750	1080	620	370	
Do. in mountain country	5850				
Gravelled roads[a]	2040	2170	2490		90
Metalled roads[a]	4040	5800	⎱7460	1540	140
Additional costs for bituminizing metalled road	1930[c]	2900	⎰	1060	150[b]
Additional costs for macadamizing unmetalled road				1360	
Concrete road				3850	
Additional cost for concreting macadamized road				3500	

[a] Specified as 3·65 metres width in Pakistan.
[b] Hawkins estimates 115.
[c] £440 each for two coats of tar surfacing plus £1050 for a carpet of 3·8 cm. (half that cost if carpet 2·5 cm.). The above however are all for a road of 3·65 m. width — well trafficked bituminous roads should be widened to 6 m. (20 feet).

The essential role of transport is to permit the exchange of goods between the cultivators and urban centres, whereby it becomes possible (and without which it is impossible) for the economic position of the cultivator to rise above subsistence level, consuming locally grown food and simple handicrafts produced in his own village, and practically nothing else; while in the absence of transport towns could not exist at all.

Before we consider the growth of towns, and their dependence upon transport, we should bear in mind certain effects of the lack of transport on the agricultural sector itself. The extraordinary differences between villages in the same region found by Buck in

[1] The costs and advantages of improving roads have been studied in the North-West Frontier Province of Pakistan and were privately communicated by the Provincial Government Offices. The prices quoted were converted at the old exchange rates of 13.3 rupees/£ and then raised 25 per cent to bring them up to date.
[2] E. K. Hawkins, Roads and Road Transport in an Underdeveloped Country, A case study of Uganda, 1962, p. 203.
[3] At new exchange rate of 21 rupees/£. Data from Healey, The Development of Social Overhead Capital in India, p. 94.

China, with some villages starving and others with an obvious surplus of food, can only be explained in terms of an almost complete lack of transport. In Thailand, where transport is very inadequate, Zimmerman[1] found that the fertile delta region of the Menam Plain suffered violent fluctuations in the local price of rice, which threatened to disrupt the whole social economy, which arose from the fact that certain areas almost entirely lacked normal marketing and transport facilities. There appeared to be many regions in Thailand, at present almost uninhabited, which could be made very productive; others, such as the fertile alluvial soil region in central Thailand, are already very densely populated. A transfer of labour from one region to the other would benefit everybody; but this cannot be considered till transport has been improved. Within a single village in West Bengal[2] there was evidence that, as access to markets improved, a larger proportion of the crop was offered for sale, even by the poor cultivators. The comparatively low income elasticity of demand of Japanese cultivators for the food which they had produced themselves, and the correspondingly high income elasticity of demand for other goods, could not have been possible except in a country with good transport and communications.

It is clear that the origin of urban settlements depends upon transport; not only their food, but also their fuel and building materials, constituting loads of similar orders of magnitude, have to be brought from a distance. The cities established by the Aztecs, the Incas and the Maya, who had no means of transport except head-loading, are the exception which proves the rule. They appear to have required a very authoritative form of society, and the imposition of heavy duties upon all able-bodied men, just in the performance of transport; and we have Gourou's opinion that the Maya civilization broke down through soil exhaustion, consequent upon the attempt to go on growing maize without fertilizers in the areas immediately adjacent to their cities, presumably because they could not face the prospect of having to transport it from a distance.

The first towns were (and we can say of some parts of the world today, still are) military strongholds, seats of kings or administrators, and religious centres. The performers of these functions required an inflow of substantial quantities of food, fuel and build-

[1] C. C. Zimmerman, *Siam Rural Economic Survey*, 1930–31.
[2] Mandal, 'The Marketable Surplus of Aman Paddy in East Indian Villages', *Indian Journal of Agricultural Economics*, January–March 1961, p. 51.

H

ing materials. Rather later, towns have developed their commercial functions, calling also for an outward movement of certain types of goods. Nevertheless, the early urban civilizations tended to grow up, not only where good sea and river transport was available, but also on arid (and therefore fertile) land where perennially high yields could be obtained by irrigation (e.g. Jericho, Egypt, Iraq and the Indus valley).

One of the great technical improvements of the classical world was in the building of ships, though it did not shine in land transport. In mediaeval Europe the techniques of land transport, and also of ploughing, were potentially considerably improved by the invention of the horse collar (whose date is uncertain); though in fact most subsistence cultivators were too poor to keep horses, and oxen with their heavy yokes continued to be used both for ploughing and for transport until comparatively recent times. But the improvements in shipbuilding made possible the transport over considerable distances, not only of goods whose value was high in relation to their weight, such as hides, wool and metals, but also of grain, wine and timber. But away from waterways the average village still depended upon high-cost land transport, could not therefore in fact sell any substantial proportion of its agricultural product, and had to rely upon its own handicrafts for most of its non-agricultural requirements.

This examination of the economics of mediaeval Europe is more than an academic exercise. If for the concept of waterways we substitute that of waterways plus a limited number of lines of modern rail and road transport, the economy of many Asian and African villages today, if they are more than a few miles removed from railways and main roads, remains very similar to that of the more backward villages of mediaeval Europe.

It was not until the mid-eighteenth century in western Europe that a road system as good as that of the Roman Empire was again in use. This is illustrated in an interesting manner by the fact that horse-drawn sleeping cars were in widespread use in the third century A.D. Apparently the Very Important Persons of those days travelled with a speed and comfort not subsequently equalled till a sleeping car was built for Napoleon, and he probably had to put up with much rougher roads. This improvement in roads made possible the replacement of pack horses by wagons, with consequent reduction of goods transport costs.

While efficient transport is a condition necessary for the growth of cities, we must not assume that it alone is sufficient. There is also an implicit political condition, which is of more fundamental importance. The complex economic network necessary to support a city cannot be constructed except under conditions of political stability and security. The cultivator, trader, and craftsman cannot safely enter into a system of mutual economic dependence until they can trust the rulers of the city to protect them alike from invasion from without and disturbances from within. Recurring wars and revolutions create an atmosphere of insecurity which eventually makes men unwilling to take the risks involved in any form of economic specialization. Society then slips back into a simpler form of household economy or, at best, a village economy, as it did in Europe at the break-up of the Roman Empire — and on many other occasions in history.

In England, even in the days of pack-horse transport, small manufacturing centres had sprung up in Birmingham and Sheffield, from which high valued metal goods were distributed by pack horse. But generally speaking manufacture, as we understand the word, namely the continuous processing of goods for distribution to a large market, is absolutely dependent upon reasonably cheap transport.

A transport economy depending primarily upon wagons travelling along improved roads, as in the later eighteenth century, made possible the growth of quite large cities. But their growth was certainly held in check by transport considerations. From information given by Arthur Young, it is possible to draw contours showing steadily rising prices as London was approached. This in turn necessitated considerably high money wages (though probably not real wages) in London than elsewhere; which factor in turn checked the growth of manufactures there.

Railway transport (mechanical road transport in the modern world) brings about the greatest *relative* reduction in the costs of transport of heavy and bulky goods. Its effects upon agriculture are more immediate than upon industry; it becomes feasible to transport away from the producing areas even comparatively low-valued crops. From the proceeds of these sales the cultivator is able to buy numerous cheap manufactured goods, and to dispense with the high-priced products produced by the village weavers and other craftsmen, who are thus forced to seek urban employment, or remain persistently underemployed. We can see this tragic but unavoidable process occurring in England about the 1830s, in

India about fifty years later, as the railways spread, and we can see it happening in some parts of the world now.

Of equal importance, however, is the fact that, while subsistence agriculture had to produce all the local requirements of food and fibre, once modern transport has been introduced geographical specialization of agriculture rapidly follows, with consequent further increases in productivity.

CHAPTER XIII

The Role of Agriculture in National Economic Development

As a subsistence economy develops, (a) it consumes more of its own food, (b) it is able to divert a gradually increasing proportion of its labour force to non-agricultural tasks, and (c) it trades more with the rest of the world. In low-income countries, a high proportion of the whole labour force is engaged in agriculture.

In China, Buck recorded that 20 per cent of the men had occupations other than agriculture, and that a further 14 per cent, though predominantly agricultural, also followed some other activities. A total of 83½ per cent of the working population occupied in agriculture, forestry and fishing was shown for Japan in 1872.[1] The Census for Thailand showed 84 per cent occupied in agriculture in 1929. For Nicaragua it was 84 per cent in 1920 and 78 per cent in 1940, for Bulgaria 81 per cent in 1910 and 78 per cent in 1934. There may, it is true, be a certain ambiguity in these figures, with the inclusion in agriculture of some who have part-time activities elsewhere.

The causes explaining a decline in agricultural employment are complex. We have to take into account the declining income elasticity of demand for food, in comparison with other products, as real income rises, and also the increasing efficiency of agricultural production. But international trade in agricultural products has also to be taken into account.

The time has not yet come for the preparation of a full economic model, or system of equations, to describe the inter-relationship between these phenomena. The rise in food consumption depends upon the income elasticity of demand for food which, we have seen, is very variable between different times and communities, and itself appears to depend upon the availability, and price, of other goods. We should expect increasing productivity to increase demand for imports; but it does not do so in a manner precisely

[1] Kimura, *Annals of the Hitotsubashi University*, April 1956.

predictable. The amount imported may be influenced by the exchange rate and by the terms of trade, for there are also certain possibilities of substitution between imports and home-produced goods. Moreover, as we shall see below, some countries, at a given level of real income per head, require considerably more imports than others.

Nor do we yet know how relative preferences for goods and leisure are affected by rising productivity. At subsistence levels of production labour in economic activity is very limited, and indeed a certain amount of ceremonial or leisure activity is regarded as socially necessary. But linkage with the exchange economy has raised the demand ceiling because it has brought a wide range of consumer goods within reach of individual producers, inducing increased productivity even among the poorest families, who badly want money to purchase these goods. After all, a somewhat similar leisure-preference relationship now prevails in the western world, with the wealthiest company directors working about 1500 hours/ year in all, while heads of poor families will continue working overtime to bring their year up to 2500 hours or more.

One or two useful empirical relationships between these variables have however been discovered, which enable us to carry the analysis a stage further.

Following de Vries, stages of economic development were first measured by computing grain equivalents of agricultural (including non-food) production/population. In the least-developed communities, the ratio of agricultural population to total population is high, and can be assumed not to vary significantly. But as we advance up the income scale, the proportion of agricultural population may be reduced considerably. Here the figure (grain equivalent of all agricultural production/agricultural population) appears more suitable for our purpose.

In a preliminary analysis, in which an attempt was made to relate the above variable to imports (also expressed in grain equivalents/population) certain discrepancies were noticed in countries having large exports of minerals or forest products. It became clear that such exports can directly 'substitute' for agricultural products in purchasing required imports, thus setting more of the agricultural production free to feed industrial workers in the country, or for other purposes. The same applies to the small quantities of manufactured exports which some of these countries produce (though in measuring these we should exclude their raw-material content, otherwise we may count it twice). These non-agricultural exports are therefore converted to grain equivalents on the basis of current world prices, and added to agricultural production to give what is best defined as 'exportable product (though most of the food produced is not in fact exported). The production of minerals, forest products and manufactures for internal use cannot at this stage be measured, and has to be left out of the calculation.

While census data for countries with a large proportion of subsistence agriculturists generally give precise information of the numbers actually at work in non-agricultural occupations, they often show for the agricultural community only the total numbers supported by agriculture, without any very clear distinction between workers and dependants — which would in any case be very difficult to obtain, in view of the large amount of part-time

TABLE L. NON-AGRICULTURAL EXPORTS
EXPRESSED IN KG. ECONOMIC WHEAT EQUIVALENT/
PERSON/YEAR

	Timber and Forest Products	Minerals	Manufactured Goods
North Africa			
Algeria	—	59	44
Egypt	—	11	28
Ethiopia	—	—	1
Libya	—	6	9
Morocco	4	185	7
Sudan	—	—	4
Tunisia	5	137	51
Rest of Africa			
Angola	10	66	33
Cameroun	22	45	—
Congo and Ruanda Urundi	4	170	7
Former French Equatorial Africa	110	27	—
Former French West Africa (excl. Guinea)	14	—	—
Ghana	95	155	4
Guinea	—	20	—
Kenya	3	16	3
Liberia	—	276	—
Nigeria and British Cameroons	6		2

	Timber and Forest Products	Minerals	Manufactured Goods
Rhodesia and Nyasaland	—	468	35
South Africa	23	354	271
Tanzania	5	22	4
Togo	—	—	—
Near East			
Iran	—	226	14
Iraq	—	1189	—
Israel	—	11	543
Jordan	—	27	4
Lebanon	—	16	103
Syria	—	—	79
Turkey	1	17	4
Far East			
Burma	8	7	5
Ceylon	—	1	4
India	—	5	18
Indonesia	—	55	1
Japan	4	12	407
Malaya	15	274	47
Pakistan	—	—	5
Philippines	46	33	19
South Korea	—	5	3
Taiwan	—	1	17
Thailand	10	10	9
Latin America			
Bolivia	—	270	—
Brazil	12	23	5
Chile	13	645	24
Colombia	—	84	6
Costa Rica	—	—	29
Cuba	—	64	43
Dominican Republic	2	4	6
Ecuador	6	3	6
El Salvador	—	1	27
Guatemala	4	—	—
Haiti	—	—	5
Honduras	54	24	5
Mexico	1	83	41
Nicaragua	33	—	3
Panama	—	—	—
Paraguay	118	—	18
Peru	—	182	—
Venezuela	—	5227	—

Source: U.N. Yearbook of International Trade Statistics, 1960.

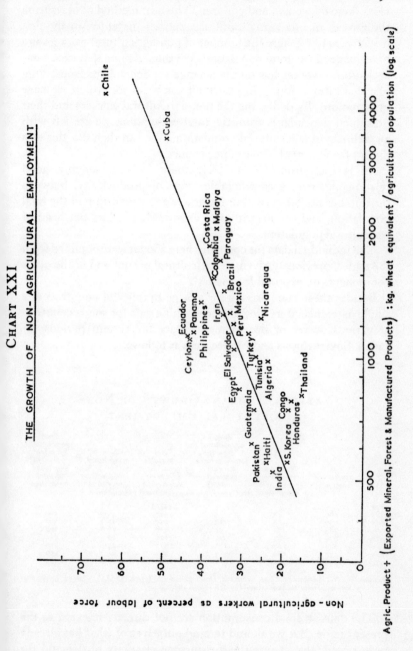

CHART XXI

THE GROWTH OF NON-AGRICULTURAL EMPLOYMENT

work done by women and children. The best method of measuring
the growth of non-agricultural occupations therefore, in the first
instance, is to measure the number of non-agricultural workers as a
percentage of the total population. We then assume that each non-
agricultural worker has on the average 1·5 dependants (something
like this ratio is found in nearly all countries for which we have
information). By deducting the non-agricultural workers and their
presumed dependants from the total population, we are left with
an estimate of 'agricultural population'. We can then use this as a
divisor for figures of 'exportable product'.

As is seen from Chart XXI, there is a reasonably good
relationship, over a considerable range of productivity, between
the number of non-agricultural workers as a proportion of the total
population, and the logarithm of exportable product per head of
agricultural population.

The individual data for countries here shown were obtained from
the tables, previously given, of agricultural output and of the other
components of 'exportable product'.

Besides these comparisons for a large number of countries at a
single date, it is interesting also to examine data for single countries
at various stages of development. Data for certain periods for
Japan, Soviet Russia and France were as follows.

TABLE LI.   JAPAN: GROWTH OF NON-AGRICULTURAL EMPLOYMENT

Year	Food production (incl. fish)	Non-food agricultural production	Non-agricultural exports (manufactures less raw material content)	Total 'exportable product' (sum of 3 previous cols.)	Non-agricultural workers as % of total population	Food consumption kg. wheat equivalent/ year/head of total population
		kg. wheat equivalent/year/head of agricultural population				
1872				(450)	7·7	
1885-9	469	45	4	518	12·6	310
1895-9	630	58	22	710	16·2	361
1905-9	785	71	54	910	18·6	387
1910-14	971	85	73	1129	19·8	442
1920-4	1380	127	210	1717	21·4	531
1925-9	1537	180	263	1980	21·3	556
1934-8	1759	212	522	2493	23·0	529

Sources: W. W. Lockwood, *The Economic Development of Japan*, O.U.P., 1955; League of
Nations, *Industrialization and Foreign Trade*, 1945.

The data on food consumption are not directly relevant to the
present issue. But we should remind ourselves of what has already
been stated, that it was the low-income elasticity of demand for

food, as income increased, which enabled Japan to divert labour to industry, and to import equipment, to so great an extent.

TABLE LII. SOVIET UNION: GROWTH OF NON-AGRICULTURAL EMPLOYMENT

Year	Population m.	Non-agricultural wage and salary workers (incl. Forces) m.	Non-agricultural wage and salary workers as % of population	Agricultural production bill. kg. wheat equivalent	Agricultural population[a] m.	Agricultural production per head of agricultural population kg. wheat equivalent
1913	139·3	9·9	7·1	147·2	114·5	1289
1926	147	9·1	6·2	141·3	124·6	1135
1939	170·6	28·5	16·7	168·9	113·6	1488
1956	200	48·3	24·1	229·9	103·4	2220

[a] Assuming 1½ dependants/worker to 1926, 1 subsequently.
Source: The Real Product of the Soviet Union, U.S. Senate publication, 1961.

N.B. Considerable boundary changes took place in 1918-21 and 1940-5. Figures for 1913 refer to 1921-40 boundaries; for 1956 refer to contemporary boundaries.

CHART XXII

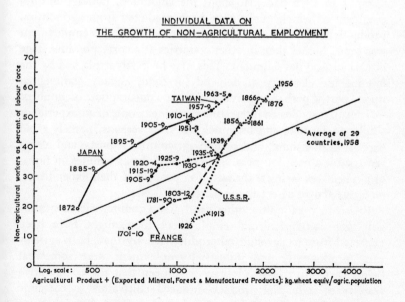

INDIVIDUAL DATA ON
THE GROWTH OF NON—AGRICULTURAL EMPLOYMENT

TABLE LIII. FRANCE: GROWTH OF NON-AGRICULTURAL EMPLOYMENT

Year	Productivity kg. wheat equivalent per head of agricultural population	Non-agricultural workers as % of total population
1701–10	680	4–6
1781–90	976	8·8
1803–12	1104	9·2
1856	1656	19·1
1861	1772	19·3
1866	1912	22·6
1876	2024	22·3

Source: Toutain, *Cahiers d'ISEA*, No. 115, Tables 141 and 145 (1 Franc of 1905–14 purchasing power equivalent to 4 kg. wheat). *Études et Conjoncture*, May 1953 (for non-agricultural workers from 1856).

Japan in 1872 had just about the amount of non-agricultural employment which might have been predicted from agricultural productivity. In the subsequent decades however this employment was much higher than in other countries at a corresponding stage of agricultural development. This may be partly explained by the low income elasticity of demand for food, already commented upon, partly perhaps by relatively low consumption of imports.

Taiwan provides an interesting further example of an experience similar to Japan's, and for much the same reasons, namely rapid expansion of fishing, and of non-agricultural exports, and also a remarkable abstemiousness. Shen (p. 295) shows families on farms of 1–2 hectares saving at the rate of 11 per cent of their expenditure, on farms of over 2 hectares 23 per cent.

Russia in 1913, on the other hand, was a country with considerably *less* non-agricultural employment than might have been expected from its agricultural productivity. By 1926, both agricultural productivity and industrial employment were somewhat below their 1913 levels. It may have been that the comparative scarcity of industrial products induced cultivators to consume more of their own produce. In the subsequent decades these

TABLE LIV. TAIWAN: AGRICULTURAL PRODUCTIVITY AND NON-AGRICULTURAL EMPLOYMENT

	1905–9	1910–14	1915–19	1920–4	1925–9	1930–4	1935–9	1951–3	1957–9	1963–5
Population millions[a]	3·15	3·37	3·57	3·88	4·36	4·90	5·54	8·14	10·05	12·07
Percentage of male labour force engaged in agriculture, forestry and fishing[ab]	69·9	69·6	68·0	66·2	65·6	64·4	62·6	51·5	47·7	(42·5)
Millions of tons wheat equivalent:										
Agricultural production[c]	1·62	1·73	2·04	2·20	2·84	3·44	4·16	4·50	6·29	7·79
Fish production[d]	0·16	0·17	0·20	0·22	0·28	0·34	0·40	0·42	0·80	1·23
Non-agricultural exports[e]				(0·10)	0·21	0·22	0·23	0·04	0·65	3·13
Agricultural and 'substitutes' production total	1·78	1·90	2·24	2·52	3·33	4·00	4·79	4·96	7·74	12·15
Do. per head of agricultural population kg.	810	810	838	856	993	1091	1384	1075	1310	1518

[a] Earlier data interpolated from census results of 1905, 1915, 1920, 1930, 1935 and 1940.

[b] Last three columns based on 1956 census and interpolated and extrapolated from agricultural population data from *Taiwan Agricultural Yearbook*, quoted Shen, *Agricultural Development of Taiwan*, p. 354.

[c] Based on 1958 (data in Chapter V), extrapolated by FAO Production Index and by Ho's index (*Agricultural Development of Taiwan, 1903–60*). Seed and fodder excluded.

[d] Shen, loc. cit, pp. 70, 252. Most recent figures from FAO Consumption Statistics. Before 1935 assumed proportional to agriculture.

[e] Excluding raw-material content of textiles. The 1964 total includes 20 per cent of forest products and 17 per cent of the manufacturing component of refined sugar exports.

relationships were violently transformed; though Soviet Russia does not appear to be any more 'above the line' now than Japan has been.

Eighteenth- and early nineteenth-century France also shows industrial employment 'below the line'; though even in the 1780s France was not so far below as Russia in 1913 or 1926. Lack of transport and communication, in each case, must be regarded as the principal cause.

The violent upward shift of the relationship in Russia in the 1930s was brought about by the forcible 'collectivization' of farming. Japan also showed a strong upward shift in the 1870s, brought about in this case by the imposition of a very severe land tax. In France, on the other hand, a similar climb, though less rapid, took place in the ordinary course of commercial development. Some say that the widespread industrialization of any country can only be brought about by an impulse of somewhat violent and, from the point of view of those living at the time, unpleasant character. If we have to choose between a land tax and compulsory collectivization, a land tax is probably the lesser evil. It is no use, however, attempting to apply it in those parts of Africa where population densities are so low that land in consequence has little, if any, selling value.

CHAPTER XIV

Trade, Aid and Development[1]

Alarger country is more likely to find opportunities of production within its own borders, and therefore to require
less imports per head, than a smaller. To state the issue
more precisely, if country B has only half the real income per head
of country A, but twice the population, so that the aggregate real
incomes of the two countries are the same, then their imports may
also be expected to be about the same in volume. Attempts to
explain volume of imports per head for various countries at
different times as a function of real income per head have not
proved very satisfactory. But an analysis[2] by one of the authors of
imports as a function of total national product, irrespective of
whether its size was due to population or to high per head income,
proved satisfactory. (After all, it is the scale of the market which
determines the possibility of establishing a greater variety of
industries in a country, largely irrespective of whether the market
has arisen through size of population, or through level of real
income per head.) A range of cases in which aggregate net real
product, measured in dollars of 1950 purchasing power, ranged
from less than 1 billion (Norway and Finland in 1913) to 350
billion (United States at the present time), showed in general
imports varying about with the three/fourth power of national
product, subject to certain qualifications for particular countries,
explainable in terms of their geographical situation, or tariff
policy.

This conclusion was confirmed in quite an interesting way for
Japan by a time-series analysis of the 1924–37 data.[3] It was found
that changes in the logarithm of the volume of imports were well
explained by 0·74 times the logarithm of real national income plus

---

[1] Much of this chapter is reproduced, by kind permission, from 'Too Much
Food?' by Colin Clark, *Lloyds Bank Review*, Jan. 1970.
[2] *Monthly Bulletin of the Banque Nationale de Belgique*, July 1953.
See also Lynden Moore, *Bulletin of the Oxford Institute of Statistics*, Nov.
1964.
[3] Tatemoto, Institute of Social and Economic Research, Osaka University,
Discussion Paper No. 9.

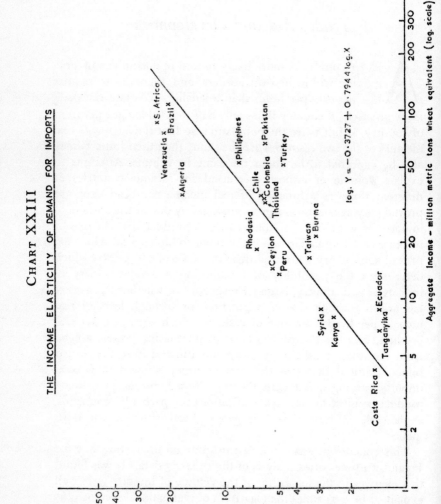

CHART XXIII

THE INCOME ELASTICITY OF DEMAND FOR IMPORTS

Aggregate Income – million metric tons wheat equivalent (log. scale)

Aggregate Imports – million metric tons wheat equivalent (log. scale)

$$\log. Y = -0.3727 + 0.7944 \log. X$$

0·279 times the logarithm of the terms of trade. The coefficient of 0·74 agrees well with that estimated from inter-country comparisons.

For the subsistence agriculture countries, however, the income elasticity of demand for imports appears to be higher than the figure of approximately three-quarters deduced for the richer countries. The comparatively low imports of India in relation to production, shown on the diagram, are to be explained, not in terms of high income per head, but of large population and high *total* product. We should, however, also bear in mind, in India's case, the very severe official restrictions placed upon imports, and the over-valuation of the rupee. It must be repeated once again that this analysis is not based on incomes per head, but on aggregate income.

The countries included in this diagram were those for which the United Nations give national product statistics. It is in respect of agricultural production, in subsistence agriculture countries, that there are the greatest discrepancies in methods of valuation. For agricultural production therefore we have used our own values, converted directly into wheat equivalents. For non-agricultural production we have taken the United Nations figures, in local currency, and converted to dollars at the current exchange rate (using the free market exchange rate where a system of multiple exchange rates prevailed). This method is crude and subject to very large errors.

The acute economic problem for the developing countries arises from their urgent need to import manufactured goods, most of which have to come from the developed countries. Machinery and chemicals are of predominant importance. The demand for chemicals is rising nearly as rapidly as the demand for machinery, and in both these sectors all but a very small proportion of the supply has to come from the developed countries.

A justifiable grievance of the developing countries arises from the fact that in order to pay for these urgently needed imports they have to export food and raw materials, in face of steadily deteriorating terms of trade. The economic difficulties of these countries are accentuated by the fact that many of them are also substantial importers of food, raw materials and fuel, as well as of manufactures.

All the values quoted in Table LV are deflated by the price index of manufactures imported into the developing countries. In other

CHART XXIV

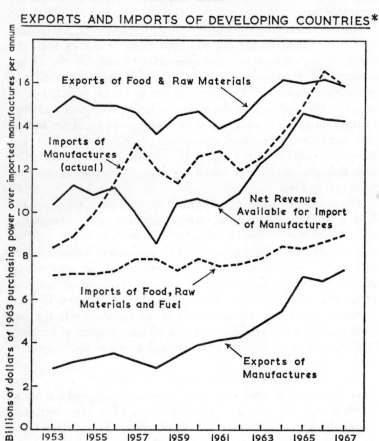

EXPORTS AND IMPORTS OF DEVELOPING COUNTRIES*

*Excluding exports of fuel (i.e. almost entirely oil) and imports purchased therewith, assumed to be 20% food and raw materials and 80% manufactures (from the experience of leading oil-exporting countries)

words, each line shows the physical quantity of manufactures purchaseable from the source specified.

It is true that imports of food, raw materials and fuel into the developing countries have been rising comparatively slowly, at the rate of only about 1·6 per cent per year, in real terms. The large imports of food into India and Pakistan which have been necessary in recent years (and which, it is hoped, will soon be unnecessary)

TABLE LV. TRADE OF DEVELOPING COUNTRIES
(ALL VALUES EXPRESSED IN TERMS OF THEIR PURCHASING POWER OVER
MANUFACTURED IMPORTS)

Billions of Dollars at 1963 Prices[a]

	1953	1954	1955	1956	1957	1958	1959	1960	1961	1962	1963	1964	1965	1966	1967	Rate of growth % per year (calculated from 1953-5 and 1965-7 averages)
Exports of food and raw materials	14·7	15·4	15·0	15·0	14·7	13·7	14·5	14·7	13·9	14·4	15·4	16·2	16·0	16·2	15·9	0·6
Exports of manufactures	2·8	3·6	3·3	3·5	3·2	2·9	3·4	3·9	4·1	4·3	4·9	5·5	7·1	6·9	7·4	7·3
Deduct imports of food, raw materials and fuel	7·1	7·2	7·2	7·3	7·9	7·9	7·4	7·9	7·6	7·7	7·9	8·5	8·4	8·7	9·0	1·6
Balance available for import of manufactures	10·4	11·3	10·9	11·2	10·0	8·7	10·5	10·7	10·4	11·0	12·4	13·2	14·7	14·4	14·3	2·4
Actual import of manufactures[b]	8·4	8·9	10·0	11·5	13·2	12·0	11·4	12·6	12·9	12·0	12·6	13·7	15·0	16·6	15·9	4·7

a Excluding exports of fuel (i.e. almost entirely oil) and imports purchased therewith. These latter are assumed to be 20 per cent food and raw materials and 80 per cent manufactures (proportions obtained from the experience of leading oil-exporting countries).
b F.O.B. value.

have helped to keep the figure up. There are some important trading countries, such as Hong Kong and Singapore, which unavoidably have to import nearly all their food supplies. There are other countries, such as Ceylon and Malaysia, which have to import food because their own agriculture is so highly specialized towards export production; and also some of the urban and mining districts in Africa, which have to live on imported food, simply because their internal transport system is insufficient to enable them to live off the produce of their own country's agriculture. Strenuous efforts are being made by the developing countries concerned to reduce their dependence on imported food, and also on imported fuel if they are lucky enough to strike oil or gas. Some reduction in this total may eventually be possible.

The encouraging feature of the situation is the increasing exports of manufactures from the developing countries. It is true that Hong Kong and Singapore account for 22 per cent of the total, and that the figures have been a little distorted by the political separation of Singapore from Malaysia. But there are some other encouraging success stories, particularly Taiwan and South Korea, which until recently were exporting only agricultural produce, and are now rapidly developing industrial exports. In Taiwan, industrial exports developed rapidly as American financial aid began to taper off, and it is hard not to see here cause and effect.

To industrialize to sell in a protected internal market, as India and Australia have done, is one thing; it is quite a different matter to produce industrial exports which the world market will accept.

Returning to the table, we see that industrial exports of the developing countries do not yet, however, pay for their imports of food, raw materials and fuel, quite apart from their requirements of manufactures.

By adding the two sources of export revenue and deducting the imports of food, raw materials and fuel, we obtain the net real revenue remaining for the purchase of manufactured imports. This figure shows an upward trend of only 2·4 per cent per year.

The actual imports of manufactures into the developing countries, ever since 1955, have been higher than the amount available to pay for them from these sources. In the middle 1950s the developing countries, considered collectively, were still paying some of their export proceeds into reserves; but the excess imports in subsequent years have been paid for partly by drawing on

reserves, and partly by grants and loans from the developed
countries and from international organizations.

It is this discrepancy, which has now persisted for a decade and
a half, which is leading us towards a crisis. The whole precarious
system of aid to the developing countries may break down, as the
burden of interest and repayments on past loans inexorably
increases.

The rate of growth of the developing countries' imports of
manufactures, largely machinery and chemicals, which they
cannot hope to produce for themselves for many years to come, of
4·7 per cent per year in real terms, is a very modest one. Their
imports as a whole, including food, raw materials and fuel, have
been rising at the rate of 3·5 per cent per year, also in real terms.
This is exactly the rate of growth of volume of imports we should
expect if we take the rate of growth of real national product of the
developing countries at 5 per cent per year (this was the United
Nations objective, which has in fact nearly been attained), and
apply to it a factor of 0·7. The reasons for expecting demand for
imports, in real terms, to rise at a rate (expressed in per cent per
year) of seven-tenths of the rate of rise of total national product,
also expressed in per cent per year, have already been given.

Planners in the developing countries, almost without exception,
have suffered from the delusion that they would be able to replace
the greater part of their manufactured imports with home products.
They failed to realize that every new industry established generates,
particularly in its early stages, an inordinate demand for imported
components and equipment. There have been some deplorable
cases, particularly in Pakistan and Argentina, where careful calculations have shown that excessive protection for certain products
has even led to an actual net loss of foreign exchange. Even industrially advanced countries such as Australia have found that rising
national product leads to a whole host of new demands, many of
which can only be satisfied by imports.

We should be fully aware of the desperate urgency for the
developing countries to increase their export revenues. They have
been raising the quantum of their exports of food and raw materials
at the rate of 2·5 per cent per year. But they have been selling them
at steadily worsening terms of trade, and the purchasing power of
these exports over manufactured imports has risen on the average
at the rate of only 0·6 per cent per year.

We do not have to look long at Table LVI or Chart XXV to see the principal factor at work. The world demand for food and raw materials internationally traded has in fact been rising at the quite respectable rate of 4·4 per cent per year, measured in volume. But the lion's share of this market has been taken by exporters from the developed countries who are now exporting nearly *twice* as much food and raw materials as the developing countries.

If we are taking a long view, we may begin to discuss in which

CHART XXV

FOOD AND RAW MATERIALS EXPORTS

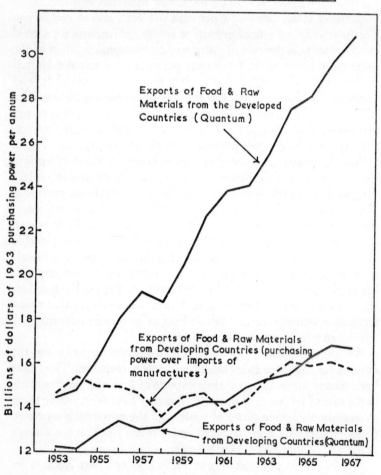

TABLE LVI. QUANTUM OF FOOD AND RAW MATERIALS EXPORTED (BEFORE TAKING INTO ACCOUNT CHANGE IN TERMS OF TRADE AGAINST MANUFACTURES)

$ billion at 1963 prices

	1953	1954	1955	1956	1957	1958	1959	1960	1961	1962	1963	1964	1965	1966	1967	Rate of growth % per year (calculated from 1953–5 and 1965–7 averages)
Developing countries	12·2	12·1	12·8	13·4	13·0	13·1	[13·9	14·3	14·3	15·0	15·4	15·7	16·4	16·9	16·8	2·5
Developed countries	14·4	14·8	16·3	18·2	19·3	18·8	20·5	22·8	23·9	24·2	25·7	27·7	28·3	29·8	31·0	5·8
World	26·6	26·9	29·1	31·6	32·3	31·9	34·4	37·1	38·2	39·2	41·1	43·4	44·7	46·7	47·8	4·4

parts of the world increased production can be most economically carried out. But for the next decade or so, whatever arguments may be advanced against it, most of this increase in agricultural production will have to come in the developing countries. They will not be able to increase their manufactured exports much faster than they are now doing, and there is no prospect of their receiving greatly increased loans and grants; so we are left with the inescapable conclusion that it is only through increased agricultural production that they can produce enough exports to buy their urgently needed imports.

The amount of agricultural produce which the subsistence agriculture countries will seek to sell on the world market will certainly increase during the coming decade. As is shown below, with the lowest assumption about productivity, and the highest assumption about their internal elasticity of consumption, the quantity offered for sale (including certain quantities of minerals, forest products, etc.) will rise from ten billion to thirteen billion dollars of present-day purchasing power. On the opposite assumptions however, of rapid productivity increase and low internal elasticity, the rise will be to over twenty-three billion dollars.

Another empirical discovery, which greatly simplifies analysis, is that in the early stages of development from subsistence agriculture it is permissible to treat average real income per head for the whole country as not very different from the agricultural productivity figure. It is true that average incomes per head in the non-agricultural pursuits are generally somewhat higher, but an important study by Umemura[1] for Japan, concerning the period of rapid economic growth from 1900 to 1920, shows comparatively slight differences, over this period, between average earnings of wage-earners in agriculture and in manufacture. The ratio between the earnings of labour in agriculture, and average net income produced per person engaged in agriculture, did not change much over the period, even though there were considerable oscillations in the rate at which labour was flowing from agriculture to industry. The principal effect of these temporary oscillations in the net rate of flow of labour into industry was to change wage-earnings (relative to profits) in industry. This study gives us a valuable idea of the mechanism of the flow of labour out of agriculture in a country emerging from subsistence economy. It appears to be, to a considerable extent, a self-regulating flow; if it becomes too rapid,

[1] Umemura, *Economic Survey of Japanese Agriculture*, 1956.

industrial wages fall strongly, and discourage it for the time being.

From the relationship between the logarithm of agricultural productivity, and the number of non-agricultural workers as a proportion of the population, we can do some interesting algebra relating
the rate of improvement of agricultural productivity, the rate of
growth of population as a whole, and the absolute increase or
decrease of agricultural population. During the period of the most
rapid increase of Japanese agricultural productivity, between 1900
and 1925, agricultural production per head of rural population was
rising at about 3·5 per cent per year; and agricultural population
was about stationary. Rural population having been about 60 per
cent of the whole at the beginning of the period, it can be shown
that this stationariness of the absolute number of rural population
would not have been compatible with a rate of general population
growth much higher than 1 per cent per annum. In other words,
the rates of population growth in the neighbourhood of 2 per cent
per annum or more now prevailing in many parts of the world are
not compatible with stationary or declining absolute numbers of
agricultural population, except in countries where the agricultural
population is already a small proportion of the whole. Where it is
30 per cent or more, as it is in all the subsistence agriculture
countries, further increases in the absolute numbers (though
decreases in the relative numbers) of people engaged in agriculture
must be expected for a long period to come, however high the rates
at which agricultural productivity is increasing.

We may make some tentative predictions for a decade of growth
on two widely varying assumptions, namely of the productivity of
the agricultural population growing by 1 per cent and by 3 per cent
per year. (Each country's output of non-agricultural 'exportable
products' is, for convenience, included here.) The calculation
includes all the low-income countries of the world, not only the
subsistence economies, but also those others whose exports for the
next decade may be expected to be predominantly agricultural.
Countries which have already reached a considerable degree of
industrialization, such as Mexico, Japan, Chile, South Africa and
Australia, are, however, excluded. For convenience in calculation,
India and mainland China are shown separately, and the other
countries grouped in ranges of exportable production/head of
agricultural population, measured in kg. grain equivalent/person.

Within each of the two differing assumptions about the rate of
growth of productivity, two further alternative assumptions are

TABLE LVII. EXPECTED INCREASES IN AGRICULTURAL PRODUCTION AND EXPORTS OF THE SUBSISTENCE AGRICULTURE COUNTRIES ON VARYING ASSUMPTIONS OF INCOME ELASTICITY OF DEMAND FOR FOOD AND RATE OF PRODUCTIVITY INCREASE

	Mainland China	India	Countries of Productivity: kg. economic wheat equivalent/head of population/year								TOTAL	Total $ bill. of 1960 purchasing power
			below 550	550–675	675–826	826–1012	1012–1240	1240–1520	1520–1861	over 1861		
Population growth 1953–60, % p.a.	1·7	1·9	1·9	2·0	2·1	1·3	3·0	3·1	2·5	3·0		
1960 population (m.)	677	433	103	166	219	67	90	125	31	7	1918	
1960 agricultural population	547	366	84	124	163	48	60	81	19	4·4	1496	
1970 expected population (on above growth rate)	800	521	124	202	269	76	121	169	40	9·4	2331	
In m. tons wheat equivalent:												
1960 production	184	174	42	79	128	44	68	112	30·6	9·0	870	
1960 net export	–6	21	1	15	28	11	18	34	12·9	5·3	137	10·1
On 1% p.a. productivity increase:												
1970 agricultural population (m.)	633	397	99	147	196	53	79	107	23·7	5·8	1740	
1970 production	235	228	55	104	170	54	98	163	42·4	13·1	1162	
1970 net export (elasticity 0·7)	–5	31	2	20	38	14	27	50	18	8	203	13·1
1970 net export (elasticity 0·3)	4	38	3	23	40	16	30	54	19	8	227	14·6
On 3% p.a. productivity increase:												
1970 agricultural population (m.)	605	378	95	140	187	50	74	101	22·3	5·5	1657	
1970 production	273	264	64	120	197	62	113	187	48·5	15·0	1343	
1970 net export (elasticity 0·7)	–2	38	3	24	46	16	31	57	21	9	243	15·6
1970 net export (elasticity 0·3)	28	63	10	35	63	22	40	72	24	10	367	23·6

Countries Included with Population in Millions

Productivity below 550		Productivity 550-675		Productivity 675-826	
Libya	1	Former French West Africa	20	Former French Equatorial Africa	4
Guinea	3	Tanganyika	9	Nigeria	35
Somaliland	2	Togo	1	Egypt	26
Haiti	4	Kenya	7	Congo and Ruanda-Urundi	20
Afghanistan	14	Ethiopia	20	Madagascar	5
Former Indochina	37	Uganda	7	Sierra Leone	2
Korea	33	Jordan	2	Guatemala	4
Nepal	9	Lebanon	2	Honduras	2
		Pakistan	93	Indonesia	93
		Yemen	5	Thailand	26
				New Guinea	2

Productivity 826-1012		Productivity 1012-1240		Productivity 1240-1520	
Angola	5	Liberia	1	Ghana	7
Sudan	12	Morocco	12	Brazil	71
Cameroons	4	Mauritius	1	Iran	20
Tunisia	4	El Salvador	3	Philippines	28
Algeria	11	Nicaragua	1		
Basutoland	1	Panama	1		
Mozambique	6	Ecuador	4		
Bolivia	3	Peru	11		
Burma	21	British Guiana	1		
		Ceylon	10		
		Taiwan	11		
		Cyprus	1		
		Syria	5		
		Turkey	28		

Productivity 1520-1861		Productivity over 1861	
Rhodesia-Nyasaland	8	Malaya	7
Costa Rica	1		
Dominican Republic	3		
West Indies	3		
Colombia	14		
Paraguay	2		

made, of a maximum of 0·7, and a minimum of 0·3, for income elasticity of demand for food.

In every case, it will be seen, a large increase in the agricultural population is expected during the decade. The higher assumption about the productivity growth, as we have postulated, requires a lesser rate of growth in agricultural population, but a greater rate of growth in total product.

What then can we best do to help the developing countries economically?

The first possibility is to continue aid in the form in which it is mainly being given now, namely loans (often at concessional rates of interest) and grants to their governments, sometimes through international organizations, generally through direct country-to-country agreements. Besides the difficulty that obligations for interest and repayment on past loans will soon swallow up the whole incoming aid, there are further objections to this method. In the first place, such governmental aid is far from fairly distributed among the developing countries, but is concentrated on countries occupying strategic positions, either military or political. If we list the developing countries according to the amount of aid received per head of population, countries such as Afghanistan, Jordan and Libya stand out far ahead of the others. Secondly, much of the aid will be wasted on 'prestige projects'.

As an alternative, more private investment might be encouraged in the developing countries.

There remains as a method of aiding the developing countries a policy of helping them to increase their exports by causing funds to flow to businessmen rather than to governments. It may be objected that businessmen in the developing countries are already too wealthy, in the light of the poverty which surrounds them. But it is necessary, whether we like it or not, to offer fairly substantial incentives, at any rate in the early stages, if we are to create a class of active businessmen; a critical factor limiting the rate of growth of the developing countries is not shortage of capital, but lack of enterprise.

The first step towards promoting exports should be the removal of the present tariff and quota restrictions. Special preferences on the exports of developing countries are indeed now being considered by the United States and Japan, and have been enacted, on a small scale, by Australia.

But this is only a first step. We should do more than remove restrictions on the developing countries' exports; we should positively encourage them. The larger countries should agree to pay a subsidy, as an *ad valorem* proportion, on all exports from the developing countries, other than staples such as sugar, coffee and cocoa, where the market is inelastic and facing over-supply.

For several reasons, it would be desirable for the wealthier countries to agree to pool the resources which they are able to give for economic aid into a common fund. From this the subsidies would then be paid at a uniform rate on all the developing countries' exports to the wealthy countries (subject to the exceptions specified above). Provision would have to be made to check re-exports of these subsidized products to other countries not parties to the agreement. In other words the wealthy countries would have to accept the burden — comparatively slight — of readapting their own industrial structure to accept substantial quantities of subsidized exports of manufactured products from the developing countries. There would remain a number of middle-income countries, who probably would not agree to accept such an obligation, though they should also agree not to impose quota restrictions, or tariffs above a certain limit, on exports from the developing countries. In return for these concessions, the developing countries should be asked to agree to mutual free trade in each other's products.

Appendix

Grains

Wheat	1·00
Wheat-flour	1·43
Rice, rough	0·80
Rice, clean	1·19
Rye	0·75
Barley	0·65
Oats	0·65
Maize	0·75
Millet	0·68
Sorghum	0·60
Buckwheat	0·65
Other grains (as maize)	0·75

Starchy roots

Potatoes	0·65
Sweet potatoes	0·30
Cassava	0·23

Vegetable oils and oilseeds

Coconuts, shelled	2·52
Groundnuts, shelled	1·83
Groundnuts, unshelled	1·10
Linseed	1·45
Cotton seed	0·87
Soybeans	1·30
Vegetable oils	3·00

Sugar

Sugar, raw	1·03
Sugar, refined	1·10
Sugar-cane	0·147

Pulses

All pulses	1·12

Fish	3·50

Fruit

Citrus	0·92
Other fresh fruit	0·68
Bananas	0·32
Cider fruit	0·10
Raisins	2·50
Dates	1·30

Vegetables

All vegetables	0·65

Wine	0·90

Livestock products

Beef and veal	6·00
Pork	7·61
Mutton and lamb	7·25
Poultry	9·86
Milk	1·30
Eggs	5·80

Fibres

Abaca	2·20
Cotton, ginned	6·50
Cotton, unginned	2·94
Flax	6·08
Hemp	5·43
Henequen	1·90
Jute	2·00
Sisal	2·20
Wool, greasy basis	11·9
Silk cocoons	12·5

Other crops

Cocoa	4·50
Coffee	5·60
Tea	9·00
Tobacco	8·00
Rubber	5·18

The weighting system is based on data given in 'International Index

Numbers of Food and Agricultural Production' by M. I. Klayman, *FAO Monthly Bulletin of Agricultural Economics and Statistics*, Vol. IX, March 1960.

ELATIVE PRICES IN AFRICA (BASED ON WHEAT = 100, OR LINKED ON OTHER GRAINS AS INDICATED)

	Cameroun	East Africa	Haute Volta	Kenya	Madagascar	Nigeria	Senegal	Tanzania	Uganda
ins									
Vheat									
Rice, rough			80					80	
Rice, clean					119				
Maize		75	60	75	32	75		53	
Millet	46		52				68		68
Sorghum	60	74	48		75			57	
rchy roots									
Potatoes				71	63		82		
weet potatoes			48		24		48	57	
Cassava		49	48		24	45	41	148	12
etable oils and oilseeds									
Groundnuts, unshelled	116	118	72		99	129	57		
Linseed									
Soybeans									
Vegetable oils							271		
gar									
Sugar, raw							177	95	
Sugar, refined				243	238				
Sugar cane					16				
ses	160				151	195	95	181	68
it	275				143		136		
Citrus					178			76	
Bananas				32	20			38	12
etables			200	71	83		98	95	
stock products									
Meat	184		380	1518	372		366		
Poultry			668		333		406		
Milk				82	79		231		
ggs					286				
es									
Cotton, unginned		190	200			145		200	
ute									
Wool, greasy basis									
er crops									
ea				1143					
obacco	511		200						

ELATIVE PRICES IN AMERICA AND ASIA (BASED ON WHEAT = 100, OR LINKED ON OTHER GRAINS AS INDICATED)

	U.S.A.	Guatemala	Mexico	China	India	Uttar Pradesh	New Guinea	Pakistan	U.S.S.R.
ins									
Vheat	100		100	96	100	100		100	
ice, rough	161	158		80	93	73		110	
ice, clean			117				112		
Maize	55	75	102	68	71	69	75	101	
Millet					92			95	
orghum					89	63		90	
rchy roots									
otatoes	45	152	84						25
weet potatoes	123						75		
assava									
etable oils and oilseeds									
roundnuts, unshelled	364				127		188		
inseed					146			187	
oybeans	114			92					
egetable oils									200

	U.S.A.	Guatemala	Mexico	China	India	Uttar Pradesh	New Guinea	Pakistan	U.S.S
Sugar									
Sugar, raw	138	139			198			171	103
Sugar, refined									
Sugar cane							75		
Pulses	208	123			88			88	
Fish		1300			73		225	265	
Fruit									
Citrus	110								
Bananas							75		
Vegetables	78								15
Livestock products									
Meat	1300	415	563	280	760			345	460
Poultry	878	660							
Milk	141				267	123		167	25
Eggs	841	870	800				600	828	400
Fibres									
Cotton, unginned				362	411			247	
Jute					172			254	
Wool, greasy basis								500	
Other crops									
Tea					1460			710	
Tobacco					530			845	

Notes to Tables of Relative Prices:

Cameroun Guillard, *Golonpoui*. Refer to an inland village. Linked on sorghum. Further data obtained f
 Le Niveau de Vie des Populations de l'Adamaoua, Ministère de l'Économie Nationale, linked
 millet (16 fr. CFA/kg.) as follows: maize 72, millet 68, sweet potatoes 34, cassava 30, groundr
 unshelled 149, bananas 68, meat 234, milk 64, butter 421.

East Africa Fuggles Couchman, *East African Journal of Agriculture*, Mar. 1939, refer to 1930s. Linked
 maize.

Haute Volta Gérardin, *Le Développement de la Haute Volta*, Institut de Science Économique Appliqué, S
 plement 142, 1963. Linked on rough rice. Other price relative, cotton seed 108. Further
 obtained from *Aspects Agricoles du Développement dans une Zone d'Action Intégrée*, Région
 Ouagadougou, Ministère de l'Économie Nationale, linked on rough rice (25 fr. CFA/kg.
 follows: rough rice 80, clean rice 187, maize 48, millet 59, sorghum 54, sweet potatoes 32, grou
 nuts unshelled 61, cotton seed 198, refined sugar 294, fish 595, meat 288, haricot 51, tomatoes
 onions 96.

Kenya Odero Ogwel, Ph.D. thesis, London University, 1969. Refer to Nyeri District, 1963. Linked
 Maize (21c./lb.). Other price relatives: bread 214, beans 143, onions 107, fat 475, salt 71.

Madagascar *Budgets et Alimentation des Ménages Ruraux en 1962*, Tome 3, Ministère des Finances et du C
 merce. Rural markets, linked on clean rice (30 FMG/kg.). Other price relatives: wheat flour
 bread 182, butter 1745.

Nigeria Upton and Petu, *Journal of Tropical Agriculture*, July 1966. Linked on maize.

Senegal *Besoins Nutritionels et Politique Économique*, Institut de Science Économique Appliqué, 1
 Linked on millet. Other price relative: coffee 271. Further data obtained from *Aperçu su*
 Recettes et Dépenses d'un Carré du Cayor, Linked on millet (20 fr. CFA/kg.) as follows: clean
 170, millet 68, refined sugar 238, fish 510, meat 374, coffee 510, tea 3400.

Tanzania *Nordic Tanganyika Project*, Dar-es-Salaam. Linked on rough rice. Other price relatives: sisal
 other fruit 76.

Uganda Pudsey, private communication. Refer to Fort Portal district. Linked on millet.

Guatemala Sol Tax, *Penny Capitalism*. Linked on maize.

Mexico *Memoria de Labores de la Secretaria de Agricultura y Ganaderia*, 1965. Rural prices 1965, based
 wheat at 0·92 peso/kg.

China Professor Chombart de Lauwe, private communication. Linked on rough rice.

India Rao, *National Income of British India*, referring to 1931. Other price relative: barley 75.

Uttar Pradesh S. P. Dhondyal, D.Sc. thesis, private communication. 1963–4 prices, based on wheat at 505 Rs.

New Guinea Fisk, private communication. Village prices 1961–2. Linked on maize (2 Australian pence
 Other price relatives: yams 94, sago 112, tapioca 75, pineapple 225, crocodile meat 75.

Pakistan Official 1948–9 prices. Other price relatives: barley 69, hemp 315.

U.S.S.R. Malin, *World Population Conference*. Based on 'all grains'. Vegetables include fruit and mea
 cludes fish.

CONVERSION FACTORS

1 kilometre	= 0·621372 miles
1 mile	= 1·609 kilometres
1 hectare	= 2·4711 acres
1 acre	= 0·4047 hectares
100 hectares	= 1 square kilometre
640 acres	= 1 square mile
1 square kilometre	= 0·3861 square miles

1 square mile	= 2·590 square kilometres
1 kilogramme	= 2·2046 lb.
1 lb.	= 0·4536 kilogrammes
1 metric ton	= 1000 kilogrammes
1 long ton	= 2240 lb.
1 short ton	= 2000 lb.
1 long ton	= 1·016 metric tons
1 short ton	= 0·9072 metric tons
1 metric ton	= 0·9842 long tons
1 metric ton	= 1·1023 short tons
1 metric ton kilometre	= 0·6116 long ton miles
1 metric ton kilometre	= 0·6849 short ton miles
1 long ton mile	= 1·635 metric ton kilometres
1 short ton mile	= 1·460 metric ton kilometres

DEFINITIONS

Economic rent: takes account only of payments for the use of land. Normal 'contract rent' also includes payment for the use of buildings or other fixed equipment. Taxes, rates, tithes etc. payable on land to be *included* in computing economic rent.

Average product per man-hour: total product divided by the total number of hours of labour applied to the same land.

Marginal product per man-hour: the additional product obtained when an additional man-hour of labour is applied to the same land.

Disguised unemployment: the state of affairs which exists when the same output could be produced using *less* labour. In this case the marginal product of labour is zero. A less extreme form of disguised unemployment is found when labour continues to work on family farms (or, sometimes, in certain other types of business) at a marginal productivity which, while not zero, is well below wages currently payable for such work.

Income elasticity of demand: the proportional change in the quantity of a good bought divided by the proportional change in income, price remaining the same.

Marginal propensity to consume: the proportion of an increment in income which will be consumed on a given commodity. For example, suppose income rises from £100 to £110 and expenditure on food changes from £70 to £75. Income elasticity of demand is $5/70 \div 10/100 = 0·714$. The marginal propensity to consume food is $5/10 = 0·5$. The two concepts must not be confused.

Price elasticity of demand: the proportional change in the quantity of a good bought divided by the proportional change in the price of the good, money income remaining the same. If the proportional change in quantity is less than the proportional change in price,

I

demand is said to be inelastic; if the proportional change in quantity is greater than the proportional change in price, demand is said to be elastic. If price falls (rises) the total amount spent on a good will fall (rise) when demand is inelastic, and rise (fall) when demand is elastic. Price elasticity depends upon the possibilities of substitution. It is generally greater when substitution is easy. In low-income groups, however, there are few substitution possibilities.

Real income: the goods and services which a person can buy with his money income. With a *given* money income, real income will be higher when prices are low and vice versa.

Total product: the total money value of all goods (including services) which are produced, valued either at factor cost, that is by summing the costs of all factors of production which were required to produce them; or at the market prices consumers pay for them. Total product at factor cost equals total product at market prices less indirect taxes levied on the goods *plus* any subsidy payments.

Real product: total product corrected for price changes. A rise in the money value of total product as between two periods does not necessarily mean that real product has increased — it may simply represent the result of increased prices. Real product is essentially a *volume* concept.

Wheat equivalent: this is the natural unit for measuring real product in communities in which the greater part of the output is grain, grown for subsistence consumption with only a small and unrepresentative part of it traded for money. Since the output of other products is comparatively small and uncertainties about their valuation unlikely to affect the result appreciably, these are converted into grain equivalents at the rate at which they exchange against grain in local markets.

Select Bibliography

ABRAHAM, T. P. and BOKIL, S. D., *Indian Journal of Agricultural Economics*, January–March 1966

AGRAWAL, G., *Indian Journal of Agricultural Economics*, March 1950

AKEHURST, B. C., and SREEDHARAN, A., *East African Agricultural and Forestry Journal*, Jan. 1965

ALLAN, W., *The African Husbandman*, 1965

ALLAN, W., *Rhodes-Livingstone Journal*, 1945

ALLARD, *Bulletin Agricole du Congo Belge*, 1960

Analyse de la Structure des Prix et des Circuits Commerciaux Internes, Madagascar, Ministry of National Economy, Tananarive, 1962

ANDREEV, V. N. and SAVKINA, Z. P., *International Grassland Conference*, 1960

ANYANE, S., *Ghana Agriculture*, O.U.P., 1963

BAER, G., *A History of Landownership in Modern Egypt*, 1962

BALDWIN, K. D. S., *The Niger Agricultural Project*, Blackwell, Oxford, 1957

BANERJEA, *Indian Journal of Medical Research*, Vol. 47, 1959

BAXTER, *Journal of the Royal Statistical Society*, 1866

BECKETT, W. H., *Akosoaso*, London School of Economics Monograph in Social Anthropology, No. 10, 1944

BENNETT, M. K., 'British Wheat Yield Per Acre for Seven Centuries', *Economic History*, February 1935

BENNETT, M. K., *The Food Economy of the New England Indians, 1605–1675*. Repr. from the *Journal of Political Economy*, Vol. LXIII, No. 5, October 1955

BENNETT, M. K., *The World's Food*, New York, 1954

BERNARD, *Le Progrès Agricole*

BICANIC, R., *Geographical Review*, January–February 1944

BILLINGS, W. D., 'Physiological Ecology', *Annual Review of Plant Physiology*, Vol. VIII, 1957

BITTERMAN, E., *Die Landwirtschaftliche Produktion in Deutschland, 1800–1950*, 1956

BOEKE, J. H., *Economics and Economic Policy of Dual Societies*, H. D. Tjeenk Willink, Haarlem, 1953

BONNÉ, A., *Archiv für Sozialwissenschaft*, 1933

BONNÉ, A., *Economic Development of the Middle East*, 1943

BOSE, S. R., *Pakistan Development Review*, Autumn 1968

BOSERUP, E., *The Conditions of Agricultural Growth*, 1965

BOURNE, J., *Railways in India*, 1848

BOWDEN, *Agrarian History of England and Wales* (edited by Finberg), Vol. IV

BOYD ORR, LORD, *Scientific American*, New York, August 1950

BRASS, W., *The Estimation of Total Fertility Rates from Data for Primitive Communities*, *World Population Conference*, 1954

BRESCIANI-TURRONI, *Weltwirtschaftliches Archiv*, October 1933

BUCK, J. L., *Land Utilization in China*, Vol. I, 1937

BUCK, J. L., *Land Utilization in China*, Vol. III, Statistics, 1937

Les Budgets Familiaux des Salariés Africains en Abidjan, Côte d'Ivoire, August–September 1956

BURGESS, R. C. and MUSA, L., *A Report on the State of Health, the Diet and the Economic Conditions of Groups of People in the Lower Income Levels in Malaya*, Institute for Medical Research, Report No. 13, Federation of Malaya, 1950

CAIRD, J. *English Agriculture in 1850–51*, 1852

CHAYANOV, A. V., *The Theory of Peasant Economy*, Irwin, 1966

CHILDE, G., *What Happened in History*, 1954

CHISHOLM, M., *Rural Settlement and Land Use*, 1962

CIPOLLA, C. M., *The Economic History of World Population*, 1962

Circuits Commerciaux de Produits et Biens Essentiels, Ministère des Finances, des Affaires Économiques et du Plan, République du Dahomey

CLARK, COLIN, *Population Growth and Land Use*, Macmillan, 1967

CLARK, GRAHAME, *Archaeology and Society*, 2nd ed., 1947

CLAYTON, E. S., 'Economic and Technical Optima in Peasant Agriculture', *Journal of Agricultural Economics*, May 1961

COCHRAN and MILLAR, *The Age of Enterprise*

COLLINSON, M. P., *Development Programme for a Rural District* (Geita), Ministry of Economic Affairs and Development Planning, Tanzania, July 1966

COMBE, *Niveau de Vie et Progrès Technique*, 1956

CONKLIN, H. C., *Hanunóo Agriculture*, a Report on an Integral System of Shifting Cultivation in the Philippines, *FAO Forestry Development Paper* No. 12, 1957

CULWICK, G. M., *A Dietary Survey among the Zande of the South-Western Sudan*, Ministry of Agriculture, Sudan Government, 1950

CUMBERLAND, KENNETH B., 'Moas and Men: New Zealand about A.D. 1250', *Geographical Review*, April 1962

DACCA UNIVERSITY, Report on the Marketing of Jute in East Pakistan, 1961

D'AVENEL, *La Richesse Privée Depuis Sept Siècles*

DAVENPORT, F. G., *The Economic Development of a Norfolk Manor*, 1906

DAYAL, R., *Indian Journal of Agricultural Economics*, July–September 1964

DEANE, P. and COLE, W. A., 'The Long-term Growth of the United Kingdom', International Association for Research in Income and Wealth Conference, 1959

DE ARLANDIS, *Weltwirtschaftliches Archiv*, September 1936

DE COURCEY-IRELAND, M. G., HOSKING, H. R. and LOEWENTHAL, L. J. A., *An Investigation into Health and Agriculture in Teso, Uganda*, Entebbe, 1937

DE FARCY, H., *Revue de l' Action Populaire*, April 1962

DE FOVILLE, *La Transformation des Moyens de Transport*

DE LA PENA, H. F., *World Population Conference*, Rome, 1954

DE VRIES, E., *World Population Conference*, Rome, 1954

DE WILDE, J. C., *Agricultural Development in Tropical Africa*, Vols. I and II, 1967

DE YOUNG, J. E., *Village Life in Modern Thailand*, 1955

DHEKNEY, *Hubli City*, Karnatak University, Dharwar

DHONDYAL, S. P., D.Sc. Thesis, University of Delhi

DISKALKAR, P. D., *Resurvey of a Deccan Village*, Indian Society of Agricultural Economics, 1960

DITTMER, C. G., 'An Estimate of the Standard of Living in China', *Quarterly Journal of Economics*, Vol. XXXIII, November 1918, No. 1

DORE, R. P., *Land Reform in Japan*, O.U.P., 1959

DOVRING, F., *Land and Labour in Europe, 1900–1950*, The Hague, 1956

DUNSDORF, E., *The Australian Wheat-Growing Industry*, 1956

East African Royal Commission, 1953–55, Report, on measures necessary to achieve an improved standard of living, including the introduction of Capital to enable Peasant Farming to develop, Cmd. 9475

EDEN, F. MORTON, *The State of the Poor*, 1797

EDWARDS, D., *An Economic Study of Small Farming in Jamaica*, Institute of Social and Economic Research, Kingston, Jamaica, 1961

EL TOMY and HANSEN, B., *Seasonal Employment Profile in Egyptian Agriculture*, Institute of National Planning, Memo. No. 501, 1964

Family Budgets of Nineteen Cultivators in the Punjab, 1953–54, Punjab Board of Economic Enquiry, Publication No. 39

FAO NUTRITIONAL STUDIES, *Calorie Requirements*; No. 5, 1950; No. 15, 1957

Farm Management, Land Use and Tenancy in the Philippines, Central Experiment Station Bulletin No. 1, 1957

FEI, HSIAO and CHANG, CHIH-I *Earthbound China. A Study of Rural Economy in Yunnan*, Routledge & Kegan Paul, 1949

FINNEY, *Lahore Symposium on Water Resource Development*, 1969

FIRTH, R., *Malay Fishermen, Their Peasant Economy*, Institute of Pacific Relations, 1946

FISK, *Economic Record*, June 1964

FLEURE, H. J., *Geographical Review*, October 1945

Les Flux de Transport dans la République du Sénégal, Campagne d'Études Industrielles et d'Aménagement du Territoire, Paris

Foreign Agriculture, U.S. Department of Agriculture, June 1945

FOX, *A Study of Energy Expenditure of Africans engaged in Various Rural Activities*, London University Ph.D. thesis, 1953

FRAENKEL, Centraal Planbureau, The Hague, Overdrukken 62

FRANÇOIS, P. J., *Budgets et Alimentation des Ménages Ruraux en 1962*, Ministère des Finances et du Commerce, République Malgache

FRASER, J. M., 'The Character of Cities', *Town and Country Planning*, November 1955

FREEMAN, J. D., *Iban Agriculture*. Colonial Office Research Study No. 18, 1955

FRIEDMAN, M., *The Theory of the Consumption Function*, Princeton, 1957

FRYER, G. E., 'A few words concerning the hill people inhabiting the forests of the Cochin State', *Journal of the Royal Asiatic Society*, Vol. 3, 1868

FRYER, G. E., 'On the Khyeng people of the Sandoway district', *Journal of the Asiatic Society of Bengal*, Vol. XVIV, Part 1, 1875

FUGGLES COUCHMAN, N. R., *Some Production-Cost Figures for Native Crops in the Eastern Province of Tanganyika Territory, East African Journal of Agriculture*, March 1939

FUKUTAKE, T., *The Social and Economic Structure of the Indian Village*, 1962–3

GALLETTI, R. with BALDWIN, K. P. S. and DINA, I. O., *Nigerian Cocoa-Farmers. An Economic Survey of Yoruba Cocoa-Farming Families*, O.U.P., 1956

GAMBLE, S. D., *Ting Hsien, A North China Rural Community*, 1954

GASSON, R., *Geography*, 1966

GEDDES, W. R., *The Land Dayaks of Sarawak*. Colonial Research Study No. 14, H.M.S.O., 1954

GÉRARDIN, B., *Le Développement de la Haute Volta*, Institut de Science Économique Appliqué, 1963

GHATGE, M. B. and PATEL, K. S., 'Economics of Mixed Farming in "Charotar" (Bombay Province)', *Indian Journal of Economics*, 1942–3

GHOSH, A. and DAS, A., 'Problems of Sub-Marginal Farming in West Bengal', *Indian Journal of Agricultural Economics*, Vol. V, No. 1. March 1950

GIGLIOLI, E. C., *East African Agriculture and Forestry Journal*, Jan. 1965

GLYN-JONES, M., 'The Dusun of the Penampang Plains in North Borneo', Report to the Colonial Office (unpublished)

GOKHALE INSTITUTE, *Poona, A Resurvey*, 1953

GOLDSMITH, R. W., *International Association for Research in Income and Wealth*, Hindsgavl Conference, 1955

GOUROU, P., *Annuaire du Collège de France*, 1959–60, 1961, 1968–9

GOUROU, P., *Impact*, 1964, No. 1

GOUROU, P., *The Standard of Living in the Delta of the Tonkin*, Institute of Pacific Relations, 9th Conference, French Paper No. 4, 1945

GOUROU, P., *The Tropical World*, 3rd edn., 1961

GRAY, M., *The Highland Economy, 1750–1850*, Edinburgh, 1957

GROVE, *Essays on African Population*, ed. Barbour, Routledge, 1961

GUILLARD, J., 'Essai de Mesure de L'activité du Paysan Africain: Le Toupourri', *Agronomie Tropicale*, Vol. XIII, No. 4, July–August 1958

GUILLARD, J., *Golonpoui*, 1965

HABIB, I., *Journal of Economic History*, March 1969

HABIBULLAH, M., *Pattern of Agricultural Unemployment*, 1962

HANCE, WILLIAM A., *African Economic Development*, O.U.P., 1958

HANSEN, B., *Journal of Development Studies*, July 1966

HANSSON, LINDHOLM and BIRATH, *Men and Tools in Indian Logging Operations*, Stockholm, 1966

HARTWELL, R., *Journal of Economic History*, March 1966

HASWELL, M. R., 'Economics and Population in Africa', *The Month*, November 1960

HASWELL, M. R., *Economics of Agriculture in a Savannah Village*, Colonial Research Studies No. 8, 1953

HASWELL, M. R., *The Changing Pattern of Economic Activity in a Gambia Village*, Department of Technical Co-operation Overseas Research Publication No. 2, 1963

HASWELL, M. R., *Economics of Development in Village India*, Routledge, 1967

HAWKINS, E. K., *Roads and Road Transport in an Underdeveloped Country. A Case Study of Uganda*, Colonial Office Research Study No. 32, 1962

HAWKINS, E. K., *Road Transport in Nigeria*, O.U.P., 1958

HAY, *Europe in the 14th and 15th Centuries*

HEADS, J., 'Urbanization and Economic Progress in Nigeria', *South African Journal of Economics*, Vol. 27, No. 3, September 1959

HEALEY, J. M., *The Development of Social Overhead Capital in India*, 1965

HERLIHY, DAVID, *Agricultural History*, April 1959

HICKEY, *Village in Vietnam*, Yale, U.P., 1964

HIGBEE, EDWARD C., 'The Agricultural Regions of Guatemala', *Geographical Review*, April 1947

HIGGS, J. W. Y. with KERKHAM R. K. and RAEBURN, J. R., *Report of a survey of problems in the mechanization of native agriculture in tropical African colonies*, Colonial Office, 1950

History of Transport in U.S.A. before 1860, Carnegie Institute, 1917

HOLMBERG, A. R., *Nomads of the Long Bow: The Siriono of Eastern Bolivia*, Smithsonian Institution of Social Anthropology, Publication No. 10, 1950

HOPPER, W., *Journal of Farm Economics*, August 1965

HSIEH, S. C., and LEE, T. H., *World Population Conference*, 1965

HSIEH, S. C., and LEE, T. H., *Economics Digest Service No. 17*, 1960, Chinese-American Joint Committee on Rural Reconstruction

INTERNATIONAL ASSOCIATION FOR RESEARCH IN INCOME AND WEALTH CONFERENCE, De Pietersberg, 1957

INTERNATIONAL BANK FOR RECONSTRUCTION AND DEVELOPMENT, *Economic Development of Ceylon. Report of a Mission Organized ... at the Request of the Government of Ceylon*, Johns Hopkins Press, 1953

INTERNATIONAL BANK FOR RECONSTRUCTION AND DEVELOPMENT, *Economic Development of Tanganyika. Report of a Mission Organized by the I.B.R.D. at the Requests of the Governments of Tanganyika and the United Kingdom*, Johns Hopkins Press, 1961

International Symposium on Desert Research, Jerusalem, 1952

IRAQ GOVERNMENT DEVELOPMENT BOARD, *Diyala and Middle Tigris Projects*, Report No. 3, 1959

ISHIKAWA, S., *Economic Development in Asian Perspective*, Hitotsubashi University, Economic Research Series No. 8

ISOBE, H., *Farm Planning with special reference to the Management and Improving of small-scale family farming*, Japanese Ministry of Agriculture, October 1956

ISSAWI, C., *Egypt at Mid-Century, An Economic Survey*, O.U.P., 1954

Italian Statistical Abstract (English version), 1954

IZIKOWITZ, K. G., *Lamet: Hill Peasants in French Indo-China*, 1951

JACKMAN, *Development of Transport in Modern England*, 1916

JANLEKHA, K., *Saraphi: A Survey of Socio-Economic Conditions in a Rural Community in North-East Thailand*, Geographical Publications Ltd., World Land Use Survey, Occasional Paper No. 8, 1968

JASNY, NAUM, *Wheat Studies* (Stanford), March 1944

JOHNSON, A. C., Volume on Egypt in the Series *Economic Survey of the Roman Empire*

JOHNSTON, BRUCE F. and MELLOR, JOHN W., *The Nature of Agriculture's Contributions to Economic Development*, Stanford University, Food Research Institute Studies, Vol. I, No. 3, 1960

JONES, G. T., *Farm Economist*, Vol. X, No. 11, 1965

JONES, G. T., and BASU, D., 'International Pattern of Demand for Foodstuffs in 1954', *Farm Economist*, Oxford, 1957

JØRGENSEN, *National Museets Arbejdsmark*, 1953

KABERRY, P., *Report on Farmer-Grazier Relations*, London University, Mimeographed, April 1959

KABERRY, P., *Women of the Grassfields:* A Study of the Economic Position of Women in Bamenda, British Cameroons; Colonial Research Publication No. 14, 1952

KÄRGER, *Landwirtschaft und Colonisation in Spanischen Amerika*, 1897

KIMURA, *Annals of the Hitotsubashi University*, April 1956

KING, GREGORY, *Political Observations*

KITSOPANIDES, G., *Parametric Programming: An Application to Greek Farming*, University of Thessaloniki, Greece, 1965

KLAYMAN, M. I., *International Index Numbers of Food and Agricultural Production*, FAO Monthly Bulletin of Agricultural Economics and Statistics, Vol. IX, March 1960

KOENTJARAMINGRAT, *Villages in Indonesia*, Cornell U.P., Ithaca, 1967

KRASOVEC, STANE, *The Meaning of Technical Change in the Context of the Agricultural Economy of South-Eastern Europe*, International Conference of Agricultural Economists, 1955

KRZYWICKI, L., *Primitive Society and its Vital Statistics*, 1935

KUMAR, DHARMA, *Land and Caste in India*, Cambridge U. P., 1965

KYOTO UNIVERSITY RESEARCH INSTITUTE OF FARM ACCOUNTING, No. 1, *The Report of Investigation of Family Farm Economy in 1956, Kinki District*, Japan, 1959

LAMADÉ, WERNER VON, 'Möglichkeiten einer Maismarktpolitik in Ghana', *Zeitschrift für auslandische Landwirtschaft*, Aug. 1966

LANDRY, A., *Traité de Démographie*, Paris, 1949

LEACH, E. R., 'Some Aspects of Dry Rice Cultivation in North Burma and British Borneo', *The Advancement of Science*, Vol. VI, No. 21, 1949

LEURQUIN, P. P., *Agricultural Change in Ruanda-Urundi*, 1945–60, Stanford University, Food Research Institute, 1963

LOCKWOOD, W. W., *The Economic Development of Japan*, O.U.P., 1955

LOPES, *International Labour Review*, November 1941

LUGARD, LORD, *The Dual Mandate in Tropical Africa*, Edinburgh, 1922

LUNING, H. A., *Netherlands Journal of Agricultural Science*, November 1964

LYNN, C. W., *Agriculture in North Mamprusi*, Gold Coast Department of Agriculture Bulletin No. 34, 1937

MACARTHUR, *Journal of the Royal Statistical Society*, pt. 3, 1964

McFIE, J., *Uganda Protectorate Nutrition Surveys, A comparison of the health of six villages consuming different types of food*, 1956

McGREGOR, I. A., 'Growth and Mortality in Children in an African Village', *British Medical Journal*, 23 December, 1961

McNEILL, W. H., *The Rise of the West*, University of Chicago Press, 1963

MADRAS UNIVERSITY, Economic Series, No. 1, *Some South Indian Villages, A Resurvey*, Ed. P. J. Thomas, 1940

MALIN, K., *World Population Conference*, Belgrade, 1965

MANDAL, G. C., 'The Marketable Surplus of Aman Paddy in East Indian Villages', *Indian Journal of Agricultural Economics*, Vol. XVI January–March 1961

MANOILESCO, *Welwirtschaftliches Archiv*, July 1935

MARTIN, ANNE, *The Oil Palm Economy of the Ibibio Farmer*, Ibadan University Press, 1956

MARUTA, S., *Memoirs of the Faculty of Agriculture*, Kagoshima University, No. 1, 1956

MASEFIELD, G. B., *Agricultural Change in Uganda*, Stanford University, Food Research Institute Studies, Vol. III, No. 2, 1962

MASSELL, B., and JOHNSON, R., *Economics of Smallholder Farming in Rhodesia*, Food Research Institute, Stanford, 1968

MA YIN-CHU, *New Construction*, Peking, November 1959 (Chinese Text)

MELICZEK, H., *Socio-Economic Conditions of a Libyan Village*, Technical University of Berlin, 1964

MESZAROA, *Statisztika Szemle*, 1952

MICHELL, *The Economics of Ancient Greece*

MIHAILOVIC, K., *World Population Conference*, Rome, 1954

MILLARD, R. S., 'Road Development in the Overseas Territories', *Journal of the Royal Society of Arts*, Vol. 107, March 1959

MISAWA, *International Conference of Agricultural Economists*, 1958

MITRANY, DAVID, *The Land and the Peasant in Rumania*, 1930

MOORE, LYNDEN, *Bulletin of the Oxford University Institute of Statistics*, Nov. 1964

MOSTAFA and MAHMOUD, U.A.R. Institution of National Planning, Memo. 497, October 1964

MYRDAL, G., *The National Income of Sweden, 1861–1930*

NADUJFALVY, *Revue Hongroise de Statistique*, 1947

NAIK, B. K., *Indian Journal of Agricultural Economics*, July–September 1965

National Accounts of Less Developed Countries, 1950–66, O.E.C.D.

NAYLOR, P. E., 'A Farm Survey of the New Hawija Settlement Project in Central Iraq', *Journal of Agricultural Economics*, Vol. XIV, No. 1, June 1960

NEUMARK, S. D., *Foreign Trade and Economic Development in Africa*, Stanford, 1964

NEWMAN, *Studies in the Import Structure of Ceylon*, Ceylon Planning Secretariat, October 1958

NOUGIER, L. R., *Population*, April–June 1954

OTTINO, *Cahiers de l'ISEA*, January 1964

OWEN, W. F., *Land Economics*, August 1964

Owen, W., *Strategy for Mobility*, Brookings Institution, 1964

Patel, H., *Economic Journal*, March 1964

Patterns of Income Expenditure and Consumption of African Unskilled Workers in Mbale, East African Statistical Department, Uganda Unit, 1958

Pedler, F. J., *The Economic Geography of West Africa*, London, 1955

Pelzer, K. J., *Pioneer Settlement in the Asiatic Tropics*, New York, 1954

Penrose, E. F., *Food Supply and Raw Materials in Japan*, Chicago, 1930

Pepelasis, A. A., with Yotopoulos, *Surplus Labour in Greek Agriculture, 1953–60*, Centre of Economic Research, Athens, Research Monograph No. 2

Peters, D. U., *Land Usage in Serenje District*, Rhodes-Livingstone Paper No. 19, 1950

Petty, Sir William, *Political Arithmetick*, 1691

Phillips, P. G., 'The Metabolic Cost of Common West African Agricultural Activities', *Journal of Tropical Medicine and Hygiene*, Vol. 57, No. 12, 1954

Pillai, V. R., and Panikar, P. G., *Land Reclamation in Kerala*, Asia Publishing House, 1965

Ping-ti Ho, *Studies in the Population of China, 1368–1953*, Harvard University Press

Pirie, N. W., 'Future Sources of Food Supply: Scientific Problems', *Journal of the Royal Statistical Society*, Series A, Vol. 125, Part 3, 1962

Platt, B. S., *Nyasaland Nutrition Survey, 1938–39*, Colonial Office Library, Mimeographed

Platt, B. S., *Tables of Representative Values of Food commonly used in Tropical Countries*, Medical Research Council Special Report No. 302, 1962

Postan, M. M., *Economic History of Europe*, 1952

Primack, M. L., *Journal of Economic History*, Sept. 1966

Les Produits Vivriers au Niger, Société d'Études pour le Développement Économique et Social, Paris, 1963

Purcal, Ph.D. thesis, Australian National University

Qayum, *Conference on Research in National Income*, Delhi, 1957

Rafiq, Ch.M., *Pakistan Development Review*, Spring 1968

Rao, V., *National Income of British India, 1931–32*, 1940

The Real Product of Soviet Russia, U.S. Senate Committee on the Judiciary, U.S. Government Printing Office, 1961

Refisch, M. A. thesis, University of London

Reindorf, *History of the Gold Coast and Asante*, 1895

Renouard, *Le Transport de la Marchandise*, 1960

Renshaw, *Journal of Business*, University of Chicago, October 1960

Reserve Bank of India, *Rural Credit Follow-Up Survey, 1956–57*, Bombay, 1960

RICARDO, DAVID, *Principles of Political Economy and Taxation*, Everyman's Library Edition, 1949

RICHARDS, A. I., *Land, Labour and Diet in Northern Rhodesia*, 1939

RICHARDSON, *Outlook on Agriculture*, Winter 1960

RINGROSE, D. R., *Journal of Economic History*, March 1968

RUDOLPH, *Geographical Review*, September 1952

RUDZINSKI, *Polish Economist*, July–September 1942

SACHS, R., and GLEES, A., *Preservation of Wildlife, Utilisation of Wild Animals and Processing of Game Meat*, Government of the Federal Republic of Germany, Tanzania Project, Project FE 428

SANSOM, D.Phil. thesis, Oxford University, 1969

SARGENT, J. R., *Report on Transport Requirements in the Light of Economic Developments in North Borneo*, Colonial Office, 1960

SARKAR, N. K., 'A Method of Estimating Surplus Labour in Peasant Agriculture in Overpopulated Underdeveloped Countries', *Journal of the Royal Statistical Society*, Series A, Vol. CXX, 1957

SAUER, CARL O., 'Early Relations of Man to Plants', *Geographical Review*, January 1947

SAUVY, A., *Population*, October–December 1953

SCHULTZ, T. W., *Transforming Traditional Agriculture*, 1964

SCHUSTER, W. H. with KESTEVEN, G. L. and COLLINS G. E. P., *Fish Farming and Inland Fishery Management in Rural Economy*, F.A.O., 1954

SEN, S. R., *World Population Conference*, 1965

SHANN, *Economic History of Australia*

SHASTRI, C. P., 'Bullock Labour Utilization in Agriculture', *Economic Weekly*, 29 October, 1960

SHASTRI, C. P., 'Input-Output Relations in Indian Agriculture', *Indian Journal of Agricultural Economics*, January–March 1958

SHEN, T. H., *Agricultural Development in Taiwan*, Cornell U.P., Ithaca, 1964

SHEN-PAO NIEN-CHIN, *Year Book*, Shanghai, 1933

SHIWALKAR, R. S., 'Technique of Measuring Rural Unemployment', *Indian Journal of Agricultural Economics*, March 1954

SHORTT, J., 'An account of some rude tribes, the supposed Aborigines of Southern India', *Transactions of the Ethnological Society*, Vol. III, 1865

SINGH, K. and HRABOVSKY, J. P., *Indian Journal of Agricultural Economics*, October–December 1965

SINGH, TARLOK, *Poverty and Social Change*, 1945

SLATER, G. (Editor), *Some South Indian Villages*, University of Madras, Economic Series 1, 1918

SMITH, M. G., *The Economy of Hausa Communities in Zaria*, Colonial Research Study No. 16, H.M.S.O. 1955

SOBERMAN, R. M., *The Cost of Road Transportation in Venezuela*,

Corporación Venezolana de Guayana, 1963, quoted Fromm and others, *Transportation and Economic Development*

SORBI, UGO, *Borgo e Mozzano*, Instituto di Economica, University of Florence

SPENGLER, JOSEPH J., 'Richard Cantillon: First of the Moderns', I and II. *Journal of Political Economy*, August and October, 1954

SRINIVASAN, M. N., 'Prices and Production Trends in Agriculture', *Indian Journal of Agricultural Economics*, March 1954

STAMP, L. D., *Geographical Review*, New York, January 1958

Statistical and Economic Review, United Africa Company, March 1957

Statistical Pocketbook of Indonesia, 1950

SUHA, A., *Economic Problems of Eastern Europe*

SUKHATME, P. V., *Journal of the Royal Statistical Society*, Series A, Part IV, 1961

SWAMINATHAN, M. C., APTE, S. V. and SOMESWARA RAO, K., 'Nutrition of the People of Ankola Taluk (N. Kanara)', *Indian Journal of Medical Research*, November 1960

TATEMOTO, Institute of Social and Economic Research, Osaka University, Discussion Paper No. 9

TAX, SOL, *Penny Capitalism, A Guatemalan Indian Economy*, Smithsonian Institution of Social Anthropology, Publication No. 16, Washington, 1953

TAYLOR, *Canadian Journal of Economics and Political Science*, August 1950

TERRA, G. J. A., *Netherlands Journal of Agricultural Science*, May 1961

THOMAS, P. J. (Editor), *Some South Indian Villages, A Resurvey*, University of Madras, Economic Series 4, 1940

THOMSON, B. P., *Two Studies in African Nutrition: An Urban and a Rural Community in Northern Rhodesia*, Rhodes-Livingstone Paper No. 24, Manchester University Press, 1954

THORN, *World Population Conference*, 1954

TOBATA, SEIICHI, *Japanese Agriculture*, 1952

TOTHILL, J. D., *Agriculture in the Sudan*, O.U.P., 1948

TOTHILL, J. D., *Agriculture in Uganda*, O.U.P., 1940

TOUTAIN, J. C., *Le Produit de L'Agriculture Française de 1700 à 1958*, Vol. II, Cahiers de L'Institut de Science Economique Appliqué, Supplement No. 115, July 1961

TROWELL, H. C. 'Calorie and Protein Requirements of Adult Male Africans', *East African Medical Journal*, Vol. 32, No. 5, May 1955

TUTIYA, K., *Quarterly Journal of Agricultural Economics*, No. 1, 1955, in Japanese

UMEMURA, *Economic Survey of Japanese Agriculture*, 1956

United Nations Monthly Bulletin of Statistics, March 1962

United Nations Yearbook of International Trade Statistics, 1960

UNITED STATES DEPARTMENT OF AGRICULTURE, FAS-M 101, 104, 108, Parts II, III and IV, *Food Balances in Foreign Countries*, 1960–61

ERS-FOREIGN-34, *The Philippines: Long-term Projection of Supply and of Demand for Selected Agricultural Products*, March 1963

U.S. JOINT ECONOMIC COMMITTEE, *An Economic Profile of Mainland China*, 1967

UPTON and PETU, *Journal of Tropical Agriculture*, July 1966

USHER, D., *Economica*, May 1963 and November 1966

VAN BEUKERING, J. A., *Het Ladagvraagstuk, Een Bedrijfs — Ein Sociaal Economisch Probleem*, Mededeelingen Van Het Department van Economische Zaken in Nederlandsch-Indie, No. 9, 1947

VAN DER KOPPEL, *Die Landbouw In Den Indischen Archipel*

VANDELLOS, *Metron*, 1925

VANZETTI, *Land and Man in Latin America*, Società Italiana di Sociologia Rurale, 1961

VON THÜNEN, J. H., *The Isolated State* (P. Hall's translation), 1966

WAIBEL, LEO HEINRICH, 'Vegetation and Land use in the Planalto Central of Brazil', *Geographical Review*, October 1948

WALBANK, *Cambridge Economic History of Europe*

WANDER, H., quoting Bino Pusat Statistik, *Penduduk Indonesia*, 1959, and statistical *Pocketbook of Indonesia*, 1950

WARRINER, D., *Economics of Peasant Farming*, 1964

WARRINER, D., *Land and Poverty in the Middle East*, Royal Institute of International Affairs, 1948

WARRINER, D., *Land Reform and Development in the Middle East. A Study of Egypt, Syria and Iraq*. 1st edition, 1948, 2nd edition, O.U.P., 1962

WATANABE, *Shikoku Acta Medica*, Vol. 15, 1959

WELK, A. D., *Recent Economic Changes*, 1889

WICKIZER, V. D. and BENNETT, M. K., *The Rice Economy of Monsoon Asia*, California, 1941

WIJEWARDENE, R., 'From Bullock to Tractor', *World Crops*, Vol. 13, No. 11, November 1961

WILSON, P. N., 'An Agricultural Survey of Moruita Erony, Teso', *Uganda Journal*, Vol. 22, No. 1, March 1958

WILSON, P. N. and WATSON, J. M., 'Two Surveys of Kasilang Erony, Teso', *Uganda Journal*, Vol. 20, No. 2, September 1956

WILSON, T. B., *Economics of Paddy Production in Northern Malaya*, Malayan Department of Agriculture, 1958

WINFIELD, G. F., *China, the Land and the People*, 1948

WINTER, E. H., *Bwamba Economy*, East African Institute of Social Research, 1956

WINTER, M., *Le Niveau de Vie des Populations de l'Adamaoua*, Ministère de l'Économie Nationale, République Fédérale du Cameroun

World Population Conference, 1954

The World Today, Institute of International Affairs, March 1947

WYCLIFFE, *Indian Journal of Agricultural Economics*, January–March 1959

YAJIMA, T., *World Population Conference*, 1965

YASIN, *Punjab Board of Economic Enquiry*, Bulletin No. 114, 1956

YONG SAM CHO, *Disguised Unemployment in Under-developed Areas*, 1963

ZIMMERMAN, C. C., *Siam Rural Economic Survey, 1930–31*

Index